THE AMERICAN NEWSPAPERMAN

The America

THE CHICAGO HISTORY OF AMERICAN CIVILIZATION

Daniel J. Boorstin, EDITOR

ewspaperman

By Bernard A. Weisberger

THE UNIVERSITY OF CHICAGO PRESS

CHICAGO AND LONDON

International Standard Book Number: 0-226-89138-0

Library of Congress Catalog Card Number: 61-8647

The University of Chicago Press, Chicago 60637
The University of Chicago Press, Ltd., London

To Walter and Tom

Editor's Preface

Even before the end of the eighteenth century, European travelers to the United States were astonished that in these remote parts there were more newspapers printed per capita than in the cultivated nations of Europe. In the second half of the twentieth century, newspapermen from abroad are amazed at the supra-constitutional powers of our Washington correspondents who question the President of the United States in regular conferences and call him to account in ways elsewhere reserved for the elected representatives of the people. The American newspaperman has played an intimate and leading role in American life. At least since the days of James and Benjamin Franklin, he has had an influence both in our households and in our capitals, in the forming of opinion and in the making of decisions.

The lively story of the American newspaperman which Mr. Weisberger tells in this volume is full of a distinctively American drama and variety. It is full of self-made men, men-on-the-move, grand failures, and unexpected successes. The American newspaperman is a touchstone of American civilization. But the newspaperman's definition of what is noteworthy does not match that of the history books. He cannot delimit his subject quietly in his study or choose to write only on topics where reliable documents are available. The unexpected currents of daily life define the newspaperman's subjects for him. He must be on the spot after an earthquake or a tornado or a fire; he must recount decisions and debates in Washington, conferences and crises in Yalta, Casablanca, Paris, Tokyo, or the Congo. But he must also report the details of any brutal hometown murder, the human interest story behind any remarkable swindler or pickpocket. He must report the scandals in the private lives of entertainers. He must report a presidential inauguration, yet not fail to note the current Community Fund drive, a local sermon, a PTA protest meeting, a high school commencement, or a banquet honoring a businessman on retirement. He must be full and unfettered and frank in his reporting, yet he must be cogent and readable, avoiding the offensive or the libelous. His task is in many ways more difficult than that of the historian.

The historian looks at experience with the eye of posterity. He picks it over to see what still interests us after the participants are dead. But the newspaperman writes about the living and for the living. While he consciously records "news" for today's paper he also unwittingly records the daily concerns of his age in a form which survives for future historians. His work takes him everywhere, among all sorts of people, at all times of the day and night, and his product goes everywhere, to keep people solaced and occupied at any odd moment. For this reason, any history of the American newspaperman like Mr. Weisberger's cannot fail to be a history of what has interested the American people.

The careers of American newspapermen raise important recurring questions about our public life. In a democracy, leaders are accustomed to apologize for their weakness by explaining that they must be able to "sell" their ideas to the people. The leader, we are often told, cannot run too far ahead if he expects the crowd to follow him. The newspaperman faces these questions even more frequently and more literally than our elected representatives. He must "sell" his product every day, or even several times a day. If it does not appeal, nobody will know him, he cannot continue to be a newspaperman. Yet if he only gives the public what it wants, if he does not somehow help shape public demands, we consider him weak and insignificant—certainly not an important newspaperman. He must be both a mirror of public tastes and a beacon for public desires. The careers of American newspapermen are parables of democratic leadership. They show us both how far a democratic leader must follow the public and how far he can lead.

In still another way the newspaperman has been at the heart of American life. For the history of American newspapers has been shaped by the decisive changes in our economy, our technology, our social history: by the invention of the telegraph and the telephone, the improvement of mass-production techniques, the rise of photography, the growth of cities and suburbs. It has been much affected by every spectacular change in our daily life in the twentieth century: the radio, the automobile, the airplane, television. When we study the history of transportation in the United States, we see ages

Editor's Preface

dominated by the railroad, by the automobile, or by the airplane. The future historian will find it much harder to delimit an Age of the Newspaper. Of course there was a heyday of the newspaper, when it offered its reports of latest events without competition from radio or television. But one of the most impressive facts in the history of the American newspaperman has been his flexibility, his ability to adapt his job to the competition of radio and television, and to find a new career for himself, to become, if necessary, not only a writer but a familiar voice and a familiar image.

Mr. Weisberger's volume, vividly surveying the many lives of the American newspaperman, suggests the many meanings of these lives for the life of all Americans. In this he admirably serves the purpose of the "Chicago History of American Civilization" which aims to make every aspect of our past a window to all our history. The series contains two kinds of books: a *chronological* group, which provides a coherent narrative of American history from its beginning to the present day, and a *topical* group, which deals with the history of varied and significant aspects of American life. This book is one of the topical group. Nineteen titles in the series have now been published, and twenty-odd are in preparation.

DANIEL J. BOORSTIN

Table of Contents

I. The Colonial Printer and the Public Business / 1

II. Politics and Press in the Infant Republic / 33

III. Special-Audience Papers in the Early Nineteenth Century / 64

IV. Democracy, Technology, and Profits: Mid-century Modernism / 88

V. Empires in Newsprint: The Century Closes / 121

VI. Legmen, Wits, and Pundits: The World of Reporting / 156

VII. The Vanishing Newspaperman? / 185

Important Dates / 204

Suggested Reading / 207

Acknowledgments / 217

Index / 219

Illustrations

The colonial hand press at work   *facing page* 20

A flat-bed cylinder press of 1845   20

Front page of the *Boston News-Letter*, 1704   21

Front page of the *Pennsylvania Gazette*, 1776   52

The Hoe "lightning press" of 1847   53

A web-perfecting, stereotyping press of 1875   53

Front page of the *New York Times*, 1865   148

Front page of the *Chicago Tribune*, 1898   149

Front page of the *Chicago Tribune*, 1912   180

Printing plant and city room of the
  Chicago Sun-Times today   181

I

The Colonial Printer
and the Public Business

The first American newspaper was in some ways as contemporary as yesterday's late edition. To residents of Boston on September 25, 1690, it brought news of an epidemic, a suicide, two fires, the mutilation of two Indians by an English captain in the course of battle with the French in Canada, and the prospects of King William against the Irish rebels. There is no record of any Bostonian complaint that such a chronicle of smallpox, self-destruction, torture, and bloodshed was too sensational, or too trivial, for the reading public. Perhaps there might have been, if Benjamin Harris had put out a second number of *Publick Occurrences Both Forreign and Domestick*. But the governor of Massachusetts and his council found in the three six-by-ten-inch pages of the "paper," certain "reflections of a very high nature," printed without the required official license. They suppressed the venture, and journalism in the English colonies had to await the test of the market place for another fourteen years.

Though Harris may have suffered personally by the dashing of his hopes, he was not unfamiliar with official displeasure. In London, which he had left for Boston in 1686, he had been a violently opinionated bookseller and publisher, and for the crime of issuing a "seditious" pamphlet he had been fined five pounds. Once, too, he had stood in the pillory. Coming to Massachusetts to mend his fortunes, he had set up a bookstore and a coffee house, and *Publick Occurrences* was a logical venture for a man in his position. The coffee house was a place of commercial gossip, and among the ancestors of the newspaper were the newsletters circulated among merchants of the sixteenth and seventeenth centuries. Harris promised, in that lonely single number of *Publick Occurrences*, that its purpose would be, in part, to help people comprehend the "Circumstances of Publique Affairs" so as to assist "their Businesses and Negotiations." Moreover, unlike the one-shot and one-sheet news broadsides occasionally run off by printers for quick profit—Boston had just seen one in 1689, entitled *The Present State of the New-English Affairs*—Harris' paper would appear with businesslike regularity and continuity. It would be printed once a month, something to count upon, or even oftener if there should be a "Glut of Occurrences." The publisher also struck a note of religious uplift and community improvement. The printing of the news, he promised, would help to fix in mind "Memorable Occurrents of Divine Providence," and also to cure "that Spirit of Lying, which prevails amongst us."

There is a certain pugnacity in that last promise, suggesting that Harris was a man given to tweaking the noses of his peers. He found no permanent home in Boston, but returned to London in 1694 to undertake further adventures in publishing, selling patent medicines—and, one suspects, gossiping and having arguments with officialdom as well. He left behind him a journalistic vacuum long unfilled. The man who finally penetrated it was far different from Benjamin Harris. John Campbell, an orderly Scot, a government functionary—postmaster of Boston—and a cautious promoter, made certain that his *Boston News-Letter*, first issued in April, 1704, was printed "by authority." Speaking in the very broadest terms, it might be said that Benjamin Harris founded one prototype of the American newspaper—racy, aggressive, and independent. Campbell gave birth to another—solid, careful, and slightly bent under a sense of official responsibility. The conflicts and compromises between these two styles in journalism fill a good portion of the annals of the press in the United States.

The newspaper came to the colonies, therefore, only with the eighteenth century. The seventeenth was the century of the founders, the first migrants, the great planters of ways of work and worship, and the rule of commonwealths in the New World. The eighteenth was the time of growing maturity, complexity, sophistication—of more of everything: more trade, more money, more migrants, more schools, more churches, more roads, more books. Such an age could afford to nourish the newspaper. From 1719 to 1783 no fewer than sixty-seven publishers tried to follow in Campbell's footsteps, and some thirty-odd papers survived to greet the age of national independence. Some of these journals had urged, and some had tried to stem, the American Revolution. But their very existence was a portent of that Revolution. They were evidence in themselves that British North America had out-grown the framework of a colonial system designed to deal with "plantations" on remote and savage shores. The colonial journals were proof of ripened commerce, widened interests, fresh thought, easier social interchange, and, above all, urban-ism in the colonies. Their editors were men of the town, de-pending on the town for skills, materials, and markets, learning to cherish it, and teaching its own people to be aware of it. Already the newspaper was both actor and narrator in the drama of history, playing a sometimes confusing double role.

The barest record of highlights is instructive of this truth. It was in Boston, with its handful of printers, its nearby col-lege in Cambridge, and its nearly ten thousand souls that Campbell's *News-Letter* made its bow. The royal government, becoming aware of the need for co-ordinating colonial ac-tivities, had begun to lay the foundations of an intercolonial postal system late in the seventeenth century. The same aware-ness led, in the 1690's, to the establishment of the Board of Trade, in London, to synchronize economic policies for the several colonies. Campbell, a bookseller, was one of the first contractors appointed under the new postal law. He knew that its purpose was in part to speed the interchange of com-mercial and legal tidings among the settlements, and he was faithful to his trust. He began to send out handwritten news-letters to selected correspondents, along with his regular pouches. These contained digests of intelligence which the postmaster picked up from the letters, documents, orders, pamphlets, and occasional English gazettes which he handled and unabashedly read. When the burden finally grew too great for his pen, he turned to Bartholomew Green, printer, to put out the *News-Letter* for him.

4

The Colonial Printer and the Public Business

Thus the newspaper came into existence in part as a public service, and indeed legend has it that the first copy was taken, damp from the press, by Chief Justice Samuel Sewall to show to the president of Harvard. Campbell, in addition, did not charge himself anything for distributing copies through his postal service, and neither, for many years, did any other postmaster-publisher. Spreading intelligence to outlying parts was simply one of the postal system's tasks, not expected to pay for itself. Those who bought the *News-Letter* were supposed to pay twopence a copy, and for this sum they got, each week (with occasional lapses), a sheet approximately twelve by seven inches, printed on both sides in a small, crowded type. The working model for the paper was the *London Gazette*, begun in 1665; the news consisted of brief items of political and military gossip culled from recent letters—some two months old—arrived from England and Europe, together with short notices of ship clearances and arrivals, piracies, storms, fires, sermons, court actions, official decisions, freaks of nature, and whatever else Campbell thought might please and instruct his two or three hundred subscribers.

The *News-Letter* was apparently satisfactory to Boston's preachers, traders, and public servants. It continued for fifteen years without competition, and might have continued longer in single majesty, if a political misfortune had not befallen John Campbell. He lost his position as postmaster. Promptly he stopped the delivery of his paper through the mails, apparently assuming that it was no longer his responsibility to provide news to the outlanders beyond Boston's town limits. The *News-Letter* remained available only to those subscribers who could call for it at the printer's office. The new postmaster, William Brooker, however, did not intend that Campbell should prevent him from doing *his* duty in enlightening the hinterlands. He went to James Franklin, printer, and got him, late in 1719, to run off the first number of the *Boston Gazette*. Campbell, bitter at the loss of both his position and his newspaper monopoly, sneered in print that the new paper smelled more "of beer than of midnight oil," and thus Boston moved into journalistic maturity with *two* papers, striking attitudes of combat.

Brooker continued the *Gazette* until the summer of 1721, when he, too, was removed as postmaster. Among the properties of the office which he turned over to Philip Musgrave was the *Gazette*, which he apparently felt by this time to be one of the responsibilities of the appointment itself. Musgrave willingly continued the paper, but he chose to transfer the printing contract to Samuel Kneeland. James Franklin thus became the first printer of a newspaper to feel the sting of losing official patronage. Unwilling to submit tamely to misfortune, Franklin at once made himself the first printer in Boston to publish his own paper. He began the *New-England Courant*, a sprightly departure from the *Gazette* and *News-Letter*, containing more purely literary and irreverently humorous matter. Its liveliness was aided at first by the anonymous contributions of James Franklin's younger brother, Ben, then working as an apprentice in the shop, and it had some support from Bostonians who were hostile to the town's ruling clique. Possibly discouraged by the appearance of still another competitor, John Campbell soon turned the *News-Letter* over to Bartholomew Green, its printer. In 1727 the *Courant* went out of business, an early casualty in a line of endeavor which was always to be noted for a high mortality rate. But in the same year a new postmaster took the *Gazette* away from Samuel

Kneeland's printing establishment, and Kneeland followed Franklin's example and began a paper of his own, the *New-England Weekly Journal*. For a time, then, Boston had three newspapers, two of them owned by their printers.

Elsewhere in the colonies, postmasters and printers also acted as the midwives of newspapers. Andrew Bradford, postmaster of Philadelphia and a printer-bookseller as well, began the *American Weekly Mercury* in 1719. Bradford's father, William, had been a Philadelphia printer himself from 1685 to 1693, when he left for New York, where an appointment as official printer to the governor's council awaited him. This elder Bradford, one of whose duties was to give printed circulation to royal and provincial decrees, decided to improve his position by embodying them in the new medium of a newspaper. He began the *New-York Gazette* in 1725—and soon discovered that a newspaper publisher, unlike an official printer, had to face the problem of competition. In 1733 a former apprentice to Bradford, John Peter Zenger, began the *New-York Weekly Journal*. Zenger had a promise of support from certain New Yorkers dissatisfied with the rulership which employed Bradford; political and business hostility were merged in the rivalry between the two papers. By the 1730's Philadelphia was also a two-newspaper town. Samuel Keimer, a Philadelphia press owner full of religious zeal and literary ambitions, began in 1728 a newspaper hopefully named the *Pennsylvania Gazette and Universal Instructor in All the Arts and Sciences*. After a year in which Keimer floundered in unfamiliar depths, Benjamin Franklin appeared, now graduated from his Boston apprenticeship and seeking his fortune in Pennsylvania. He took the journal off Keimer's hands, pruned its title of the final nine words, and commenced to make it pay.

The American Newspaperman

Bit by bit, journalism spread. In 1727 printer William Parks began the *Maryland Gazette* in Annapolis, and in 1736 he started the *Virginia Gazette* in Williamsburg. Thomas Whitemarsh launched the *South Carolina Gazette* in Charleston in 1731. In 1732 James Franklin, who had also forsaken Boston by that time, founded the *Rhode Island Gazette* in Newport. The popularity of "Gazette" as a name was more than accidental. The publishers were frequently public printers to the colony, and a gazette, by definition, was a kind of official record. All these new journals were located in seaports or provincial capitals—Boston, Newport, New York, Philadelphia, Annapolis, Williamsburg, and Charleston. They were meant originally for the convenience of those who governed and those who trafficked in goods, and if the publishers chose to put advertisements and literary miscellany into their four pages, these were marginal extras to lure new custom. Only when cities enlarged and politics became more factionalized, around the middle of the century, did the center of gravity in the successful papers begin to shift toward political essays and news of the town, of which advertising was, after all, a part—revealing who had entered the community and wished to buy a farm or a home; who was leaving and had farms and homes to sell; who had lost horses, dogs, and servants and who stood in need of them; who wished to commit a cargo to the seas and who had imported goods in ships newly arrived at the wharves.

The first thrust of newspaper founding took place, then, in the major colonial towns between 1705 and 1740—years of increasing migration, economic specialization, and a kind of general, though uneasy, peace on the military, political, and religious fronts. The next wave of foundings came in the two decades before the Revolution, when fresh colonial wars, the

8

The Colonial Printer and the Public Business

Great Awakening, and efforts at imperial reorganization by London had lit the fires of controversy—and when settlement was moving inland. The year 1755 was a landmark in Boston journalism, for it was then that printers Benjamin Edes and John Gill took over the thirty-six-year-old *Boston Gazette.* In time they were to make it the vigorously antiroyalist organ of the Sons of Liberty. But great things were happening to journalism outside of Boston. A *North Carolina Gazette* emerged in New Bern in 1751, and a *Georgia Gazette* in 1763 in Savannah, capital of the thirty-year-old colony. The *New Hampshire Gazette* appeared in Portsmouth in 1756, and the *Providence Gazette* began to enlighten Rhode Island in 1762. In 1761 a *Wilmington Courant* was founded in Delaware; and Wilmington, North Carolina, was endowed with the *Cape Fear Mercury* in 1769. Salem, Massachusetts, was the birthplace of the *Essex Gazette* in 1768. Hartford witnessed the start of the *Connecticut Courant* in 1764. Journalism was moving into the smaller seaports and into the back country. Actually the process was speeded up by the British occupation of the coastal ports during the Revolution. Isaiah Thomas, to name only one, had begun a Patriot paper, the *Massachusetts Spy*, in Boston in 1770. When the redcoats fully occupied Boston in 1775, he moved the paper inland to Worcester, renamed it the *Worcester Spy*, and launched it on a long and honorable career.

The publishers were opportunists, moving in wherever culture had aged sufficiently to give them a market—first in the coastal towns which queened it over colonial trade, and later in the growing centers above the fall line. The westward movement carried journalism with it, as it did all else in American life. By the time of that westward drift, the newspaper had made a place for itself as an institution of the colonial town.

9

The American Newspaperman

So had the newspaper's owner. His place was unique, shaped by the nature of his printer's craft, the business which grew out of it, and his relationship to government.

The colonial printer was something more than a "mere" artisan. He was the master of a craft which was exacting, rare, and essential. As early as 1638 the fathers of Massachusetts recognized that salvation was by ink no less than by water. They authorized a search for a press and printer, and finally got Stephen Daye to settle in the colony, rewarding him not only with printing patronage but ultimately with three hundred acres of land. Daye taught the craft to other men whose imprints were to become collectors' items—Samuel Green, for one. Green, in turn, taught James Glen, John Foster, Marmaduke Johnson, and others. He also passed on the art to his sons, as did other early printers, so that by the middle of the eighteenth century there were dynasties of printers—among them the Greens, the Bradfords, the Christopher Sowers of Pennsylvania (who pioneered both German-language publications and type-founding in America), and the Franklins. Benjamin Franklin not only trained sons and grandsons at the press but took a fatherly interest in his generations of apprentices. When their training had been completed, he set many of them up in business in other towns, thus retaining a partial interest in a virtual chain of newspapers. The men who worked the crude, flat-bed hand presses of the day knew what it was to dirty their hands with ink and oil. Yet as owners of their shops, agents of authority, and men of property, they quickly acquired status in a society where status came easily with an increasing share of the world's goods.

They sought prosperity with as much energy as any of their

contemporaries. Printers not only sold books and stationery but took advantage of the popularity of their shops as gathering places to offer other than printed goods for sale. Samuel Keimer, Franklin's predecessor on the *Pennsylvania Gazette*, advertised "bayberry wax candles, and fine white Liverpool soap" at his establishment; Andrew Bradford offered whalebone, goose feathers, pickled sturgeon, chocolate, and Spanish snuff; Hugh Gaine, of New York, dealt in patent medicines, flutes, and fiddle strings as a sideline. As a printer became successful, he was apt to sink his profits into town lots and houses. Thus he was clearly a member of his community's "establishment." Guarding a tradition-rich craft, he had within him the makings of a conservative. Yet there was the other side of the coin. The printer was still linked to the world of manual labor, and he was still a tradesman who had to work lustily at selling both his arts and his wares in order to stay solvent. He was both merchant and mechanic, and neither station fitted into an aristocratic pattern. Besides, mobility in the calling was high. A hardworking apprentice had every right to expect that he might one day own his own shop, what with new settlements opening up, and the cost of a used press and font of type within the reach of a careful man's savings, supplemented by a friendly loan. Benjamin Franklin himself was a stellar example of such possibilities. Isaiah Thomas was a hungry apprentice, six years old, in 1756; in 1770 he was part-owner of a newspaper in Boston; in 1810 he was a wealthy publisher and philanthropist of Worcester, Massachusetts. Such stories, which could be multiplied, show that for all the pull of respectability, the printer also had a stake in keeping colonial society fluid and fast-moving. The contradictions of his role found their way, to some extent, into the newspapers which came out of his shop. If newspapers owned by men on the make tended, until 1765, to lean unduly toward the side of order, this was partly because of the special relationship between printers and governors in the provinces.

For one thing, the printer who, like William Bradford, had a monopoly on publishing the colonial statutes, notices, and court decisions had therewith a substantial source of income. He needed no reminding about the relationship between orthodoxy and bread and butter. If he put out a newspaper in his shop, criticism of authority was not likely to be its staple. It was much easier for the newspaper-owning "publick printer" or postmaster to be studiously loyal and to praise his public patrons to his private ones, thus letting one hand wash the other. It was, however, more than judiciousness in business that held newspapers in line. Almost all the colonies had explicit or implied statutory power to license the operation and output of presses. It was under such a law that Massachusetts had silenced Benjamin Harris, and it was under the shadow of censorship that new journals were founded in Boston. The censor's power was not always exercised, and as printers found support for their papers in the town, they flirted with criticism, but always at some risk.

James Franklin was the first to feel the rod in Boston after it became the home of his *Courant*. Franklin was something of an innovator, substituting a bold and witty style for the cautious approach of Campbell's *News-Letter* and the postmaster-owned *Gazette*. He was legally on thin ice to begin with, having undertaken the paper without official sanction (although his precedent gradually became the rule), and he increased his perils by running squibs which poked fun impartially at the royal governor and at the leading members of his Boston opposition. In 1722 Franklin sarcastically attacked official torpor in policing the coast. A pirate had been reported in the vicinity of Boston, he noted, and a ship was being prepared for pursuit. It would sail "late in the month, wind and weather permitting." The governor's council got the point clearly enough and summoned Franklin for an explanation and an apology. Franklin was outspokenly unrepentant, and was jailed for a month. During his absence brother Ben happily and competently ran the paper. Released from imprisonment, Franklin continued on his peppery way, until the colonial assembly, by now as irritated as the governor, forbade him to print anything more without supervision. James Franklin took refuge in Yankee trickery. He publicly announced that he was turning the *Courant* over to his younger brother and canceled Benjamin's apprenticeship. Then he made a secret agreement with young Ben to continue their original relationship. But the future Poor Richard also knew a trick or two. Realizing that the secret contract could not be enforced, he walked out on James and departed Boston to find his future in Philadelphia. Somewhat subdued, the older Franklin took up the *Courant* once more, but avoided head-on collisions with the government for the remainder of its life.

Andrew Bradford of Philadelphia's *American Weekly Mercury* also learned wariness. He was twice threatened with suppression, once for petitioning the assembly to revive the "dying credit" of the province and once for running an essay, over the signature "Busy Body," extolling the virtues of the ancient Romans and hinting broadly that the rulers of contemporary Pennsylvania had plenty to learn from them. (The essay was the work of the ubiquitous Benjamin Franklin.) Thomas Fleet of the *Boston Evening-Post* was haled before the council in 1741 for printing a rumor that Sir Robert Walpole was to be arrested in London. Elsewhere printers from time to time found themselves in official disfavor. Although actual prosecutions were few, they undoubtedly had some effect in encouraging some printers to be cautious. With official patronage to keep the publicly supported presses in line, and an occasional threat as a reminder to those printers without government contracts, the governors did not have much to fear from hostile newspapers. Still, unruly men like James Franklin had set an example of partial independence and laid foundations to be built on. Moreover, a governor confronted with really massive public distemper could find the weapons of patronage and prosecution useless. Enough customers might be found for a "seditious" paper to make it independent of official support, and a fractious jury might refuse to convict an outspoken but popular editor on a charge of seditious libel.

This was precisely what happened in the celebrated case of John Peter Zenger. Zenger's *New-York Weekly Journal* had been founded to give a voice to the party of landowners and merchants who opposed the administration of royal governor William Cosby. Zenger willingly gave space in the paper to a number of lampoons of royally appointed officials. They not only served the interests of the *Journal*'s sponsors, but they made the paper a much livelier competitor to the *Gazette* of public printer Bradford. After a few abortive attempts to get Zenger indicted for seditious libel by a grand jury, the gubernatorial council finally issued its own warrant for his arrest. The high-handed nature of this proceeding immediately made the issue something larger in the public mind than the liberty of a printer, a reaction which had much to do with the final result. Zenger languished in jail for months, although he was allowed to communicate freely with outsiders and to edit his paper "thro' the hole in the door," as he put it.

When the case came to trial in 1735, it presented curious legal aspects. Under the law as then applied, the truth of the alleged libel was not a defense. Moreover, the jury was not permitted to decide whether the offending material was actually seditious. That was up to the judge—appointed by the governor—and the jury was supposed to find only as to the facts. It could consider only whether or not Zenger had printed the lampoons, a point which was beyond argument. Zenger's backers had hired Andrew Hamilton, a brilliant old Philadelphia lawyer, who, confronted by this impossible case under the law as it stood, chose to appeal on sweeping grounds to the discontents of the jurors. Drawing on the whole body of anti-authoritarian doctrine developed in the English revolutions of the seventeenth century (and therefore charged with considerable emotional voltage for his audience of English-minded colonials), he defended the right "publicly to remonstrate against abuses of power in the strongest terms." The cause, he declared, was "not the Cause of the poor Printer, nor of *New York* alone." It was

the Cause of Liberty; and I make no Doubt but your upright Conduct, this Day, will not only entitle you to the Love and Esteem of your Fellow-Citizens; but every Man who prefers Freedom to a Life of Slavery will bless and honour You, as Men who have baffled the attempt of Tyranny; and by an impartial and uncorrupt Verdict, have laid a Noble Foundation for securing to ourselves, our Posterity and our Neighbors, That, to which Nature and the Laws of our Country have given us a Right,—the Liberty—both of exposing and opposing arbitrary Power . . . by speaking and writing—Truth.

No jury could withstand such oratory when launched against an already unpopular administration, and it took only a few moments for Zenger to be found not guilty. He and Hamilton were both lionized for a time, but in the uproar over the case, then and subsequently, certain points were obscured. Hamilton's defense did not touch the question of the government's right to license the press, a much more effective muzzling device (if applied) than any libel prosecution. Moreover, Hamilton's insistence upon the truth of a libel as an exculpation of the offense was not accepted in British law and was not to be firmly established in American practice until some three-quarters of a century later, when it was, curiously, written into the "infamous" Sedition Act of 1798. Zenger's trial was important not so much as a legal precedent but as an emotional and symbolic triumph for a doctrine of "freedom of the press" which few contemporaries had thought of applying to newspapers.

What Hamilton did prove was that, in the face of really widespread disloyalty, a colonial administration liberal enough to grant trial by jury could not count on winning verdicts against rebellious subjects. But extensive resistance to British rule did not begin to develop until the Stamp Act crisis of 1765. It was only then that the newspapers began to become major voices of revolution. Before 1765, the Zenger trial's outcome notwithstanding, few newspaper owners dared to play public gadfly. Nevertheless, they were preparing themselves for that new journalistic role all through the eighteenth century, by winning public acceptance.

Slowly the printer-publishers experimented with the newspaper, the awkward child among their family of enterprises, until it grew up and arrogated to itself the very name of "the press," of which it was originally only a single product. Gradually the owner-editors shaped it to fit the ways and needs of the community, matching it to their own temperaments and the hard logic of the market.

The early newspapers were not things of beauty. The old-fashioned hand presses became cranky after long use and had to be replaced from England if at all. Almost no presses were built in the colonies before the Revolution. The first successful American type foundry was not begun until 1772, in Pennsylvania. A paper mill was put up as early as 1690 in Pennsylvania, by William Bradford and William Rittenhouse, but while it had a few successors in the eighteenth century, paper in the colonies was almost always in short supply. Thus, when the Townshend taxes of 1767 laid a stiff import duty on paper, the British government grew even less popular with American printers. The colonial journal generally consisted of a single sheet folded over to make a four-page paper about ten by fifteen inches. The print was often faded and uneven, and maddeningly small. Occasionally a woodcut decorated the title page—an arthritic-looking bird, fish, Indian, or nymph—and in later years a silhouette of a runaway servant or a sailing ship might call attention to an advertisement. The newspaperman worked within closely confining technical limitations. He had only eight to twelve columns a week, as a rule, in which to make his offerings. The surprising thing was how much variety he sometimes got into that narrow compass.

The news itself was primary. However small a percentage of the paper it occupied, or however trivial or stale it might appear by the standards of later generations, it was the distinguishing mark of the newspaper as opposed to the magazine. Defining the news was one of the tasks of the first generation of newspapermen, and from the start the idea took root that tidings must be current. Even John Campbell went so far as to print an extra sheet to his *News-Letter*, now and then, to make the news "newer and more acceptable." Campbell was a thoroughgoing editor, who felt that news should be a kind of history of the times, with no instalment left out. He tried to print whatever came to his hand concerning politics, war, trade, and diplomacy abroad and in the colonies. But the little *News-Letter*, even as early as 1719, could not accommodate all postmaster's information. What he left out of one issue, Campbell put into the next, even if it meant displacing more recent items, and gradually he fell further and further into arrears—as much as thirteen months behind the times. Plaintively he requested delinquent subscribers to pay their bills; with the extra funds, he said, he could enlarge the paper and catch up. It was at least a recognition of the fact that the news, as a kind of history of the times, was incomplete until brought up to the most recent possible date. Later colonial editors sometimes continued the practice of bringing stories to readers only in strict chronological sequence—a logical procedure if one viewed the newspaper as a species of historical tract—but by the eve of the Revolution a few began to run lately arrived dispatches to the exclusion of older ones.

In the search for news the printers did not hesitate to borrow freely and without credit from one another and from foreign journals. Most of the notices were brief and dealt with acts of the governors and assemblies, new campaigns against the Indians and colonial enemies, the commencement of new stores, mills, or other enterprises, late movements of shipping, possible political changes in Europe, and wars and rumors of wars. The foreign news came from the European papers, which arrived by sea after a two-month voyage. The other news came out of the mailbags (when the printer happened to be the postmaster) or the gossip of tavern and market. Local items such as storms, fires, epidemics, bountiful crops, cases before sheriffs and justices, accidents, weddings, births, and deaths—the staple of the country press for generations thereafter—generally came to the editor by word of mouth. It was generally served up without much order, in a fashion plainly suggesting that, as the entire paper would be read, it did not matter at which end one began.

When both foreign and local items were lacking, clippings from the "exchanges" filled the gap. These gradually came to play an important social and political part in colonial life. The mail service slowly expanded throughout the eighteenth century, hampered always by execrable roads, casual postboys, nonexistent ferries and bridges, and, occasionally, highwaymen. By 1753, when Benjamin Franklin and William Hunter were made joint deputy postmaster for the colonies, a system of postal routes linked the settlements from Georgia to New Hampshire, and the mail went through, even though the time between major cities like Charlestown, Philadelphia, Boston, and New York varied from five days to five weeks, depending on the distance. Many of the original postmaster-printers sent their own papers through the mails free of charge, a competitive advantage which they were not at all backward about exploiting. In 1758, however, Franklin and Hunter ordered that subscribers should pay postage for papers carried through the mails regardless of ownership, but papers "exchang'd between printer and printer" should go free.

This practice encouraged still further borrowings back and forth among the newspapers, and news of affairs in Savannah began to appear, however belatedly, in Philadelphia, New

York, and Boston, while observations on the state of affairs in Rhode Island would ultimately be pored over by Virginia's burgesses in Williamsburg. Through the exchanges, in the absence of any regular newsgathering system, the papers were beginning to create a kind of "national" news and to foster the first seeds of an intercolonial outlook. The newspaper in a postboy's saddlebag was an unsuspected "Americanizing" force.

If letters, gossip, and exchanges all failed, the printer could always borrow something for the impending edition from the almanacs, ready reckoners, legal handbooks, medical books, ballads, and sermons which lay in the office waiting to be run off. The tendency to make the newspaper something of a useful and amusing miscellany—a kind of little magazine with current news included—sprang from the owner's role as job printer. Often these extras considerably enlivened the newspaper, and the subscribers shared the educational advantages of the printer's apprentice, who spent his boyhood surrounded by a variety of topical reading matter.

The mere assembly of the "brief chronicles of the times" did not exhaust journalism's possibilities. Two or four pages of items running down the columns in unruffled summary of the week's news gave no sense of personality in a journal or its owner. There were tonalities and colors to be explored. James Franklin was one of the first to test the range of the new instrument. Early in the career of the *New-England Courant*, he undertook to insert a series of articles crisply attacking Increase and Cotton Mather, the learned but arrogant deans of Boston's clerical aristocracy. From a modern standpoint the printer chose the wrong issue. The Mathers were advocating the newfangled idea of inoculation against smallpox, and in opposing them the *Courant* was matching questionable preju-

The colonial hand press (*top*) could print, at most, two hundred copies hourly of such papers as the *Boston News-Letter* and the *Pennsylvania Gazette*. A flat-bed cylinder press like this one (*bottom*), made about 1845, when powered by steam could put out many copies of large journals. (From *The Growth of Industrial Art* [Washington, D.C.: Government Printing Office, 1886].)

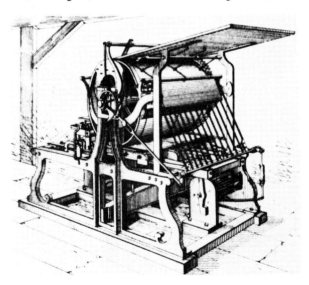

Ω. C.   Numb. 1.

The Boston News-Letter.

Published by Authority.

From Monday April 17. to Monday April 24. 1704.

London Flying-Post from Decemb. 2d to 4th. 1703.

LEtters from *Scotland* bring us the Copy of a Sheet lately Printed there, Instituted, *A seasonable Alarm for* Scotland. *In a Letter from a Gentleman in the City, to his Friend in the Country, concerning the present Danger of the Kingdom and of the Protestant Religion.*

This Letter takes Notice, That Papists swarm in that Nation, that they traffick more avowedly than formerly, & that of late many Scores of Priests and Jesuites are come thither from France, and gone to the North, to the Highlands & other places of the Country. That the Ministers of the Highlands and North gave in large Lists of them to the Committee of the General Assembly, to be laid before the Privy-Council.

It likewise observes, that a great Number of other ill-affected persons are come over from *France*, under pretence of accepting her Majesty's Gracious Indemnity; but, in reality, to increase Divisions in the Nation, and to entertain a Correspondence with *France:* That their ill Intentions are evident from their talking big, their owning the Interest of the pretended King *James* VIII. their secret Cabals, and their buying up of Arms and Ammunition, wherever they can find them.

To this he adds the late Writings and Actings of some disaffected persons, many of whom are for that Pretender, that several of them have declar'd they had rather embrace Popery than conform to the present Government; that they refuse to pray for the Queen, but use the ambiguous word Soveraign, and some of them pray in express Words for the King and Royal Family; and the charitable and generous Prince who has shew'd them so much Kindness. He likewise takes notice of Letters not long ago found in Cypher, and directed to a Person lately come thither from *St. Germains.*

⌐ He says that the greatest Jacobites, who will not qualifie themselves by taking the Oaths to Her Majesty, do now with the Papists and their Companions from St. *Germains* set up for the Liberty of the Subject, contrary to their own Principles, but meerly to keep up a Division in the Nation. He adds, that they aggravate those things which the People complain of, as to *England's* refusing, to allow them a freedom of Trade, *&c.* and do all they can to foment Divisions betwixt the Nations, and to obstruct a Redress of those things complain'd of.

The Jacobites, he says, do all they can to perswade the Nation that their pretended King is a Protestant in his Heart, tho' he dares not declare it while under the Power of *France*; that he is acquainted with the Mistakes of his Father's Government, will govern us more according to Law, and endear himself to his Subjects.

They magnifie the Strength of their own Party, and the Weakness and Divisions of the other, in order to facilitate and hasten their Undertaking; they argue themselves out of their Fears, and into the highest assurance of accomplishing their purpose.

From all this he infers, That they have hopes of Assistance from *France*, otherwise they would never be so impudent; and he gives Reasons for his Apprehensions that the *French* King may send Troops thither this Winter, 1. Because the *English & Dutch* will not then be at Sea to oppose them. 2. He can then best spare them, the Season of Action beyond Sea being over. 3. The Expectation given him of a considerable number to joyn them, may incourage him to the undertaking with fewer Men if he can but send over a sufficient number of Officers with Arms and Ammunition.

He endeavours in the rest of his Letters to answer the foolish Pretences of the Pretender's being a Protestant, and that he will govern us according to Law. He says, that being bred up in the Religion and Politicks of *France*, he is by Education a stated Enemy to our Liberty and Religion. That the Obligations which he and his Family owe to the *French* King, must necessarily make him to be wholly at his Devotion, and to follow his Example; that if he sit upon the Throne, the three Nations must be oblig'd to pay the Debt which he owes the *French* King for the Education of himself, and for Entertaining his supposed Father and his Family. And since the King must restore him by his Troops, if ever he be restored, he will see to secure his own Debt before those Troops leave *Britain.* The Pretender being a good Proficient in the *French* and *Romish* Schools, he will never think himself sufficiently aveng'd, but by the utter Ruine of his Protestant Subjects, both as Hereticks and Traitors. The late Queen, his pretended Mother, who in cold Blood when she was *Queen of Britain*, advised to turn the West of *Scotland* into a hunting Field, will be then for doing so by the greatest part of the Nation; and, no doubt, is at Pains to have her pretended Son educated to her own Mind: Therefore he says, it were a great Madness in the Nation to take a Prince bred up in the horrid School of Ingratitude, Persecution and Cruelty, and filled with Rage and Envy. The *Jacobites*, he says, both in *Scotland* and at St. *Germains*, are impatient under their present Straits, and knowing their circumstances cannot be much worse than they are, at present, are the more inclinable to the Undertaking. He adds, That the *French* King knows there cannot be a more effectual way for himself to arrive at the Universal Monarchy, and to ruine the Protestant Interest, than by setting up the Pretender upon the Throne of Great *Britain*, he will in all probability attempt it; and tho' he should be perswaded that the Design would miscarry in the close, yet he cannot but reap some Advantage by imbroiling the three Nations.

From all this the Author concludes it to be the Interest of the Nation, to provide for Self defence; and says, that as many have already taken the Alarm, and are furnishing themselves with Arms and Ammunition, he hopes the Government will not only allow it, but encourage it, since the Nation ought all to appear as one Man in the Defence

The Boston News-Letter *of 1704 was small, homely, and prosaic. (Courtesy, University of Chicago Libraries.)*

dices against sound scientific instinct. But Franklin's satiric little squibs exposed the pedantry and self-importance of Increase Mather in particular, who took to the columns of the *Gazette* to denounce Franklin and his impious young friends as members of a "Hell-Fire" club and to warn readers of the "libellous" *Courant* that they were in peril of brimstone. Franklin avoided direct attacks on the patriarch, but he did not hesitate to jab at some of the writers who took up the Mather case; young Mather Byles, for example, was denounced as "a young scribbling collegian, who has just learning enough to make a fool of himself." Eventually the battle died out, but James Franklin had been the begetter of a full-scale debate in the newspapers. He had shown how a community dispute could be brought into sharp focus in the columns of the weekly press, and he had blown both life and fire into the little world of Boston periodicals.

In 1722 the *Courant* blossomed out with a series of letters over the signature of "Silence Dogood," the anonymous work of Benjamin Franklin. Franklin admitted in his autobiography that they were frank imitations of the pieces run in the *Tatler* and the *Spectator* of Richard Steele and Joseph Addison, pieces which had amused a large London readership between 1709 and 1714. They also owed something to the journalistic writings of Daniel Defoe, occasional samples of which must have appeared in Boston by 1722. Like their British predecessors, Franklin's essays dealt ostensibly with a variety of subjects, trivial or serious, such as fans, drunkenness, coaches, widowhood—all in a style befitting the ephemeral nature of a newspaper. In an intimate tone they laughed at foibles which readers could easily observe in the daily life around them. It was as if a small circle of close friends were being addressed, and the few hundred readers of the *Courant* did indeed form a kind of club. They recognized each other in Franklin's caricatures, much as fashionable Londoners caught the personal nuances and allusions of Addison. The essays were short and therefore had to make their points quickly and pungently. They were shrewd and clear-eyed, turning the light of practical, middle-class common sense on men and manners; they aimed at correction and reform if need be, but above all at amusement. Both Franklins were forerunners of a chatty and personal journalism, admirably suited to win not merely subscribers but friends and adherents.

When Benjamin himself took over the *Courant* during James's imprisonment, he made his aim explicit. He created a mock figure, whom he called "the Author" (the term "editor" not then being in use), who would endeavor "to entertain the Town with the most comical and diverting Incidents of human Life," with an occasional "interspersion of more serious Morals." Yet "the Author" was to be more than an impresario at a carnival. He must understand the significance of the news which he retailed; as Franklin later wrote, he needed "an extensive Acquaintance with Languages, a great Easiness and Command of Writing and Relating Things clearly and intelligibly and in few Words," and he must be "well acquainted with Geography, with the History of the Time, with the several Interests of Princes, and States, the Secrets of Courts, and the Manners and Customs of all Nations." Franklin, in short, was outlining a creative and positive function for both editor and paper, eventually to flower in other hands besides his own.

The same vision of the newspaper as a vehicle of instruction and entertainment appeared elsewhere. Samuel Kneeland, in

The Colonial Printer and the Public Business

the *New-England Weekly Journal,* promised to solicit correspondence with "the most knowing and ingenious Gentlemen in the several noted Towns," who would send in "Pieces of History that may be profitable & entertaining both to the Christian and Historian." Samuel Keimer's *Pennsylvania Gazette and Universal Instructor in All the Arts and Sciences* took its educational job with deadly seriousness and began to reprint, piecemeal, a complete encyclopedia. It had only reached "Air" when Keimer went out of business. In 1731 Jeremy Gridley, "a young man of fine literary acquirements," founded the *Boston Weekly Rehearsal* with lofty intentions of making it a repository of beautiful letters. Gridley's style was mincing and full of grace notes, hardly suited to the mundane realities of newspaper publishing. After two years he turned the paper over to Thomas Fleet, a practical printer, who changed the name to the *Evening-Post,* dispensed with the rhetoric, and put the sheet on a sound footing. Franklin and Fleet, stepping in to retrieve the failures of Keimer and Gridley, both showed that the newspaper could not be purely didactic or artistic. It had to go beyond the bounds of the traditional book-reading class, reaching further out and deeper down into society.

As the newspaper accumulated years and acceptance, many subscribers began to send communications to it for publication. The editors were not sure what to do with these contributions. Thomas Fleet printed one of Wesley's sermons in 1741. When chided by an anti-Methodist Bostonian for this, he replied that several "Gentlemen of Learning and good Sense" had desired to have it printed, and he had done so because he had a "Prospect of getting a Penny by it, as I have by all that I print." But Benjamin Franklin, elsewhere, denied that "a Newspaper was like a Stagecoach, in which anyone who would pay had a Right to a Place." The argument over whether a newspaper was a public or a private vehicle for ideas would long continue, but significantly, as the century progressed, men with an argument at their pen's end began to look for newspaper outlets. It was cheaper, easier, and more influential to publish in a journal than to get a pamphlet printed. Gradually the newspaper-carried essay began to displace the pamphlet as a weapon of political warfare, and the papers ultimately fell heir to the pamphleteering tradition.

By 1760, then, the colonial newspaper had taken a recognizable form. One could expect to find in it a column of "Occurrences, or The History of the Times," an essay or two of local or imported origin on any subject from astronomy to turnip culture, a list of advertisements running from prosaic requests to buy so-and-so's fine laces to a modern-sounding claim for the wonders of some nostrum like Dr. Bateman's Pectoral Drops, the infallible destroyer of "Fluxes, Spitting of Blood, Consumption, Small-Pox, Measles, Colds, Coughs, and Pains in the Limbs or Joints." And always, poetry, the unfailing recourse of the eighteenth-century writer in the grip of mirth or malice—doggerel on the appearances of comets, the visits of dignitaries, the fall in paper currency, or the sins of rival printers. Perhaps the most important of all these rhymed flights of fancy, from a journalistic point of view, was the one which began: "A Newspaper is like a Feast; some Dish there is for every Guest."

For the newspaper had indeed become a unique kind of popular literary creation—something of a handbill, something of a public forum, something of a school of every subject on a down-to-earth level. Its model was English, but in England a

The Colonial Printer and the Public Business

stiff tax kept prices up and readership down. In the colonies the newspaper caught on because it so deftly suited the needs of busy men with a great thirst for practical information of every sort in plain terms. Subscriptions to the eighteen colonial weeklies in 1760 probably numbered only in the hundreds, but copies were read aloud in taverns or passed from hand to hand until dog-eared. All that was needed for the newspaper to emerge prominently from among the printer's enterprises was something to make the owners fully aware of the power of their creation. The British obligingly supplied such a catalyst in 1765 with the Stamp Act.

Colonial publishers felt the Stamp Act not merely as an abstract question of taxation without representation but immediately and drastically in their pocketbooks. The law, which laid taxes on various kinds of printed work running from a halfpenny on a "half sheet" upward, would have throttled the business of many printers if they had tried to issue their works only on paper to which the proper tax stamps were affixed. Few cared to try; any who did were threatened with mob action. Some papers disappeared for a time; others boldly appeared on unstamped paper, breathing execrations on the Stamp Act. William Bradford temporarily closed down his Philadelphia *Pennsylvania Journal*. His last number before the new tax went into effect carried black-bordered columns, a death's-head over the title, and the notice: "Expiring: In Hopes of a Resurrection to Life again." It was an effective device, often copied elsewhere. The *Journal* later reappeared, though not as colorfully as the *Maryland Gazette*, which put out successive numbers announcing that it was "not Dead but only Sleepeth," then "Reviving," and finally "Revived." The papers rivaled each other in running letters condemning the Act, with the *Boston Gazette* and the *New-York Journal* proving especially mettlesome, which was natural enough, since their owners were ardent Sons of Liberty. For the first time, liberty of the press was talked of widely and enthusiastically, and a patriotic New Yorker put his finger on more than one truth when he wrote that newspapers were "the Ark of God, for the Safety of the People. Their Fullness of general Entertainment, small Bulk and Price, recommend them to everyone, and . . . awaken the Minds of many to a solid Inquiry of interests they would not otherwise dream of." Many townships felt as Worcester, Massachusetts, did when it instructed its representatives in the assembly to "take special care of the liberty of the press." And when, after a bitter year of argument, resistance, stamp-burning, and boycotting, the Act was finally repealed, many were ready to ponder the words of another observer who declared that had it "not been for the continual informations from the Press, a junction of all the people . . . would have been scarcely conceivable."

The printers had not in any sense engineered the public resistance to the Act. But they had discovered how powerful the newspaper could be in consolidating, encouraging, and articulating such resistance. As members of the colonial business classes, they were of course sympathetic toward the "Patriot," or anti-British viewpoint. Their willingness to use their columns for revolutionary propaganda was not lessened by the discovery that circulation increased with the tempo of debate. By the eve of Lexington, some successful papers had circulation lists approaching two thousand. So in the long battle of words with crown and ministry, from 1765 to 1775, they became doughty allies of the leaders of insurgency. Their presses, as one historian has put it,

> trumpeted the doings of Whig [pro-revolutionary] committees, publicized rallies and mobbings, promoted partisan fast days and anniversaries, blazoned patriotic speeches and toasts, popularized anti-British slogans, gave wide currency to ballads and broadsides, furthered the persecution of Tories, reprinted London news of the government's intentions concerning America and, in general, created an atmosphere of distrust and enmity that made reconciliation increasingly difficult.

A hard-hitting group of printers found themselves becoming editors and propagandists. In Boston, Edes and Gill of the *Gazette* worked hand in glove with John Adams, Joseph Warren, John Hancock, James Otis, and Sam Adams, the Revolution's peerless propagandist. The *Gazette* printed innumerable letters by these men under such pen names as Candidus, Vindex, Valerius, Poplicola, and Mentor; the editor did not yet speak his opinion in his own person. The paper also knew how to appeal to a lower intellectual level. After the "Boston Massacre" of 1770, the front page featured a crude engraving (by Paul Revere) of four coffins, surmounted by grinning skulls, each bearing the initials of one of the Bostonians killed by British soldiers. Only the hopelessness of getting an indictment kept the governor from snaring Edes and Gill in the toils of a libel prosecution.

In 1770 Isaiah Thomas began the *Massachusetts Spy*, after a wandering career as printer and editor in Boston, Halifax, and Charleston. Quickly abandoning an intention to remain "Open to all Parties, but Influenced by None," expressed in his original masthead motto, he filled the *Spy* with such incendiary material that it was necessary for him to flee for his life when the British army took over Boston in April, 1775. From Worcester, however, where he began the *Spy* anew, he struck back with a "news" account of the Battle of Lexington, which began: "AMERICANS! forever bear in mind the BATTLE OF LEXINGTON! where British Troops, unmolested and unprovoked, wantonly and in a most cruel manner fired upon and killed a number of our countrymen, then robbed them of their provisions, ransacked, plundered and burnt their houses!"

In New York, James Parker, a one-time business partner of Benjamin Franklin, preached Patriot doctrine in his *Weekly Post-Boy*, fortified by previous experience in newspaper publishing in Connecticut and New Jersey. John Holt had begun a new *New-York Journal* in 1767 (John Peter Zenger's celebrated paper of that name having expired), and in it he printed such choice titbits as an alleged "Journal of Occurrences" in Boston in 1768, detailing the rapes and robberies perpetrated on the citizenry by the redcoats of the British garrison. In Philadelphia the two leading Patriot organs were the *Pennsylvania Journal* and the *Pennsylvania Chronicle*. The *Journal* belonged to William Bradford III, grandson and namesake of Pennsylvania's first printer. Bradford had large holdings in other business ventures, which he protected, in his view, not only by espousing the American cause in his paper but by later joining the Revolutionary army and rising to a colonelcy on his merits as a hard fighter. The *Chronicle* belonged to William Goddard, an able and independent newspaperman, who had already made a mark in Rhode Island and New York journalism and who was to move on to Baltimore and the ownership of the *Maryland Gazette* in 1773. Goddard was a fiercely free spirit. His contribution to the Revolution consisted of printing in 1767 John Dickinson's influential *Letters of a Pennsylvania*

The Colonial Printer and the Public Business

Farmer in the *Chronicle*. These cool and sensible strictures against British taxation of the colonies were widely reprinted in other journals. In 1773 Goddard grew dissatisfied with Benjamin Franklin's handling of the British postal network in the colonies. Promptly he organized his own excellent private system, only to see the Continental Congress ignore him when it set up an independent government, by making Franklin the first postmaster general of the United States. In 1777 and in 1779 he published criticisms of both the Continental Congress and General Washington and defied Baltimore mobs and Maryland judges to do their worst. A superbly unbossed man, he was one of the best of the scarce breed of really brave and original editors.

The Tories were generally unable to match the output or quality of the Patriot press, although this was partly due to the fact that the risks were considerable. John Mein and John Fleeming tried to found a Boston "royalist" organ in the *Boston Chronicle* in 1767, but Mein was hanged in effigy, beaten on the streets, and finally forced to fly to England. Mein and Fleeming insisted, it must be noted, that they were not Tory but neutral, and historians may be willing to give this claim more credit than it got from irate Bostonians in 1770. Hugh Gaine of the *New-York Mercury* practiced a perilous neutralism during the crisis. A frugal immigrant from Belfast and a New Yorker from 1753 onward, his obvious desire was to run his affairs without any trouble. When the British occupied the city in 1776, the best way to do this seemed to be to collaborate, and poor Gaine was lampooned throughout the colonies as a turncoat. The liveliest Tory editor, however, was James Rivington, a somewhat exotic figure among the practical printers of the time. Rivington was a well-educated

Londoner who had gambled away a fortune and come to the colonies to get it back in bookselling and publishing. Unabashedly aristocratic, he strutted among his bookstore patrons in a velvet purple coat and full wig, and in his *New-York Gazetteer* he swung freely at the "demagogues" of the popular party. Presently he was one of the best-hated men in the colonies. He was insulted, boycotted, and hanged in effigy; James Madison, in private correspondence, yearned to get his hands on him for only twenty-four hours; and the governor of New Jersey declared during the war that if Rivington was captured, he wanted one of his ears, the governor of New York should have another, and Washington, "if he pleases, may take his head." Rivington stood up to this stoutly enough and replied in kind, dubbing Edes and Gill's *Gazette*, for example, "Monday's Dung Barge." He could not hold out against the mobbing of his office in 1775, however, and he took refuge in England. With the British seizure of New York he returned to rename his paper the *Royal Gazette* and carry on the battle. There must have been something likable in him, after all, for when the fighting was over he remained in New York as a successful bookstore owner. So did Gaine, suggesting that good booksellers were scarce enough to have their sins forgiven. Though he met defeat, Rivington, too, had contributed much to the tradition of editorial independence, and he was entirely right in his claim that for many Patriots the love of a free press applied only to papers which agreed with them.

The Revolution itself was a valley of desperation for some papers and of opportunity for others. There were thirty-seven in the course of publication on April 19, 1775. Seventeen of them perished during the war. Eighteen more, begun between 1775 and 1781, died in infancy. But fifteen other new journals survived to bring the total to thirty-five when Cornwallis laid down his arms. The editors who remained in business struggled with paper shortages, a war-ravaged postal system, and, occasionally, military occupation. Where the British were in control, Patriot papers gave up the ghost. Where they were not, Tory papers were hounded into oblivion. The "American" journals which outlasted these vicissitudes continued to perform valiantly as agents of propaganda and unification. They printed accounts of battles and campaigns which gave their readers a sense of participation in a widespread effort. They publicized the acts of the new state legislatures and of the Continental Congress, gave space to appeals for recruits and supplies, and ran such important essays as Thomas Paine's papers entitled *The Crisis,* besides printing the texts of important documents like the Declaration of Independence. The circulation of the outstanding sheets increased impressively. The *Connecticut Courant* of Hartford temporarily claimed an astounding eight thousand readers in 1778. The appetite of the people for newspapers had increased by what it fed on. "One is astonished," a British official in New York wrote in 1776, "to see with what avidity they are sought after, and how implicitly they are believed, by the great Bulk of the People."

Everywhere there were stirrings of things to come. The seeds of the editorial column lay ungerminated in the comments with which publishers headed their columns of "late dispatches." Embryonic efforts to manufacture American types, presses, and paper were stepped up. Freedom of the press was less freely spoken about wherever the British had left—it was too handy a weapon, after all, for Tory editors to use. Nevertheless, the new constitutions of nine states embodied clauses guaranteeing it. The newspaper had come to stay. Many of its features were already hardening—its tendency to strike at a common level of understanding, its heavy reliance on advertising for revenue, its miscellaneous character, its dependence on freshness, and its tendency to succeed best in large cities. Other features were to change as it became something more than a mere sideline of the postmaster or public printer. Like the new nation itself, the newspaper of 1781 was ready to enter a period of experiment, innovation, growth—and dissension.

II

Politics and Press
in the Infant Republic

The United States in 1781 was something more than a geographic expression and something less than a completed experiment. For thirty-five years its chosen leaders wrestled with the job of mating bookish ideals and well-reasoned schemes of rule to non-literary and unreasonable realities. The questions involved grew out of the mighty choices to be made. In whose interest should government operate? What should the form of government be? Under the best of conditions those choices were racking, and they were not to be made under the best of conditions. Combustible social tensions of colonial days, smothered by six years of war, were reignited by postwar economic misery. In 1798 ten centuries of European feudalism began to collapse. The resulting shock wave of world war rocked American society, too. So Hamilton, Jefferson, Randolph, Taylor, Marshall, Gerry, Quincy, and Dwight flung arguments at one another, while pro-French and pro-English cliques, Federalist and Republican, planter and merchant, aristocrat and democrat, dueled in toast and ballad, in convention and legislature. Debate was hot, continuous, and needed. While it went on, restless men in the backwoods or on ocean trade routes added new imponderables of growth to the terms of argument.

The newspaper was part of this growth, responding to it and nurturing it. The newspaper, being a form of social communication, went wherever society was going, to the very limits of settlement. The newspaper served as a handmaid of commerce, and as commerce increased, the newspaper page grew in size, and in the largest towns daily publication became the rule. Above all, the era of the Revolution had made the newspaper a forum, and as a forum it had most to do. The newspaperman became not so much the printer as the editor, the publicity-making arm of political faction in the process of crystallizing into party. The best-known journals from 1789 to 1816 were partisan organs—more partisan than party—and their editors, for a time, gave the United States the nearest thing it ever had to a journalism of political debate. If the debate was finally muddied by insult, it was nonetheless conducted, often enough, with literary grace and intellectual boldness. The *Federalist* papers themselves originally ran as weekly letters to a newspaper, the *New York Independent Advertiser*. The "partisan organ" of Jefferson's day was apt to be the creation of an editor with a firm point of view, which he was willing to put at the disposal of gentlemen in public life who thought as he did. A money subsidy might discreetly change hands, if necessary, to keep the paper solvent, but only to buy ink and types, not ideas. This set it off from the later party sheets of the Jacksonian era. The latter, appealing to a larger and less literate electorate, aimed to provide common ground for disparate groups mutually hoping for better things to come, political or otherwise. There were really two stages of party journalism, just as there were two kinds of party system, one stamped with the mark of Jefferson and Hamilton, the other built by the rivals and heirs of Jackson. The difference between Philip Freneau's *National Gazette*, founded in 1791, and Thurlow Weed's *Albany Evening Journal*, founded in 1830, is the difference between the legislative caucus and the convention.

Boston, the birthplace of the American newspaper, found its journalistic scene full of ghosts and wreckage at the Revolution's end. The *Massachusetts Spy* remained at Worcester, Benjamin Edes carried on a *Gazette* which was only a shadow of its former self, and the *Evening Post, Post-Boy*, and *News-Letter* had disappeared forever. Although an *Independent Chronicle* and a *Continental Journal* had appeared, there was room for a new figure of command, and into that vacancy, in 1784, stepped twenty-three-year-old Benjamin Russell. Russell was in the tradition of the journalist trained at the composing-stick. He had learned his craft from Isaiah Thomas himself, served long enough in the army to acquire the title of "Major," and returned to Boston as a devoted apostle of nationalism and commercial progress. Gathering together a small stake, he began publication of the *Massachusetts Centinel*, and for more than forty years he made it the assertive voice of Boston Federalism. Begun as a biweekly, the paper eventually became a daily, like other emergent journals in the major seaports between 1784 and the end of the century. Russell kept the needs of Boston's mercantile group in mind, and the *Centinel* was always well up on shipping news and prices current. But the major had other ideas, too. His prospectus not only promised whatever might be "of public utility, or private amusement" but continued the grab-bag tradition of the preceding century. Variety was to be "courted in all its shapes, in the importance of political information—in the sprightliness of mirth—in the playful levity of imagination—in the just severity of satire—in the vivacity of ridicule—in the luxuriance of poetry—and in the simplicity of truth."

True to this promise, the paper contained not only liberal extracts from Massachusetts and Federal laws but excerpts from Goldsmith, Gray, Cowper, Cook's *Voyages,* and other staples of a gentleman's English library, along with sermons of diverse origins. But it was in the political department that Russell made his name. An enthusiastic advocate of the Constitution, he took down the proceedings of the Massachusetts ratifying convention with his own hand and published a series of crude cartoons of a temple called "the Federal edifice," with a new pillar being raised into place as each additional state ratified. He underscored the national outlook of his sheet by changing its name in 1790 to *Columbian Centinel,* and in the succeeding ten years he defended the acts of Washington and Adams with crusty vigor and poured out the vials of his wrath, in squibs, essays, poems, and letters, on the Jeffersonian Republican opposition—those "Jacobinic foxes, skunks, and serpents." The election of 1800 sent him into a frenzy of despair, and the *Centinel* published an epitaph for the "Federal Administration" wantonly done to death by the "Secret Arts and Open Violence of Foreign and Domestic Demagogues."

Russell recovered his spirits sufficiently to carry on his war with Republicanism for another sixteen years, when the "era of good feelings"—a phrase which Russell claimed to have coined—temporarily quieted the national political warfare. Until he retired in 1828 he could be observed in Boston streets in eighteenth-century smallclothes, carrying a gold-headed cane. Although he became a venerable institutional figure, he was not above occasional resort to the roughhouse tactics of a brawl between printers' devils. Once, in a furious debate, he spat in the face of a Republican state legislator and willingly paid damages of twenty shillings for the privilege. But if the newspaperman saved from his printshop origins the manual laborer's privilege of using his fists without losing status, he was nonetheless a gentleman. John Adams might growl, in a letter, that many newspapers in America were run by "vagabonds, fugitives from a bailiff, a pillory, or a halter in Europe." And, on the Republican side, a budding editor might be advised by a friend that he would be "more Honorably . . . employed by the Printing of Books." Yet the press leaders were needed and accepted. Honest Benjamin Russell's horizons might be somewhat limited, but in the snug craft of Massachusetts polite society he was clearly one of the complement of officers regularly entitled to a seat at the captain's table.

No one, by contrast, would have questioned the credentials for politeness and learning of another New Englander, who went elsewhere for journalistic laurels. This was Noah Webster, graduate of Yale in the 1770's, schoolmaster, lawyer, publisher, lexicographer, grammarian, and American. Webster's forceful literary talents had been demonstrated in writings on a variety of subjects, including medicine and physics, and a group of Federalist leaders in New York City in 1793, knowing him to be free for such a task, persuaded him to take the editorship of a new daily which they would subsidize. The appearance of Webster on the journalistic scene was a novelty. The newspaper had been the printer's creature. If the printer happened, like Benjamin Franklin, to excel in literary gymnastics, that was an added bonus. But that a young man of learning, with a diploma, should voluntarily seek an editorial platform was something new, conferring added respectability on the calling and foreshadowing the emergence of the editor, not the printer, as the king among newspapermen.

Webster's paper, the *American Minerva*, began in 1793 with a prospectus appropriate enough for a man whose spellers and grammars were to instruct generations of schoolchildren. Newspapers themselves, Webster declared, deserved an "eminent rank in the catalogue of useful publications" and should "like schools . . . be considered the auxiliaries of government." Webster was true to this conception, though he gave it a thoroughly Federalist interpretation. The backbone of the *Minerva*'s contribution to learning consisted of such fare as Webster's own series of letters (signed "Curtius") defending Jay's Treaty with England against the charge that it represented a surrender of American interests. Alexander Hamilton and Rufus King also contributed discourses in explanation and palliation of Federalist actions. After serving the cause of American nationality in the *Minerva* for four years, Webster departed in search of other platforms. It is noteworthy that the paper's new management elected to change the paper's base of support from politics to trade. Renamed the *Commercial Advertiser*, it dedicated itself much more fully to market news and survived in its new form for more than a century.

The resulting gap in Federalist journalism in New York

Politics and Press in the Infant Republic

was filled in 1801 by the *New-York Evening Post*. Hamilton, the colossus of Federalism, was behind the paper's creation; he helped to raise the initial funds for the *Post* and provided, until his death in 1804, much of its inside political information and editorial material. The man chosen to edit the new paper was again drawn from the world of polite (and conservative) letters. This was William Coleman, a native of Massachusetts, a graduate of Phillips Andover Academy, a classicist, a lawyer (onetime partner of Aaron Burr), a businessman (speculator in Mississippi lands), and a friend of such early American writers as Charles Brockden Brown, Joseph Rodman Drake, and Fitz-Greene Halleck. Coleman was no puppet. He imparted to the journal a literate and intelligent tone, and, more important, he always managed to fit into his pages the legal notices, real estate promotions, shipping lists, and prices current needed by New Yorkers diligent in their business. As a result, the *Post* outlived Hamilton, outlived the battles of the Jeffersonian era, outlived Coleman, and has in fact survived until the present day. Coleman tried to prove that in the United States a man of letters could find a theater for art and action amid the hurly-burly of getting out a daily paper serving the needs of a workaday world. He created a pattern long to be followed in the *Post,* for on Coleman's death in 1829 the editorial chair passed to the poet William Cullen Bryant, who filled it for another half-century. The personal cost of editorship for Coleman was high. Readers and editors alike in his day were, in Hamlet's words, somewhat "splenetive and rash." For his views Coleman fought at least one duel and was well-nigh crippled by a beating at the hands of an enraged opponent.

For Coleman, as for others, journalism as a branch of literature had certain inherent limitations of a frustrating kind. These were best illustrated, perhaps, in Philadelphia, where the journalism of polish and polemic had its outstanding opportunity. Philadelphia in the 1790's was a major seaport. It was the home of a group of brilliant native and immigrant scholars, many of the latter in flight from political upheavals in England and France. It was also the capital of the United States. It was thus a commercial, cultural, and political capital—the kind that drew men of scientific and literary attainments into politics, as Lord Bryce pointed out a century later, and the kind that the nation lost when the government moved to Washington in 1800. Philadelphia thus was ripe for a journalism conducted by poets, pamphleteers, and "philosophers," and the experiment was briskly tried.

The life of trade already, in 1783, had procured for Philadelphia the first American daily, the *Pennsylvania Evening Post*, followed by the *Pennsylvania Packet and Daily Advertiser*, filled almost entirely with advertisements. Then in 1790 the federal government entered the town, coming from New York, and with it came John Fenno and the *Gazette of the United States*. Fenno, a Boston schoolmaster, was anxious to "endear the general government to the people," and his desire to give the newspaper a national, rather than a local, basis was underscored by his willingness to transfer the paper, begun in New York, to Philadelphia with the administration. Fenno was yet another editor subsidized by Hamilton, whose own essays had filled newspaper columns from the time of his West Indies boyhood and who thoroughly understood the uses and possibilities of publicity. The *Gazette of the United States* began as a kind of court circular, and Fenno even had utopian (and unfulfilled) hopes of conducting it without advertising. Eventually, however, the columns became crowded with Federalist arguments, including such solid fare as John Adams' *Discourses of Davila,* a challenging but heavy defense of the Vice-President's kind of conservatism. Subscribers for this sort of journalism were scarce. Fenno was beseeching Hamilton for more money in 1793 and complaining that he was $2,500 in debt. Bailed out by the party, apparently, he was able to continue his particular political service until his death in 1798.

Meanwhile, Jefferson, looking about from his position as Secretary of State, realized the need of some public carrier for his viewpoint. To break what looked like a Federalist newspaper monopoly in Philadelphia, he joined with others in sponsoring the *National Gazette* in 1791. For editor he chose Philip Freneau, an ideal spokesman for Republican principles, a delightfully versatile warrior, full of verve and vitriol. Freneau was another of the new breed of college-taught editors. At Princeton he had studied classics and philosophy with such classmates as James Madison and Hugh Henry Brackenridge, a gifted satirist, lawyer, and Republican, later to play an important part in the journalism of the West. Freneau was primarily a poet. His intensely personal lyrics of nature and emotion foreshadowed the Romantic movement to come. His satires were less influential, but they sprang from genuine gifts of verse-making and were shaped by his political ardors. He was a passionate libertarian, believing that society might shed, in America above all places, its confining skin of outworn customs, faiths, and rulerships. A vigorous Patriot in the Revolution, he peppered the pages of various journals with satires directed at British generals, Tories, and other enemies of enlightened Reason. Occasionally, fettered by the restraints of the land, he took to sea as a supercargo and captain. One of these adventures ended in disaster during the war, when he was captured by a British cruiser and confined in a prison hulk to rot away for months before being exchanged. The agony of it confirmed his strong anti-British bent. In 1791 events stirred him to partisan passion once more. The French Revolution seemed a magnificent continuation of the promise begun by America's fight for independence. At the same time, the "capture" of the United States government by the pro-British and antidemocratic Federalists seemed to be a betrayal of all that Patriot armies had bled for.

Sailor, poet, wit, and philosopher, Freneau was a kind of *philosophe* with extra blood and bile in him—ready for war when he launched the *National Gazette*. It would, he promised, support "the great principles upon which the American Revolution was founded" and would help to prove that a "pure republic" could exist in a country of vast extent. This it would achieve by the "dissemination of useful knowledge," for Freneau was just as certain as his Federalist counterparts like Noah Webster that the truly illuminated mind could not fail to support *his* side. What would such a man choose to put into a newspaper? The first number contained an essay by Thomas Paine on the establishment of a mint; the late proceedings of Congress; a letter from Jefferson to the French National Assembly; some notes on the population of the Northwest Territory; a reminder that the Secretary of State still had some copies of a report on the whale and cod fisheries available at his office; and an anonymous poem, "The Prudent Philosopher." The items of "pure" news included a letter from the Spanish governor of Florida on immigration policy; a judge's speech to a Philadelphia grand jury deprecating the use of titles of honor in a republic; a note from Richmond on the gubernatorial election in Virginia; an item from Hartford summarizing a debate on the public lands of Connecticut; a report of an alleged election fraud in Savannah; and brief notes on the revolt in Haiti and affairs in Rome. The emphasis in succeeding issues continued to be on political and economic news of special interest to Republicans and emigrants to new territories.

Freneau gained his greatest notoriety from his red-hot assaults on Federalists. He denounced Hamilton as a would-be tyrant, Fenno as a toady and a liar, and even reached out to accuse the venerated Washington of kingly ambitions. The "first magistrate," he suggested, was possibly deceived by his "court satellites" into undervaluing the nation's pure republicanism. If he did not "think it beneath his dignity to mix occasionally with the people," he might learn better. When Freneau sent three copies of the paper containing such sentiments to Washington, the President's wrath at "that rascal" exploded. His temper was not improved upon hearing that Jefferson was the original begetter of the journal, but the Secretary of State declared that he had given Freneau nothing beyond a clerkship in his department, paying him $250 a year. This was not strictly true, and the nature of politically supported journalism is revealed in the measure of the untruth. Jefferson's intent, whether carried out or not, was to show Freneau "all my letters of foreign intelligence and all foreign newspapers" and to give him "the publication of all proclamations and other public notices within my department, and the printing of the laws." The Secretary's justification for thus subsidizing attacks on the President who had appointed him would have been that only such an organ as the *National Gazette* could "save our constitution, which was galloping fast into monarchy." Freneau, in turn, would have defended his shots at Washington by the claim that he had no other way to hit the malefactors who hid in the General's awesome shadow. In any case, the anomalies of the situation were resolved by 1793. Jefferson resigned from the administration, and Freneau gave up the *National Gazette*. With some fifteen hundred subscribers and not many advertisements, it was doomed without heavy subsidy, which was not forthcoming.

The vacancy in the ranks of Philadelphia Republican editors was soon filled by a figure as colorful in his own way as Freneau. Benjamin Franklin Bache was a grandson of Benjamin Franklin. He was taken to France by Franklin as a boy of seven, during the Revolution, and sent to Geneva. In that pleasant city which managed simultaneously to be cosmopolitan and Calvinist, he received his elementary education. Then, rejoining his grandfather in Paris, he was trained in printing, by the old philosopher's loving wish, at the press of M. Didot *père*, "the best printer in France." Music, philosophy, wine, and love were added to the unique curriculum of the emerging journalist here. Returning to Philadelphia, itself a kind of American Geneva just after the Revolution, Bache studied such topics as natural philosophy, magnetism, hydrostatics, logic, and universal history at the University of Pennsylvania.

He was ready for a career, but it was questionable whether society would allow him any career other than that of Benjamin Franklin's grandson. He had a birthright entry into social circles which included men like Benjamin Rush, William Logan, Robert Morris, and David Rittenhouse, but this did not necessarily help to set a young printer on his feet. The doors of public life were not ajar, either; the "court" of the new government felt, if anything, slightly uncomfortable in the presence of someone who reminded them that the late, revered Dr. Franklin had been a pro-French freethinker. The incoming Federalist tide left Bache in a side-eddy.

Politics and Press in the Infant Republic

With recollections of his grandfather in mind, Bache launched a journal in 1790, the *General Advertiser, and Political Commercial, Agricultural and Literary Journal.* Gradually he drifted editorially toward espousing the causes of the various "out" groups in Federalist Philadelphia—artisans suffering from hard times and high taxes, religious dissenters from Quakerism and Anglicanism (turned into Episcopalianism since 1784), spokesmen for the land-hungry, defense-hungry, road-hungry West, and Irish, French, and English refugees sharing a common distaste for "Anglophile" Federalist policies. The name of the paper was shortened in 1794 to the *Aurora,* and the tempo of attacks on Washington and Adams quickened. In the great battles over Jay's Treaty, the recognition of the new French revolutionary regime, and the Whiskey Rebellion, Bache's letters and editorial paragraphs waxed hotter and hotter. By the time of Washington's retirement, he was saying:

If ever a nation was debauched by a man, the American nation has been debauched by Washington. If ever a nation has suffered from the improper influence of a man, the American nation has suffered from the influence of Washington. If ever a nation was deceived by a man, the American nation has been deceived by Washington.

Such assaults were strange manifestations of a new, enlightened journalism, conducted by scholars, nationalists, and democrats. But the times themselves were out of joint and violent everywhere. Bache's office was wrecked by a Federalist-inspired mob, and Bache himself once had a street brawl with Fenno—Boston schoolteacher and French-trained university graduate punching and caning each other in full public view. The ways of the press were novel. Neither Fenno nor Bache, however, was a match for the germs of yellow fever; the epidemic of

1798 in Philadelphia killed both of them. Fenno's *Gazette of the United States* was continued by his son. Bache was succeeded by a man like himself, William Duane. American-born and English-educated, Duane had worked for journals in London, then gone to Calcutta, where he published a paper that sharply criticized the East India Company. The company, which then governed the future jewel of empire, had the last word. It confiscated Duane's property and sent him to England, whence he returned to the United States. Ripe in discontent, he was good raw material for Jeffersonian journalism. He took over the *Aurora* and continued it for many years, meanwhile marrying Bache's widow. The *Aurora*'s heyday ended, however, when the capital moved to Washington.

The Federalists responded to the attacks of Bache and the *Aurora* letter-writers by calling in still another tempestuous editor. William Cobbett's first sojourn in the United States left a trail of sparks through American newspaper history. Disgusted with corruption and jobbery in England, he had come to the new nation in 1792, supported himself at odd teaching jobs, and then become involved in pamphlet warfare. Various rebuffs from the Republicans had inclined him to the Federalist side, although as a natural controversialist he never belonged wholly to any faction. In 1797 he began the publication of *Porcupine's Gazette* in Philadelphia. It was a four-page paper, filled partly with advertisements and partly with devastating personal attacks on Bache and all the Republicans. These were motivated by a strenuous philosophy of journalism, announced in the first issue.

Professions of impartiality I shall make none. They are always useless, and are besides perfect nonsense, when used by a newsmonger; for, he that does not relate news as he finds it, is something worse than partial; and as to other articles that help to compose a paper, he that does not exercise his own judgment either in admitting or rejecting what is sent him, is a poor passive tool, and not an editor. For my part, I feel the strongest partiality to the cause of order and good government, such as we live under, and against every thing that is opposed to it. To profess impartiality here, would be as absurd as to profess it in a war between Virtue and Vice, Good and Evil, Happiness and Misery. There may be editors who look on such a conflict with perfect indifference, and whose only anxiety is to discover which is the strongest side. I am not one of these. . . .

. . . I have not descended from the Censorial chair merely to become a news-monger; I have not made that sacrifice for the sake of augmenting the number of retailers of small-beer politics; in short, I have not taken up that cut-and-thrust weapon, a daily paper, without a resolution not only to make use of it myself, but to lend it to whomsoever is disposed to assist me.

Seldom has the credo of the pamphleteer-journalist been so explicitly stated, and seldom has anyone excelled Cobbett in vituperativeness. He accused his enemies of bribery, blackmail, venality, concupiscence, intrigue, mendacity, and whatever other crimes his fertile vocabulary could put a name to. His rancor knew no limits. In castigating Bache, for example, he referred to the *Aurora's* editor as the grandson of a "crafty and lecherous old hypocrite . . . whose very statue seems to gloat on the wenches as they walk the State House yard." He ascribed Bache's financial straits, well known in the city, to the fact that the money formerly used to bribe him was now spent "in bribing foreign traitors," and he suggested that Bache's "cure" should be confinement at public expense on water and "bullock's liver, served out with a sparing hand," together with exercise in beating hemp, until "he should be decently tucked up in his own manufacture." Even Federalist fellow editors winced at shots so incendiary, and Cobbett's victims heaped libel suits upon him. The most celebrated of these, by Benjamin Rush in defense of his medical reputation, cost the "porcupine" five thousand dollars. This blow, together with other misfortunes, drove him out of the country in 1800, although he would be back for a less sensational visit in 1818.

Cobbett cannot be written off simply as a sharp-tongued villain. He was, in fact, an excellent reporter whose best work was not done in this country. He had a keen eye for detail and a devastating ability to get quickly to the point of an argument. His indignation flared easily, but he wore no man's collar and had a brave heart beneath his thick hide. The journalistic role of common—or, rather, uncommon—scold was later to be revived in the "crusading editor." Cobbett's passion for correcting the world's rottenness by exposing it in the most merciless detail and then denouncing it was the fruit of a hopeful radicalism. If his "cut-and-thrust weapon" could become at worst a mere sounding board for party propaganda, so an "objective" newspaper, like John Campbell's early *Boston News-Letter,* could be the pallid clipping file of a cash-register-minded "news-monger." Cobbett's kind of journalism had a vitality which later newspapers were to draw on, to their profit.

With such men as Webster, Coleman, Freneau, Cobbett, Bache, and Duane in the field, American newspaperdom in the two decades after 1790 appeared to be heading toward a pattern in which a few journals, supported by parties and conducted by scholars, wits, and men of polite (and impolite) letters, would debate the issues of the nation. But, for a number of reasons this was not the way things were to develop. The nation's geographic diversity worked against the idea of a constellation of leading papers concentrated in the capital city. The expansion of the United States, especially after 1815, bred regionalism and sectionalism. Successful journals, always dependent primarily on local support, tended to be scattered through the leading towns of the different sections, and their editors were inclined to focus on matters of local import. National viewpoints, if they existed, were first beaten into shape in St. Louis, Charleston, Cincinnati, New York, and Boston.

In addition, the major market for the newspaper, throughout the first third of the nineteenth century, was to be found among those men of affairs who wanted a journal filled with "news" of immediate utility to them. The tendency after 1800 was toward the shrinking and disappearance of purely literary offerings in the daily or weekly journal. The colonial newspaperman had been a printer, and as a printer he poured the productions of his press indiscriminately into a number of forms. Thus the lines between almanac, magazine, and newspaper had been hard to make out. Statistics, history, geography, advertisements, and "publick occurrences" were all "news" of a kind, as were topical or illustrative poems and essays. All found room in the hospitable "gazette" or "courant" or "mercury." But the expansion of American book publishing meant that "literature" could find a more permanent form. Then, too, the magazine made its bow on the literary scene—some seventy-five were founded between 1783 and 1800 and several hundred in the thirty-five years thereafter. Only a few of them survived, but they all absorbed essays, poetry, and short stories inspired by the American muse. And as the printing and postal facilities of the nation multiplied, the state and national governments were able to distribute official proceedings, papers, and documents widely, without relying so heavily on the newspaper as an intermediary.

The American Newspaperman

The newspaper therefore, in order to pay for itself, had to consolidate around a hard core of immediately significant or interesting news (local, national, or foreign), interwoven with advertisements. For the editor who was a would-be littérateur, this offered little scope. Sustained literary effort was difficult when the editor had to shoulder the burden of supervising the paper's business affairs and when he had to shift his attention from subject to subject as the changing pattern of the news unfolded. There was need for good writing in the newspaper press, but good *journalistic* writing—topical, quick, pungent, and descriptive. The discursive or imaginative writer could not make a newspaper the vehicle for his work without losing income, and few American gentlemen had funds to sink in a non-profitable literary daily or weekly. Those who had made fortunes could think of more productive uses for them.

Political subsidy was a partial answer to this problem. But the political party in the United States was not long inclined to support essayists who were masters of theoretical and philosophical discourse. As parties grew into widespread and popularly based coalitions, political theory faded into the background. The political battles of the 1830's produced no *Federalist* papers, no *Discourses of Davila*, not even a *Common Sense* (although Thomas Paine might well have felt at home among Jacksonian propagandists and journalists). The editor who received party backing after 1815 was not so much an expounder of principles as a clever manipulator of catchwords and slogans aimed at convincing multitudes that *his* party best supported those great truths which all Americans took for granted.

So the scholar-wit and the pundit were not to set the final form of the American newspaper. The Freneaus and Baches had to give way to men who were more sensitive to the demands of a medium which was always, in part, a practical business undertaking. Yet the essayists of the Federalist-Republican era left their mark on the national journalism. They did much to establish the primacy of the editor over the printer as the man behind the newspaper. They also played their part in building the general popularity of the newspaper press in the nation. That popularity was evidenced not only in the continued flowering of papers in the big cities but in the spread of journalism into the rural world in the form of the country weekly.

From its coastal birthplaces the newspaper crept steadily outward. There were 70 weeklies in 1790, 178 in 1800, 302 in 1810, and 422 in 1820. Which of these can be labeled "country" papers is a matter for argument; the great majority of them were published in towns of a few thousand or less. In New York State, for example, there were 77 newspapers in 1816, 11 of which came out more than once a week. Since the latter were unquestionably concentrated in the city of New York, the rest must have been at least semirural.

Many factors encouraged this growth. Settlers who had come from newspaper-endowed cities brought the habit with them. The decentralized American political system, with its constant round of county, state, and local elections, created a demand for news, notes, and arguments on public affairs. Merchants and speculators were anxious to have a means of advertising. Moreover, the possession of a newspaper gave a township a certain consequence, important to those lawyers, would-be legislators, bankers, and builders who had a stake in its growth. Civic leaders were thus ready, in fact eager, to encourage the establishment of local papers.

Nor was it difficult to find men and materials, if proper encouragement was forthcoming. The number of trained printers was always on the increase (enough so that Philadelphia and New York printers took to forming unions in the 1790's), and as it became increasingly clear in the larger towns that not every printer's apprentice was going to end up with his own shop in his native town, a number of venturesome typesetters were willing to try their independent luck in a new locality. The capital needed was not exorbitant. The old colonial hand press was slowly being modified and improved. In 1796 Adam Ramage had strengthened it by introducing a better screw mechanism for applying pressure to type and paper. An English version of the flat-bed hand press, using more iron in the working parts, was also available in the United States after 1800. Some time around 1813 in Philadelphia, George Clymer developed his "Columbian" press, which exerted pressure still more efficiently through the use of compound levers; and after 1820 the "Washington" press, embodying further improvements in this lever principle, found its way into many printing offices. As these better models were bought by affluent operators, used presses became readily available for a few hundred dollars. Second-hand type could be bought easily, too, as well as a stock of American-made paper. As a result, three or six or eight hundred dollars was enough to set a newspaper up in business. A small number of village benefactors could easily lend such sums to a printer. With the promise of advertising, job printing, publishing official notices, and an initial subscription list of two or three hundred customers, there was no lack of inducement for prospective country editors.

Besides, the Post Office Act of 1792 encouraged the spread of journalism by fixing the postage on papers at one cent each

July 10, 1776. NUMB. 2481.

The PENNSYLVANIA GAZETTE.

Containing the Freshest Advices, Foreign and Domestic.

IN CONGRESS, JULY 4, 1776.

A DECLARATION

By the REPRESENTATIVES of the UNITED STATES of AMERICA, in GENERAL CONGRESS assembled.

WHEN, in the Course of human Events, it becomes necessary for one People to dissolve the political Bands which have connected them with another, and to assume among the Powers of the Earth, the separate and equal Station to which the Laws of Nature and of Nature's God entitle them, a decent Respect to the Opinions of Mankind requires that they should declare the causes which impel them to the Separation.

We hold these Truths to be self-evident, that all Men are created equal, that they are endowed by their Creator with certain unalienable Rights, that among these are Life, Liberty, and the Pursuit of Happiness—That to secure these Rights, Governments are instituted among Men, deriving their just Powers from the Consent of the Governed, that whenever any Form of Government becomes destructive of these Ends, it is the Right of the People to alter or to abolish it, and to institute new Government, laying its Foundation on such Principles, and organizing its Powers in such Form, as to them shall seem most likely to effect their Safety and Happiness. Prudence, indeed, will dictate that Governments long established should not be changed for light and transient Causes; and accordingly all Experience hath shewn, that Mankind are more disposed to suffer, while Evils are sufferable, than to right themselves by abolishing the Forms to which they are accustomed. But when a long Train of Abuses and Usurpations, pursuing invariably the same Object, evinces a Design to reduce them under absolute Despotism, it is their Right, it is their Duty, to throw off such Government, and to provide new Guards for their future Security. Such has been the patient Sufferance of these Colonies; and such is now the Necessity which constrains them to alter their former Systems of Government. The History of the present King of Great-Britain is a History of repeated Injuries and Usurpations, all having in direct Object the Establishment of an absolute Tyranny over these States. To prove this, let Facts be submitted to a candid World.

HE has refused his Assent to Laws, the most wholesome and necessary for the public Good.

HE has forbidden his Governors to pass Laws of immediate and pressing Importance, unless suspended in their Operation till his Assent should be obtained; and when so suspended, he has utterly neglected to attend to them.

HE has refused to pass other Laws for the Accommodation of large Districts of People, unless those People would relinquish the Right of Representation in the Legislature, a Right inestimable to them, and formidable to Tyrants only.

HE has called together Legislative Bodies at Places unusual, uncomfortable, and distant from the Depository of their public Records, for the sole Purpose of fatiguing them into Compliance with his Measures.

HE has dissolved Representative Houses repeatedly, for opposing with manly Firmness his Invasions on the Rights of the People.

HE has refused, for a long Time after such Dissolutions, to cause others to be elected; whereby the Legislative Powers, incapable of Annihilation, have returned to the People at large for their Exercise; the State remaining in the mean time exposed to all the Dangers of Invasion from without, and Convulsions within.

HE has endeavoured to prevent the Population of these States; for that Purpose obstructing the Laws for Naturalization of Foreigners; refusing to pass others to encourage their Migrations hither, and raising the Conditions of new Appropriations of Lands.

HE has obstructed the Administration of Justice, by refusing his Assent to Laws for establishing Judiciary Powers.

HE has made Judges dependent on his Will alone, for the Tenure of their Offices, and the Amount and Payment of their Salaries.

HE has erected a Multitude of new Offices, and sent hither Swarms of Officers to harrass our People, and eat out their Substance.

HE has kept among us, in Times of Peace, Standing Armies, without the consent of our Legislatures.

HE has affected to render the Military independent of and superior to the Civil Power.

HE has combined with others to subject us to a Jurisdiction foreign to our Constitution, and unacknowledged by our Laws; giving his Assent to their Acts of pretended Legislation:

FOR quartering large Bodies of Armed Troops among us:

FOR protecting them, by a mock Trial, from Punishment for any Murders which they should commit on the Inhabitants of these States:

FOR cutting off our Trade with all Parts of the World:

FOR imposing Taxes on us without our Consent:

FOR depriving us, in many Cases, of the Benefits of Trial by Jury:

FOR transporting us beyond Seas to be tried for pretended Offences:

FOR abolishing the free System of English Laws in a neighbouring Province, establishing therein an arbitrary Government, and enlarging its Boundaries, so as to render it at once an Example and fit Instrument for introducing the same absolute Rule into these Colonies:

FOR taking away our Charters, abolishing our most valuable Laws, and altering fundamentally the Forms of our Governments:

FOR suspending our own Legislatures, and declaring themselves invested with Power to legislate for us in all Cases whatsoever.

HE has abdicated Government here, by declaring us out of his Protection and waging War against us.

HE has plundered our Seas, ravaged our Coasts, burnt our Towns, and destroyed the Lives of our People.

HE is, at this Time, transporting large Armies of foreign Mercenaries to compleat the Works of Death, Desolation and Tyranny, already begun with Circumstances of Cruelty and Perfidy, scarcely paralleled in the most barbarous Ages, and totally unworthy the Head of a civilized Nation.

HE has constrained our Fellow-Citizens, taken captive on the high Seas, to bear Arms against their Country, to become the Executioners of their Friends and Brethren, or to fall themselves by their Hands.

HE has excited domestic Insurrections amongst us, and has endeavoured to bring on the Inhabitants of our Frontiers the merciless Indian Savages, whose known Rule of Warfare is an undistinguished Destruction of all Ages, Sexes and Conditions.

IN every Stage of these Oppressions we have petitioned for Redress in the most humble Terms: Our repeated Petitions have been answered only by repeated Injury. A Prince, whose Character is thus marked by every Act which may define a Tyrant, is unfit to be the Ruler of a free People.

NOR have we been wanting in Attentions to our British Brethren. We have warned them from Time to Time of Attempts by their Legislature to extend an unwarrantable Jurisdiction over us. We have reminded them of the Circumstances of our Emigration and Settlement here. We have appealed to their native Justice and Magnanimity, and we have conjured them by the Ties of our common Kindred to disavow these Usurpations, which would inevitably interrupt our Connections and Correspondence. They too have been deaf to the Voice of Justice and of Consanguinity. We must, therefore, acquiesce in the Necessity, which denounces our Separation, and hold them, as we hold the rest of Mankind, Enemies in War, in Peace, Friends.

WE, therefore, the Representatives of the UNITED STATES OF AMERICA, in GENERAL CONGRESS assembled, appealing to the Supreme Judge of the World for the Rectitude of our Intentions, do, in the Name and by Authority of the good People of these Colonies, solemnly Publish and Declare, That these United Colonies are, and of Right ought to be, FREE AND INDEPENDENT STATES; that they are absolved from all Allegiance to the British Crown, and that all political Connection between them and the State of Great-Britain is and ought to be totally dissolved; and that as FREE AND INDEPENDENT STATES, they have full Power to levy War, conclude Peace, contract Alliances, establish Commerce, and to do all other Acts and Things which INDEPENDENT STATES may of right do. And for the Support of this Declaration, with a firm Reliance on the Protection of divine Providence, we mutually pledge to each other our Lives, our Fortunes, and our sacred Honor.

Signed by Order and in Behalf of the Congress,
JOHN HANCOCK, President.

Attest. CHARLES THOMSON, Secretary.

Little change in format marked the journal of 1776. A column was added, and advertisements appeared on the front page. The document reprinted in the first column got no special featuring over the "ads." (Courtesy, University of Chicago Libraries.)

The Hoe "lightning press" of 1847 (*top*), with the type revolving on the great main cylinder, put out the journals of the Civil War era, such as the *New York Times*. The web-perfecting, stereotyping press of 1875 (*bottom*), also made by the Hoe firm, contains the seeds of modern newspaper printing machinery. Printing both sides of a continuous roll of paper from solid, curved plates, it did not need the cumbersome feeding tables of the 1847 press and could use a smaller cylinder to achieve much greater output. (From *The Growth of Industrial Art*.)

and continuing the practice of carrying "printers' exchanges" free. The latter provision meant that any country editor could help himself without charge to news from papers anywhere in the country. The postal system was thus fulfilling one of its interesting positive purposes. More than a mere service for those who wished to communicate with one another, it was also supposed to be an active agent in spreading knowledge throughout the community at public expense—part of the system of national protection and promotion of the useful arts also exemplified by the patent and copyright laws and the reservation of portions of the public domain for schools. The postal system was widening too, with the number of post offices increasing from 75 in 1790 to 4,500 in 1820, and the mileage in post roads from 1,875 to 72,492. The rural editor could now take his place in what was becoming a national communications network.

The country paper was a curious production. Half of its four or six pages went to advertisements for everything from auction sales to singing lessons. The news was in part local gossip, but a goodly measure of it consisted of stories relating to enterprises of great pith and moment on the national and international scene. The country journalist could be a potent agent in linking the countryside to the city, the nation, and the world. An item from a Paris newspaper, recopied in a New York sheet and then printed again in the local press, would make Louis XVIII a familiar name around cracker barrels in Elmira and Weathersfield. Foreign visitors were often surprised, not only at the sturdy independence of the American yeoman, but at his generous stock of information on the doings of the great world. Landownership, the common school, and the newspaper all combined to lift him far beyond the level of the peasant. Moreover, the country weekly, frankly imitative of its big-city counterpart, was a bridge to great things. The local "literary man" tried his wings in the "Poet's Corner," or "Bower," and the ambitious politician practiced his arguments by casting them in the form of letters to the editor. The editor himself, a part of the community's professional class even when he was his own pressman and delivery boy, often dreamed of rising higher by moving into large-scale journalism, and sometimes he did. All in all, he played no mean part in breathing life into nineteenth-century American democracy, though city-bred wits liked to poke fun at him.

> Abreast the inn—a tree before the door,
> A Printing-Office lifts its humble head
> Where master *Type* old journals doth explore
> For news that is thro' all the village read;
> Who, year from year (so cruel is his lot)
> Is author, pressman, devil—and what not?
>
> . . . .
>
> Three times a week, by nimble geldings drawn
> A stage arrives; but scarcely deigns to stop,
> Unless the driver, far in liquor gone
> Has made some business for the black-smith shop;
> Then comes the printer's harvest-time of news,
> Welcome alike from Christians, Turks, or Jews.
>
> . . . .
>
> Ask you what matter fills his various page?
> A mere farrago 'tis of mingled things;
> Whate'er is done on Madam TERRA's stage
> He to the knowledge of his townsmen brings;
> One while, he tells of Monarchs run away;
> And now, of witches drown'd in Buzzard's Bay.

There were, of course, printers and printers. Many showed a tendency toward the restlessness of men who were fancy-free

Politics and Press in the Infant Republic

in the knowledge that they carried a paying trade with them wherever they went. Some, possessed of a considerable thirst, created a tradition that in an itinerant printer's veins ran equal parts of ink and alcohol. Country papers were begun and then abandoned by their begetters in the hundreds. Yet rural readership was a fact that could not be denied. Even big-city dailies were beginning to bid for it by making up weekly editions, composed of cullings from their own pages, and sending them out to "the country." There were four such "country editions" in New York alone in 1816, and the number was to go on increasing until late in the century, when the railroad made possible same-day delivery of the regular city edition to surrounding small towns. The country reader insisted on his paper, and this fixing of the newspaper habit in the public consciousness had much to do with the growth of the American version of the concept of freedom of the press. The newspaper was strong enough by 1820 to prosecute a bold claim for a privileged relationship to the government. But the claim was not made good without a long and strenuous argument.

The echoes of the Revolutionary debate over freedom of the press died slowly. The First Amendment, restraining Congress from "abridging the freedom of speech, or of the press," followed the lead of nine state constitutions. But what did these guarantees mean? Did they mean, for example, that government should not tax the press? The state of Massachusetts did not think so in 1785, for it imposed a levy of two-thirds of a penny on newspapers and other reading material. The editors cried aloud in protest and brought out the ghost of the Stamp Act to walk the ramparts. Isaiah Thomas changed his *Massachusetts Spy* to a magazine, and even faithful Federalist Benjamin Russell was bitter in complaint. In 1788 the legislature retreated, the *Spy* became a newspaper once more, and peace was restored.

Did "freedom of the press" mean the unrestricted right of newspapermen to report the proceedings of Congress? Certainly no official provision for such publicity was made at first, and as late as 1800 the Senate summoned William Duane of the *Aurora* to answer a charge of publishing "false, defamatory, scandalous and malicious" accounts of the chamber's proceedings. Duane's responses were unsatisfactory, and he was cited for contempt, but he escaped punishment by hiding himself for the duration of the session. It should be noted, however, that individual newspapermen did get access to the debates. By 1802 or thereabouts they had official permission to report them and recognition of their right to seats in the galleries, but only if they represented Washington papers.

Was the press free, in the new nation, from harassment by libel suits and under the common law of seditious libel? In the 1790's the answer was not at all clear. Press debate on all subjects was so furious and so personal that opportunities to bring personal libel actions into court were abundant. A more direct method of responding to individual insults was to seek out the offending editor with a club or horsewhip—or, if one was willing to consider his traducer a gentleman, to challenge him to a duel. (Benjamin Franklin humorously suggested that liberty of the press should be kept within the bounds of due restraint by "liberty of the cudgel.") The stormy history of press brawls and duels is due, in part, to the absence of more orthodox and formal methods of correcting newspapers which did not hesitate to accuse public men of such sins as theft, bribery, wilful prevarication, physical cowardice, or sexual immorality. Eventually—late in the nineteenth century—newspapers themselves restricted personal attacks, as political debate became less passionate and society grew more formal, organized, and integrated. But in the days when Adams men and Jefferson men genuinely believed that their enemies were seriously plotting to establish an American monarchy or to foment a "Jacobin" revolution against God, state, and property, the tempestuous nature of newspaper controversy made even liberal thinkers reflect seriously about the limits of a free press.

Jefferson's debates with himself on the subject are revealing. In 1787 he believed that the "good sense of the people" would furnish a check to would-be tyrants, provided the people were furnished "full information of their affairs through the channel of the public papers." Indeed, given the choice between "government without newspapers, or newspapers without a government," Jefferson preferred the latter. His remark has often been quoted without his additional proviso, that "every man should receive those papers, and be capable of reading them." Later, under the sting of vicious Federalist press attacks, he deplored the "abandoned spirit of falsehood" which had "destroyed the utility of the press." On balance, however, he was still willing to trust in the ultimate wisdom of the people. He would, he said in 1802, protect the Federalist papers in "the right of lying and calumniating," if only to prove that Americans were capable of "conducting themselves under a government founded not in the fears and follies of man, but on his reason." This idea stayed with him; in 1807 he was declaring that he had lent himself "willingly as the subject of a great experiment, which was to prove that an administration conducting itself with integrity and common understanding" could not be "battered down even by the falsehoods of a licentious press." However, he added in the same letter, he would leave others to restore the press to its strength "by recalling it within the pale of truth." What he meant by that is possibly made clearer by recalling that during his Presidency he countenanced prosecutions for seditious libel, under the laws of New York and Pennsylvania, against two especially obstreperous Federalist editors. Jefferson himself, moreover, encouraged and subsidized editors like Bache, or James T. Callender of the *Richmond Examiner*, who had nothing to learn about calumny from anyone.

Jefferson seemed to be saying that a free press was a noble institution when it told the truth but that it might be all right to encourage it in "truthfulness" through seditious libel actions under state law, or even to meet "calumniators" head-on by setting other "calumniators" against them. If his attitude seems somewhat erratic, it is because he had to reconcile his belief in freedom of opinion under a mild government with an apparent need for press control. The Federalists, on the other hand, were hampered by no such restraints. They deplored any liberty which became mere "license," and they were willing to use the power of government, and the central government at that, to save the country from the dire threats of their imaginings. Irritated beyond judiciousness, they brought on a crisis by passing the Alien and Sedition Acts.

These acts were passed in 1798, when war with France seemed close, and they bore some earmarks of hysteria. The measures regarding aliens gave the President wide powers of arrest and deportation and were aimed at the many French, Irish, and English fugitives from revolution and reaction who found congenial homes both in the United States and in Jeffersonianism. Some of these men were editors. Newspapermen were to be primarily controlled, however, through the Sedition

Politics and Press in the Infant Republic

Act. This provided that whosoever should write, print, utter, or publish any "false, scandalous and malicious writing" against the government of the United States, or either house of Congress, or the President, tending to bring them into "contempt or disrepute" or excite against them "the hatred of the good people of the United States" might be fined up to two thousand dollars and imprisoned for up to two years. Unquestionably the law was full of dark portents, ominous enough to create what one modern writer has called a "crisis in freedom." It brought the federal government into the sphere of control of opinion, whence it could muzzle opposition within the states. Fear of such federal power, as much as any devotion to free speech, underlay the resolutions of protest passed by the Virginia and Kentucky legislatures. The Sedition Act made part of the First Amendment meaningless and threatened to crush all free discussion of public issues under a Federalist-driven steamroller.

Yet the Act deserves a little further scrutiny. Its victims, during the two years it stood in force, were relatively few. Twenty-five arrests were made under it, fifteen indictments returned, and ten convictions secured. None of these last carried the maximum penalty. Inspired by the national example, Federalists in several states brought a few editors to trial on common law sedition charges. Some of these culprits were relatively inoffensive. An attack on a man like Dr. Thomas Cooper of England, a first-class scholar and scientist temporarily editing a Pennsylvania Republican paper, seemed to show that the Federalists were enemies to freethinking intelligence. But some were born to trouble as the sparks fly upward. Matthew Lyon of Vermont, an Irish-born firebrand, was a natural public brawler who later transferred his operations to the lustier sur-

59

roundings of Kentucky and Arkansas. James T. Callender, the English refugee who edited the *Richmond Examiner* in Jefferson's interest, was convicted after a flagrantly partisan trial under Federal Judge Samuel Chase. (The Republicans, when Jefferson was President, tried to impeach Chase for this, as well as for other high crimes and misdemeanors.) Yet Callender was a scandalmonger who later turned on Jefferson and originated many vile reports about the Virginian's personal life. William Duane, indicted but not tried, had known his troubles with government in England and India. The Federalists were not necessarily justified in trying to gag such men, but neither were these editors unwilling martyrs. They were used to paying for their strong opinions.

The Sedition Act, to be sure, did contain a provision conceding the principles for which Andrew Hamilton had argued in the Zenger case. The accused could offer the truth of his statements in defense, and the jury might determine the law (that is, whether the writings were actually seditious as defined) as well as the facts of publication and authorship. This did not entirely reduce the Act's power of harassment, for the indicted editor had to prove the truth of his charge "to the marrow," as Judge Chase put it, and even if he could perform so exacting a feat, the expense and delays of trial were a threat in themselves. Nevertheless, the language of the Act and the relatively small number of prosecutions seem to show that the Federalists were less interested in a wholesale war on the press than they were in silencing a few particularly galling critics whom they thought of as dangerous liars. The press *had* its liars, in point of fact, but the artillery brought to bear against them by the Federalists was clumsy and far too dangerous.

The Jeffersonians themselves were not above retaliation

against newspapermen, though *their* weapon was state law. In 1804 an action in common-law libel was brought against Harry Croswell of the Hudson, New York, *Wasp*. The specific charge was that Croswell had falsely accused Jefferson of paying James Callender to denounce George Washington, but Croswell's real offense lay in the fact that his pro-Federalist lampoons were thorns in Republican sides. Here one of history's delicate ironies made itself manifest. Alexander Hamilton, allegedly the archfoe of freedom and friend of aristocracy, monarchy, and repression, appeared for the defense. It was but a curious coincidence that he should bear the same surname as the defense attorney in the Zenger case. The Hamilton of 1804 argued brilliantly that the truth of a statement published with good motive should be allowed as an answer to a charge of libel, but more than that, he added, the press must be allowed to turn its scrutiny on public men as well as public measures if popular government was really to be subject to salutary checks. Hamilton lost his case, but his doctrine, that a truthful statement, honestly published, could be no libel, found its way into many state constitutions and statute books. That "freedom of the press" owes more to the great Federalist than to his democratic opponents is one of the vicissitudes of politics.

But freedom of the press owed still more, perhaps, to a slow change in public opinion, which came to identify the right of change and dissent with the right of an editor to say pretty much what he pleased about public men. (If a newspaper offended the pieties of the community, it might be mobbed, of course, but that was censorship of a different order.) Although criminal libel suits speckled the dockets of a few states in the twenty years or so after 1804, their number shrank, and in 1826 and 1828 two events took place, unimportant in themselves but significant in what they disclosed about the popular temper. In the earlier instance, an editor in St. Louis published a criticism, by a lawyer, of a decision of Federal District Judge James H. Peck. Peck brought both editor and lawyer before him, reprimanded the newspaperman, and fined the attorney. For this affront to the two majesties of the press and the law, the Senate of the United States moved to impeach the judge; it failed to do so by only one vote. The second event came to pass in Detroit, when the editor of that town's *Gazette* delivered himself of some uncomplimentary reflections on a local court. He was fined for contempt and, on his refusal to pay, thrown into the community's bastille. Whereupon, a vast number of sympathizers united to make good his fine (at contributions not exceeding twelve and one-half cents per person) and, on his release, tendered him a banquet in sight of his late prison.

Through all the excitements of the first forty years of the Republic, the editor was clearly not only a community fixture but a potential community hero. His paper might be scurrilous or mendacious or inchoate or tedious, as a goodly number of them were, but his countrymen were unwilling to leave the task of judging him to public authority. So long as they had a choice among papers—and the number of papers to choose from was increasing with every decade, reaching more than a thousand by 1830—they were satisfied to manage the editors, for the most part, by giving or withdrawing support. Alexander Hamilton had been farsighted, as usual, when he wrote in *The Federalist:*

> What signifies a declaration that "the Liberty of the Press shall be inviolably preserved"? . . . I infer, that its security, whatever fine declarations may be inserted in any Constitution respecting it, must altogether depend on public opinion, and on the general spirit of the people and of the Government.

Politics and Press in the Infant Republic

The "general spirit of the people" had spoken in favor of the unregulated newspaper. Yet while this gave the American newspaperman both freedom and opportunity, it offered no sure clue to how those opportunities should be used. The newspaper of the nineteenth century's first quarter was still a sheet of a few pages, with a circulation rarely running above three thousand. To survive in a growing nation, it would also be obliged to stretch, expand, and alter. But in what way? No one seemed quite sure of the right road to unlimited press expansion. The editor-owners, lacking a mass public, called on their various heritages and tried to reach specialized and differentiated publics. From the end of the War of 1812 until the mid-1830's they were busy attempting, modifying, blending, and rejecting different styles of journalism. In the process, special-audience newspapers devoted to commerce, religion, agriculture, reform, and politics appeared on the scene. The modern newspaper and the reading public felt their way toward each other on a number of separated fronts.

III

Special-Audience Papers
in the Early Nineteenth Century

One day in 1827, a weary traveler stepped ashore at a small town in Missouri, stretched his cramped legs, and went for an after-breakfast walk. Thomas L. McKenney, the United States Secretary for Indian Affairs, was finishing a long, hard trip up the Mississippi, conducting business with the Creeks and Choctaw tribes. Missouri was far from home in those days, and McKenney's delight, therefore, was almost indescribable when he found a packet of undelivered Washington papers in the local post office. They were, he noted:

> . . . another article after which one who has been accustomed to their daily presence is no less hungry, when deprived of them for several months, than for milk. . . . I literally devoured the newspapers; and every name I saw that was known to me about Washington, and elsewhere, seemed to be invested with new charms. I read every article, in every paper, and even the advertisements, and many of them over and over again.

Special-Audience Papers

This was the kind of reading appetite which the newspapers of McKenney's day were multiplying to fill. Only a few years later, Alexis de Tocqueville noted that in America there was "scarcely a hamlet which has not its own newspaper"—perhaps an exaggeration, though certainly not a gross one. In 1830 there were some 700 newspapers in the country, 65 of them dailies. By 1840, five years after the first volume of Tocqueville's *Democracy in America* had appeared, the total was 1,404, and 138 of these were dailies. Yet the number of "urban places" containing more than 8,000 people was only twenty-six in 1830 and forty-four in 1840. These cities embraced almost all the dailies, but there was still a generous number of papers spread throughout the "hamlets."

From 1815 to 1835 purely technical progress was slow. In general, even the most outstanding journals held closely to a four-page format and were issued in editions rarely exceeding one or two thousand copies. With the form and size of their instrument more or less stable, but with its popularity and freedom from restraint assured, the editors tested new possibilities in content and new roles for themselves. Society appeared to be comfortably elastic. A man of talent and ability could stretch it to accommodate his personal quirks fairly easily, if he proved a financial or political success on terms accepted by the majority. The newspapermen of this period were not giants in their communities, for the newspaper itself was not yet a big enough undertaking to sustain giants. But they were conscious of their growing power and could just sense, without precise realization, the tantalizing possibilities ahead—like mariners catching the first offshore breeze laden with the scent of some fabled kingdom still over the horizon. The best of them were adventurous, self-centered, and articulate—not giants, perhaps, but certainly originals.

The regional muse in a growing country was a practical one; she enlisted in her service writers and printers who were clearly men of the world, as early journalism in the West demonstrated. The first trans-Allegheny newspaper was the *Pittsburgh Gazette*. Its press was perilously hauled across the mountains in a wagon, in time for a first issue in 1786, and its first stock of paper came by pack-horse train. Its owners, Joseph Hall and John Scull, were merely printers seeking a market for their skills in the new Jerusalem of the Northwest. They had been given a flattering view of the prospects for journalism in Pittsburgh by Hugh Henry Brackenridge. That scholar and novelist had moved to Pittsburgh to become a lawyer, judge, political organizer, land and townsite speculator, and propaganda-maker for the rising glory of the new territories. The *Gazette* was in part his creation, and when Scull and Hall showed an "ungrateful" independence by embracing his enemies, the Federalists, Brackenridge found himself another printer to begin a newspaper devoted to Jeffersonianism.

The links between journalism, politics, and promotion were strong, and the western journalist was not supposed to exercise a fugitive and cloistered virtue but to stir himself in advancing the fortunes of a new settlement. He was in much the same position as the editor of the country weekly in the more populous states, but the interests he served were likely to be larger in scope, commonwealth or section-sized rather than cut to the measure of a township. In 1786, for example, the settlers of Kentucky, then only the western district of Virginia, were eager for separate statehood with its promise of self-government and economic growth under a friendly legislature. Among the residents of Lexington, the largest town in the district, was John Bradford, a Virginia surveyor who decided that a newspaper was a necessary and useful testimony to a region's maturity and readiness for independence. Bradford sent one of his brothers to Pittsburgh to learn printing and ordered type and press from Philadelphia. The equipment had a hazardous trip of it, and brother Fielding Bradford may have experienced his own difficulties as an apprentice, but both press and printer were ready, in April of 1787, to issue the first number of the *Kentucke Gazette* (the spelling was modernized a few years later). Disdaining to run much local news, the *Gazette* was filled mainly with advertisements, notices of new arrivals and projects in Kentucky, political tidings bearing on Kentucky's future, and editorials demanding the blessings of statehood. Carried free through the postal system to other editors and clipped by them for reprinting, the *Kentucke Gazette* did its part in enlightening the rest of the country on the would-be commonwealth's just requirements.

Similar service in voicing the aspirations of Ohio, Tennessee, and Mississippi was rendered by other western papers of the 1790's, such as the *Centinel of the Northwestern Territory*, founded in Cincinnati in 1793, the *Knoxville Gazette*, dating from 1791, and the *Mississippi Gazette*, born in Natchez in 1799. Even after statehood had been achieved, the "western" paper was charged with the offices of publicity. It was duty-bound to note the coming of consignments of merchandise, the first sizable export of some cash crop like hemp or pork or whiskey, the change in ownership of particularly significant parcels of land or (in the Southwest) Negroes, and the initial appearances in various sections of such agents of progress as schoolmasters, preachers, bankers, doctors, and, in due time, steamboats. These were the backbone of the "news." The printers were often staked to their four or five hundred dollars' worth of used hand press and type by some aspiring politician, and if the amateur statesman was successful at the polls, then the new paper got the public printing contract. As in colonial days, this was an important source of revenue when presses were still few and laws and announcements had to be newspaper-carried. The link between pioneer printer and legislature was forged again as territories recapitulated the life-history of the original colonies, from "plantation" to state. Evidence is seen in the popularity of the title of "Gazette" for a new journal. The first editor in a territory often pre-empted both the name and the official function it suggested. The *Indiana Gazette* appeared in Vincennes in 1804, the *Missouri Gazette* in St. Louis in 1808, and the *Detroit Gazette* in the city of that name in 1817. Successors looked for other names, but their new papers were no less tightly tied than the "Gazettes" to the furtherance of local fortunes. The *St. Louis Enquirer* (founded in 1815 as the *Western Journal*) soon found an editor in Thomas Hart Benton, then beginning a long career as the political colossus of Missouri. On the national scene he was to become the leading Senate spokesman for Jackson, cheap lands, an improved internal transportation system, and other things close to western hearts. The *Illinois Emigrant*, the second paper in that state, was edited from 1820 to 1822 by James Hall. Hall was a Philadelphian who moved to Illinois to become an important precursor of "western" literature. Long before public relations was an organized business, the West had the benefit of a tireless press agent in Hall. He published a volume of letters describing the natural wonders and promises of the region; he collected its folklore and tall tales and published them in book and magazine form; he encouraged and raised funds for its founders of academies, universities, libraries, museums, and presses; and he did all this while pursuing a career in law, politics, and business.

With men like Brackenridge, Benton, and Hall guilding western newspapers even temporarily, the place of those papers in the spectrum of "promotions" is clear. Their sponsors were the men who also became, in growing communities, directors of banks and insurance companies, trustees of benevolent and educational institutions, and perennial commencement speakers. For them the newspaper was simply another device for shaping and imparting life to their adolescent cities. It might contain only a few columns of purely political and commercial news, and many advertisements, but in that form it did its necessary "booster's" job.

In the older South, a sectional journalism emerged only imperfectly, for the ways of the South were not the ways of the city, and journalism was made for the town. In Richmond, Thomas Ritchie of the *Enquirer* used that paper to assist him in a long career as a Virginia political nabob, first for the Jeffersonian Republicans and later for the Democrats. Ritchie was not only a power in legislative caucuses but a necessary part of every public meeting, ball, and banquet in Richmond—greeting, nodding, taking notes, proposing toasts, a kind of genial personification of the civic spirit but close enough to the plantation to preserve its country-squire manners. Editor, citizen, and politician were at one in him, as in Thomas Hart Benton. In 1824 Ritchie encountered opposition in the form of the *Richmond Whig*, edited by John H. Pleasants. This gave the excitement of combat to the Richmond newspaper scene, and not mere combat of words, either; in 1846 Ritchie's son killed Pleasants in a savage sword-and-pistol duel. Charleston also knew the fireworks of newspaper debate in the 1820's and 1830's when the solid, mercantile-minded *Charleston Courier*, a pro-Union organ, warred with the *Charleston Mercury*, dedicated to nullification of the national tariff even at the cost of disunion. New Orleans had a few papers filled with prices current and buyers' arrivals for the convenience of its shipping community. But by and large there was no significant southern newspaper tradition, and virtually no southern newspapermen achieved national prominence before the Civil War, unless Baltimore is considered a southern city.

While regional journalism was spreading across the land, mercantile newspapers began to take on new life in the 1820's. As the political turbulence of the century's first fifteen years subsided into the illusory calm of the "era of good feelings," stability seemed the reward of those editors primarily concerned with the life of trade. Political factions might come and go, but commercial exchange endured. Such papers as the *New York Commercial Advertiser*, successor to Webster's *American Minerva*, or *Poulson's American Daily Advertiser* in Philadelphia, enjoyed a lasting life that invited imitation. Half of all the daily papers in existence in 1810 and 1820 bore the word "Advertiser" in their names, and not inappropriately, since 60 to 80 per cent of their contents consisted of advertising matter. Their editors, too, were working on behalf of a kind of non-regional community, composed of merchants, manufacturers, and investors in trade centers such as Boston, New York, Philadelphia, and Baltimore. The size, the format, and the content of the mercantile papers all bespoke the growth and diversification of national economic life and the changing outlooks of the businessmen who furnished custom for the commercial daily press.

New York, marching resolutely toward the leadership among the nation's ports, got three new commercial organs in 1826 and 1827. These were the *New York Courier,* the *New York Enquirer* (both of which were merged into one paper in 1829), and the *New York Journal of Commerce.* The last-named began life under the ownership of Arthur Tappan, who represented a new kind of New York merchant. The old lords of Father Knickerbocker's wharves had been haughty, High-Church, and Federalist, riding to their countinghouses with chins held high and a liveried Negro boy behind the coach. Their ships were stout and slow sailers, rarely venturing beyond the West Indies or the Mediterranean. Tappan belonged to a newer age of firms like the Tappan Brothers, Grinnell and Minturn, Howland and Aspinwall, Phelps and Dodge. Their investments were wider and more adventuresome, their vessels were fast packets and clippers, and their traffic was in the teas, silks, and spices of the Orient, the coffee and fruit of Latin America, the cotton of New Orleans and Liverpool. Naturally, such men wanted bigger and better papers to bring them the latest intelligence of world markets and movements and of those political ups and downs which affected the flow of the earth's goods among her traffickers in merchandise. The newer mercantile aristocracy of New York also tended to be more sober in dress and more evangelical in their piety, as befitted the rural beginnings of many of them. Tappan, who gave generous sums to finance revival meetings in New York and the reform societies which grew out of them, accordingly designed the *Journal of Commerce* to be a paper with a high moral tone. It refused to print advertisements for liquor and the theaters (though not for villainous patent medicines) and managed to provide an air of earnestness along with prosaic notices of the latest arrivals in the Narrows of New York's lower bay.

Yet New York's journalism of trade did not belong exclusively to the devout. There was Mordecai M. Noah, who founded the *Courier* in 1826. Far from disdaining the theater, Noah loved nothing better than to attend and write plays. Far from being a revivalistic Christian, he was a Jew who had once announced his intention of founding a new homeland for the harassed children of Moses on Grand Island, in the Niagara River near Buffalo. Appointing himself the first governor and judge over Israel, he laid out on the island a city named Ararat, in 1825 solemnly dedicated the site after a procession through Buffalo's streets, and issued a proclamation inviting the world's Jewry to settle on Grand Island as the nucleus of the revived "Jewish Nation, under the auspices and protection of the constitution and laws of the United States of America." No Jew ever came, but Noah had a glorious, theatrical time of it and plenty of publicity, which he understood. He had also served, at various times, as American consul to Tunis, sheriff of New York County, and judge of the New York Court of Sessions. After three years of editing the *Courier*, Noah merged his paper with the *Enquirer* of James Watson Webb, a terrible-tempered former army officer whose street fights, duels, and arrests furnished better copy for the New York press than did many events of greater gravity.

The mercantile organs were not entirely devoid of news or opinion. The *Courier and Enquirer*, to take only one example, ran admirable reports from Washington on the future of legislation affecting currency, the tariff, and transportation. Moreover, most of the commercial papers carried brief editorial columns which yielded nothing in heat or firmness to anyone when the issues touched closely on economic life. But with the years the pressure of increasing advertising on limited space, along with a certain rigidity of old habits, made the mercantile sheets ungainly and expensive.

Part of this ungainliness was unavoidable because press technology changed slowly. The classic hand press squeezed a flat surface, or platen, down upon a sheet of paper laid on top of inked type, using either a screw or combination of levers to develop pressure. About 1811 a German, Frederick Koenig, replaced the platen with a cylinder, under which the bed of type rolled back and forth, picking up ink and fresh paper with each trip. Adding a second cylinder made it possible to print both sides of a sheet rapidly, and as early as 1814, moving the apparatus by steam added appreciably to the speed of production. Whereas hand-press operators had to grunt and strain at their levers to print a maximum of 200 impressions (on one side) an hour, the Koenig press of 1814 could print 550 sheets, top *and* bottom, in the same length of time. Modifications of the cylinder press by David Napier of England reached the United States by 1824, and by 1830 the New York firm of Robert Hoe and Son, pressmakers, had developed a version of the Napier double-cylinder, self-inking press which could deliver between one and two thousand "perfected" (printed on both sides) sheets an hour. Because the machinery for collating and folding separate sheets had not yet been developed, the most efficient way to use this new output was still the old-fashioned one of hand-folding the printed sheet in half to make a four-page paper. A press run of some three hours could thus produce as many as 4,500 completed copies of a daily in 1830—more than enough for all but the circulation "giants" like the

Courier and Enquirer, which claimed that figure at about this time.

In order to get more material into these single-sheet papers, printers enlarged the sheet to allow for more columns and reduced the size of the type. The mercantile papers, therefore, tended to become monstrosities—"blanket sheets," they were called—as much as two feet wide and a yard long, folded. Across each of these giant pages ran six to eight wide columns, and down each column ran an inky rope-ladder of advertisements set in "squares" an inch or so in depth. In minute letters the business of New York cried out to be transacted. Shipowners besought cargoes; jobbers offered to buy and sell commodities in wholesale lots; farmers described acres for sale; retailers announced the supremacy of their hats, shoes, coal, garden seeds, coffins, cork legs, and cough medicines; insurance agents, hotels, renters, carriage-makers, roof-repairers, theatrical producers, music teachers, and quack doctors all promised satisfaction. The town was growing, and its needs were increasingly catered to by specialists and furnishers of ready-made goods. There was no variety of display in these advertisements, not even much prominence given to merchant's names or any conspicuous advocacy of the merits of "brands." Essentially they were *notices* of wares on the market rather than appeals to the imagination of prospective buyers. The mercantile paper was chiefly a clearinghouse for all such notices.

Because these advertisements were still of interest to a relatively small class with free income to spend, the commercial dailies did not aim for a large, low-income reader market. The owners were seemingly content to work for a restricted audience. If their organs were not things of beauty or wit, they did what was needful for the merchants and were creatures of utility. Papers sold for five or six cents, or ten to fourteen dollars a year by subscription. The annual cost amounted to two or three weeks' pay for a workingman, effectively discouraging him as a customer. Individual copies were bought at the printing office, or carriers delivered papers to homes, with the mails used to reach outlying districts. The advertising rate policy of the blanket sheets was not aggressive. Though each "insertion" of an advertisement cost up to fifty cents, a businessman willing to let the same notice stand unchanged indefinitely could get that service for thirty-five to fifty dollars a year. For this reason commercial newspapers, while giving up to four-fifths of their space to advertisements, earned less than half their revenue from that source. These figures, like all circulation and income figures for the period before the Civil War, are at best hazy approximations. Blurred as they are, however, they do show that the various "Commercials" and "Advertisers" were primarily expensive bulletin boards for a small trading clientele. The margins of the bulletin board were given over to news and editorials, both designed to assist the reader in judging the significance of the posted notices.

Yet even on these restricted terms, the mercantile press had contributions to make. Its editors were often spokesmen for a viewpoint profoundly important in the growing nation. They trumpeted the glories of nationalism and industrialism, and involved the pride of Americans with economic expansion. The nonpareil among them was Hezekiah Niles, whose *Niles' Weekly Register* of Baltimore straddled the fence between newspaper and magazine. Niles crammed his pages with statistics, reports, tables, legislative documents, official messages, and company prospectuses, all presented with a glowing, hand-rubbing satisfaction in the progress they showed. The

Register burst into pyrotechnics of editorial praise for a newly opened canal, a recently discovered market for fish or lumber, a textile factory just commencing operations, a projected railroad from an inland coal mine to a seaport. For over a third of a century, from 1811 to 1848, it set a pattern for a national business journalism which became important as a carrier of attitudes and a spur to investment. Though the *Register* appeared in Baltimore, it did for the nation at large what some western papers did for the entrepreneurial classes of their communities, and if, like the modern *Wall Street Journal* (which it somewhat foreshadowed), it could have been simultaneously printed in several cities throughout the land, it would have lost nothing by detachment from its local base.

Elsewhere, too, the mercantile sheets gave a platform to spokesmen for a national point of view. A. S. Willington's *Charleston Courier* used whatever space it had left over from advertising ship departures and plantations for sale to battle South Carolina disunionism. In Boston, Nathan Hale's *Daily Advertiser* and Joseph T. Buckingham's *Courier* defended the viewpoint of the New England version of the Whig party which emerged during the 1830's. Since this viewpoint was national, institutional, rational, and conservative (whatever curious forms it might take at the polls), these papers found it consistent with their mercantile pursuits to leave room for the political, religious, and literary criticism of such men as Edward Everett, Jared Sparks, and William Ellery Channing. The advertising content was still predominant but did not necessarily flatten the tone set by these contributors.

Another achievement of the mercantile newspapermen was the launching of efforts to speed up the flow of news. Readers had to know as quickly as possible what favoring breezes or what storms blew upon their ventures. In 1811 Samuel Topliff, then working for a coffee house in Boston which kept a file of newspapers on hand for its businessmen patrons, began sending out a small boat to meet incoming vessels and take the mails from them. By the time the arriving ship had been piloted to her berth and cleared by customs, immigration, and quarantine officials, Topliff's customers could be comfortably scanning the latest journals from Europe over their cups and saucers. Willington of the *Charleston Courier* adopted this practice soon afterward, and by 1827 half a dozen New York papers had joined in supporting a "press boat" to collect foreign news from ships standing off the harbor's entrance. Internal quarrels in that year broke up this primitive press association, but several sheets had their individual fast little sailing craft racing each other to the docks until the era of the telegraph. A few enterprising journals occasionally arranged for special postriders to bring particularly topical items, like the text of a presidential address, from Washington faster than the mails could do the job, and all the newspapers kept up a steady pressure for improvement on the postal department. The *Courier and Enquirer* even made arrangements as early as 1828 for regular letters from a man in Washington. Two of these first Washington correspondents were James Gordon Bennett, later to stir the newspaper world in other capacities, and Matthew Davis, himself a businessman of solid social pedigree. Glimmers of things to come—quick news transmission, syndication, and special correspondents—thus were flickering even over the world of the predominantly businessmen's newspapers, for all their restricted ambitions and class-bound visions of their duty.

The American Newspaperman

The borderline between "mercantile" and "political" journalism was never boldly marked and guarded, it must be remembered. Even those newspaper owners who agreed that commercial patronage was "the best, safest, and most unchanging of any," dealt in party debate in their "editorial paragraphs." Conversely, papers whose reasons for being were transparently partisan needed the income of advertising and gave it plenty of elbowroom. Yet with the revolution in the nature of parties which took place beginning roughly with Jackson's administration, a new kind of political editor came to the fore. From the days of the colonial public printer, the newspaper had served governments as a channel of communication. The pamphleteer-journalists of the day of Cobbett and Bache had given voice to certain conceptions of public virtue and vice. The party journalist of the 1830's and 1840's did both these things, but in addition he served as the agent of an *administration*. The tasks of government itself were unchanging; but with the coming of more broadly based political coalitions and the spoils system, those tasks were carried out by a constantly changing cast of officeholders, renewed by biennial or quadrennial purges. New groups of voters had to be organized through national, state, and local committees, and standard-bearers chosen at every official level from wards and precincts upward in a bewildering series of conventions. The party paper became an element in the management of political life, and the official printer who conducted it found his way into executive councils.

A bridge between the old and the new political journalism was provided by the *National Intelligencer* of Washington. In Jefferson's first administration it belonged to his friend and kindred spirit, Samuel Harrison Smith, a Virginian full of

Special-Audience Papers

schemes for universal education and at home equally in a literary or a political circle. After some initial difficulties Smith, an excellent shorthand reporter, was given permission to record the deliberations of Congress, which he printed, in part, in the *Intelligencer*. He also got the contracts for many of the official publications of the federal government, and became something of an authorized spokesman and trial-balloon-launcher for the President. Tiring of newspaper life in the capital, in 1810 he sold the paper to Joseph Gales, Jr., and William W. Seaton, both of them well equipped to carry on in his tradition. They continued to report congressional oratory in full, and in fact their transcripts, bound and published in 1834 as the *Annals of Congress*, are the only reasonably full record of the debates in the earliest Congresses. The official printing of congressional proceedings continued to be farmed out privately until the Government Printing Office initiated the *Congressional Record* in 1873. Gales and Seaton were both large landowners, gracious hosts to Maryland and Virginia society, rich in civic responsibility (each serving for a time as mayor of Washington when it was an independent city), and well intrenched among the national-minded bureaucracy which grew up in the various departments of the government under Jefferson, Madison, Monroe, and John Quincy Adams. The *Intelligencer*, which began a daily edition in 1813, reflected this editorial background. It was heavily packed with gubernatorial messages, state legislative proceedings, and summaries of judicial and election news from all over the nation. It was to the world of government what *Niles' Register* was to commerce, a national miscellany of events, which in due time was rummaged by grateful historians. In its devotion to compiling a record, and its discreet conservatism, it foreshadowed today's *New York Times*.

The American Newspaperman

The Whiggish politics of the *Intelligencer* were unobtrusive, but still they were present, and the emerging spokesmen for Jackson wanted a Washington paper more cordial to them. Their efforts to arrange this brought some of the bravura and bellow of southwestern journalism into capital life. They first provided for the founding of the *United States Telegraph* in 1826. Its editor, Duff Green, had just come from St. Louis, where, like other regional editors, he had owned a newspaper as a useful adjunct to his operations in law, trade, land-jobbing, and politics. In the *Telegraph* Green submitted to a candid world a running compilation of news briefs and editorials showing the desperate perfidy of Adams men and the purity of the people's heroes, Andrew Jackson and John C. Calhoun. When Jackson and Calhoun were elected President and Vice-President in 1828, the *Telegraph* moved into the semiofficial position previously enjoyed by Gales's and Seaton's paper, which, except for brief periods, never again knew its former prerogatives as an insider. But in 1830, when Calhoun broke with Jackson over the joined issues of tariff and nullification, Duff Green followed the South Carolinian's star. So Jackson turned to two Kentuckians, Francis P. Blair and John C. Rives, to begin a new administration organ, the *Washington Globe*.

Blair, the better known of the two men, was a banker, planter, and speculator, one of the rising cotton aristocrats of the new Southwest, like Jackson himself. These men were of a tough breed. Natural leaders, they could win the hearts of plain people by making it appear that they had not forgotten their simple beginnings and had achieved no more than the rudest pioneer was capable of, if given the proper chances. Maintaining the outward graces of gentlemanliness, they could still duel and brawl with pistol, knife, or horsewhip as occasion required, gamble with colorful carelessness, and hold their liquor with the best. Blair was one of the most articulate of them, and as editor of the Frankfort *Argus of the Western World* he had lustily fought for Jackson, cheap lands, state banking, popular government, and the continued growth of a Union which was the rock of his salvation precisely because of the opportunities it offered to the likes of him. Blair's predecessor on the *Argus*, Amos Kendall, had already been brought to Washington as a Treasury officeholder in 1830, and the two of them, along with Rives and Isaac Hill, sometime editor of the *New Hampshire Patriot*, became members of that inner circle of advisers to the President which was called (not always with complimentary intent) the "kitchen cabinet."

Blair and Rives were members of this political planning team thanks to their control of the *Globe*, the storm center of Washington's political battles. Their job, in part, was to compose editorials furiously attacking the President's enemies, most notably Nicholas Biddle and his Bank of the United States. For that service they were rewarded with the official printing contracts, and they took over the publication of the congressional debates, retitling the bound numbers the *Congressional Globe*. But there was more to their editorial assignment than that. With the advent of spoilsmanship on a large scale, the party faithful came to include not only the voters but the army of minor officeholders—postmasters, surveyors, weighers, gaugers, bridge-tenders, lighthouse-keepers, Indian agents, purchasing commissioners, and the like—whose loyalties kept the system in motion. For them the *Globe* was not only a propaganda sheet but a kind of continuing communiqué from national headquarters. It kept them abreast of the plans of the leadership, advised them of the progress of the electoral war in states other than their own, and stiffened their sinews with a sense of cohesion and common purpose.

As owners of such a paper, Blair and Rives (and Kendall, too) had a privileged access to the presidential ear. Their contact with subscribers through letters, and especially their constant reading of "exchange papers" as they searched for reprint material, gave them an invaluable awareness of the pulse of the country. They were in a position to know what combinations were forming, whose star was rising in a given state, what sections were doubtful, and what discontents might be growing too large to handle. They were not only spokesmen for settled policies and advance agents for still untested ideas, but they were intelligence gatherers as well. Their acquaintance within the party was wide, and in case of strife among its leaders they were in a good position to act as go-betweens. For all these reasons, in addition to the personal warmth which Jackson felt for them, the onetime editors of the *Argus of the Western World* were part of the unofficial White House entourage. Moreover, until the Civil War, after which the newspapers and the parties alike tended to grow more professional and independent of each other, an "official" capital organ was part of the machinery of every national administration.

What was true in Washington was equally true in the states. Edwin Croswell of the *Albany Argus,* New York's official printer whenever the Democrats were in power between 1830 and 1850, was a key man among the members of the "Albany Regency," and in Virginia, Thomas Ritchie of the *Richmond Enquirer* carried on his role of master expediter for the Old Dominion's Democrats so effectively that he, Croswell, and Blair, were sometimes referred to as the "triumvirate" of the party at large. For the Whigs, Thurlow Weed rose from an original position as editor of the *Albany Evening Journal* to the role of kingmaker, in New York, in alliance with William H. Seward, and then in Washington, under Zachary Taylor. Later he carried his dexterity into the service of the Republicans, as did many other political newspapermen of both Whig and Democratic stripe. The chieftainship of the official paper was a prize to be fought for even among intraparty factions, and some of the bitterest battles within the states in the 1850's, when old political alliances were falling apart like the House of Usher, took place over the naming of authorized editorial spokesmen.

If the party-endowed journals, therefore, concentrated on political news to the exclusion of all other varieties, they were doing no more than was expected of them. If their editorial matter lacked style, their adherents were not disturbed. An editor who was a poor writer could always fill his columns with letters from subscribers or with reports of speeches by those with defter pens. The news was, naturally, "slanted," and nothing good was likely to be reported of the opposition. But an editor of the type of Blair or Ritchie (who moved up from Virginia to replace him as national Democratic editor, with a new paper, in 1845) saw no evil in this, any more than a county boss saw malfeasance in bestowing a job on some deserving Democrat instead of on a more qualified Whig. In the political world of the day, objective reporting was as rare a concept among newspapermen as civil service was among administrators. In any case, one-sided journalism was not a major threat to public wisdom when papers of conflicting viewpoints could be founded cheaply and flourished thickly. A reader who was so inclined had the chance to choose among many "slants." The news which went into a party paper was like the news which went into any other kind of paper in this early national period; it was limited and controlled by the needs of a specialized readership. A journal filled with impartial "general" news, if anyone could have agreed on what that was, could hardly have sustained itself, although an almost purely advertising sheet could do so. The political press was one more example of how newspapers were addressed to particular communities of interest and run by inside members of those communities.

Given the fact that a newspaper could be cheaply founded, kept alive by a small readership, and circulated through the mails at a modest cost, it was not surprising that almost any group of citizens which felt burdened by an undelivered message should try a plunge into journalism. Among the hundreds of weeklies founded before 1850, a goodly number were the property of churches and reform societies. The Baptists, for example, published the *Watchman and Reflector* in Boston, from 1819 onward. The Presbyterians were in the press fold in 1820 with their *Observer*, emanating from New York. The Methodists were not long in founding a *Christian Advocate*, the Unitarians sponsored a *Christian Examiner*, and eventually almost every denomination of any consequence had a weekly operating under the eye of its "board of publications," while the larger churches owned monthly or quarterly magazines, too. The small sects were not left out of the picture, and the titles of their papers sometimes showed a certain ingenuity. The followers of William Miller, for example, who believed that the world was going to end in the 1840's, called one of their journals the *Signs of the Times* and filled it full of omens and portents. Most of these publications were innocent of what they called "secular" news, but they contained abundant notices of denominational affairs, and under the editorial philosophy then in force they were therefore entitled to be called newspapers. Since all news was aimed at special markets, a paper for Baptists full of recent information about other Baptists was as much a journal of current events as any *Express* or *Mercury* that ever came off a press.

The denominational papers blazed no new trails in journalism, but they made the periodical press an agent in the process whereby the American churches organized and grew worldly. They printed seasonal scripture texts and Sunday-school lessons that went simultaneously into thousands of homes and classrooms; they passed the plate on a national scale for missionary activities in foreign lands; they advertised the progress of revivals and sang triumphantly over each newly added congregation; they beat the drums for the reform movements dear to them. Even their advertisers were businessmen interested in gaining a circulation that was not purely local, among them being such pioneers of a national market as book publishers, transportation companies, and patent-medicine makers.

The newspaper could be a strong right arm likewise to those with a purely earthly gospel to disseminate. In 1818 John Skinner founded the *American Farmer* in Baltimore; in 1821 Solomon Southwick launched the *Plough-Boy* in New York; Thomas G. Fessenden began to print the *New England Farmer* in 1822; the *Southern Agriculturist* appeared in Charleston in 1828. Agricultural weeklies thus spread throughout the sections of the country inside of ten years, and by 1860 there were forty of them in operation. Together they publicized new discoveries in soil science and farming machinery, giving impetus to a revolution in food production. In Europe innovations in farming came from the great owners of landed estates, who could experiment with new crops, fertilizers, or breeds of stock without explaining their motives publicly or seeking assurance from others of their good sense and modernity. In the United States new agricultural techniques had to be adopted voluntarily and more or less "sold" to the uncommitted. The county and state agricultural associations, and the journals of farming with their wide distribution, were forces designed to enlist the power of public opinion on the side of change.

The reformers of every kind who flourished in the century's second quarter turned to the special journal, just as the churchmen, the businessmen, and the farmers were doing. Such antislavery papers as Benjamin Lundy's *Genius of Universal Emancipation* and William Lloyd Garrison's *Liberator,* such labor organs as Frances Wright's *Free Inquirer* or George Henry Evans' *Workingman's Advocate* or the *Mechanics' Free Press* of Philadelphia, and such ephemeral weeklies as sprang up to champion temperance, women's rights, free gifts of public land, Mesmerism, Fourierism, spiritualism, and a dozen kindred "isms," all combined in a mighty witness to the integrating and propagandizing power of the newspaper and the magazine. Their sponsors had full confidence in their ability to rally the faithful, inspire the faint of heart, and impress lawgivers with unimpeachable truths. The thrust of reform in America would be expressed not only through the traditional channels of the oration, the book, and the sermon, but through the fragile and short-lived pages of the weekly paper. Somehow its common touch, its rapid succession of issues, and its loose inner structure seemed especially fitted to the tempo of American life.

Thus by the middle of the 1830's, journalism's physical and economic growth, together with a more aggressive and widespread democratic spirit, had already given the makers of the political, mercantile, and reform newspapers impressive public power. Further technical and social changes were now to open still vaster potentialities. A group of hard-driving men elbowed their way forward to show what those potentialities were and to start the newspaper on its way to a bigness yet undreamed of.

IV

Democracy, Technology, and Profits:
Mid-century Modernism

For sixty years after 1835 the forces of industrial change which were sweeping over the nation stretched, rolled, hammered, and squeezed the newspaper into its modern form. By 1865 the outlines of that form were visible, though the most spectacular alterations were yet to come. The great editor-owners who fought their way to the top of the journalistic ranks by the end of the Civil War succeeded in giving the daily press an independent institutional existence. Newspapers had been printers' sidelines, political pulpits, civic forums, and bridges between groups which had things to exchange, from goods to gossip. Now they were to be all this and more.

As society expanded in the early part of the nineteenth century, it had grown more specialized; the worlds of business, religion, farming and politics became, to a greater degree than in colonial days, separate provinces. Regional, political, commercial, literary, and religious newspapers had each tried to reach a particular segment of the public, a special audience. Now, a new journalism was to emerge which, in a sense, re-synthesized the newspaper-reading audience by appealing in a single paper to a wide range of interests. This new journalism would set its own boundaries, evoke its own professional loyalties, and tailor its own styles of expression. As a form of communication, it would not be a passive channel between segments of the public but would to some degree change the nature of the public in the very act of uniting it. In the growth made possible by new machinery and new audiences, the newspaper would find a fresh, stimulating freedom, although like all freedoms it had its price tag.

The potential for mass circulation was swelling like a huge carnival balloon in the cities. New York, Boston, Philadelphia, and Baltimore numbered their citizens in rising hundreds of thousands; Cincinnati, St. Louis, Louisville, and New Orleans swarmed and spread in the West. By the 1850's perplexed city fathers were wrestling with the purely physical problems of providing sewerage, water, gas, street lighting, transportation, and police and fire protection for such hives. But to create some kind of complementary emotional and social community among thousands of "fellow townsmen" who could now go through life without ever meeting one another face to face was not a task for any board or commission. A newspaper might manage the job, if it knew how to reach these new urbanites with something appealing and within their means. As more and more states took to furnishing at least a grade-school education without charge, the "laboring classes" of the cities became literate, but nobody knew exactly what use they would make of their literacy. Green pastures might well be the reward for whatever purveyors of the printed word found the right answer quickly enough.

With every passing year, too, the instruments for reproducing newspapers in quantity got better. By 1835 the Hoe firm was making a version of the two-cylinder Napier press which delivered 2,000 finished four-page papers an hour, and a company which owned two of them could easily circulate as many as 12,000 copies a day. In 1847 the Hoes unlocked the door to the real treasure house of high-speed printing when they built, from their own designs, the first of their rotary presses. In this machine the type was no longer laid on a flat bed but actually fastened to a revolving cylinder by wedge-shaped "column rules," which held the letters in place. Around the circumference of the type cylinder were four impression cylinders, at each of which a "feeder" inserted sheets of paper. One complete revolution of the type cylinder could thus run off four complete impressions, up to a total of 8,000 an hour. By the eve of the Civil War there were versions of this "lightning press" with ten cylinders and an output of 20,000 sheets printed on one side, or 10,000 printed on both sides each hour. A wealthy journal could, with two such machines, reach the streets with 60,000 eight-page papers a day, provided it had enough manpower to do the necessary collating and the folding, which was as yet unmechanized.

Toward the end of the 1860's two more inventions with spectacular possibilities began to find their way into the pressrooms of the biggest papers. One was the process for making curved stereotype plates to fit the printing cylinder. Once the type was set up, a mold was made from it and plates cast, from which the actual impressions were taken. This not only saved wear on the type but allowed a page to be duplicated quickly for running off on more than one press at a time. It also did away with the need for column rules, thus permitting the use of cuts, displays, and headlines of more than a column's width. The other innovation of the immediate postwar period was the web perfecting press, which printed both sides of a continuous roll of paper simultaneously and then cut the paper into sheets. An English version of this machine, the Walter press, was available in the United States as early as 1868. The full impact of stereotype and web perfecting presses, however, was not felt until the 1880's and afterward, partly because they were at first expensive rarities and partly because further inventions —cheap, tough paper, fast-flowing inks, and gathering and folding apparatus—were necessary before their complete capabilities could be realized.

Nevertheless, the track was cleared for a zesty acceleration of output by the middle of the century. Now there was no mechanical reason why the combination of the steam engine and the printing press, twin deities in the pantheon of progress, should not claim thousands of new subjects. In addition to providing power for the presses, steam had other uses vital to the growth of the newspaper. As the railroad network spread from some 3,000 miles in 1830 to ten times that figure in 1860, and as paddles and propellers outstripped sails on the ocean lanes, the world suddenly shrank. Europe was only twelve days away, and the most widely separated states of the Union east of the Mississippi were only half that time apart. And as if this were not miracle enough, electricity all but eliminated time and space in 1844, with the first successful test of a telegraph line between Baltimore and Washington. Some time after noon on May 27 of that year, the Washington *Madisonian* printed a note from the Maryland state Democratic convention to the effect that it had elected a chairman at forty minutes past eleven. "Telegraphic news" had come on the scene, counting its age not in days or even hours, but in minutes. Fifteen years after the *Madisonian*'s "first," there were nearly 50,000 miles of telegraph wire webbing the nation.

These developments gave the quality of novelty to the news and thus made it not only more immediately significant but more marketable. For the American of the 1840's and 1850's had begun his long love affair with speed, and somehow his confidence that he lived in the best of places and times was buoyed by the feeling that at his own breakfast table he could learn what had happened in a city fifteen hundred miles away the preceding afternoon, or in Europe only the week before last. He was better informed than kings and merchant princes had been but a few years since, and it did not particularly matter if he had no business that required him to know the latest news. He did not share Thoreau's fear, when Maine and Texas were joined by telegraph wires, that they might have nothing to say to each other. Merely to know that he could hear at once anything that might pass between them—that in a day of progress he could be, as the revealing phrase had it, *up-to-date*, was thrilling. The fast collection and publication of news, once the newspaper's way of faithfully serving its business patrons, now became its steppingstone to a circulation that would make it partly free of those patrons.

Still, there was more to capturing a mass audience than furnishing it with the digest of great events, no matter how recently torn from the telegrapher's message pad. There were new curiosities to satisfy, new tastes to explore, new sales, price, and advertising policies to be worked over and tried in practice. The editors who were shrewd and tough enough to venture upon the uncharted seas of printing, newsgathering, and audience reaction did not always know in what direction they were going. Nor, after a time, did they always recognize the shores on which they were cast.

The first attempt at journalism for the masses was made in New England. In 1830 Lynde M. Walter began the *Boston Transcript* on a plan designed to break the mold of the mammoth mercantile sheet. Walter slashed the page size back to ten by fifteen inches and, on the saving in newsprint, offered his journal by subscription at four dollars a year. The *Transcript* remained afloat at that price and within two years had two local imitators. Meanwhile, in New York and Philadelphia, other printers stirred by the promise of a large, low-priced market issued (or sometimes simply planned to issue) short-lived dailies priced at a cent or two, laying thus the foundations for later claims to monuments as founders of the "penny press." But the authentic light of cheap journalism (in all senses of the word) actually first shone on New York, in September, 1833, from the pages of a paper appropriately named *The Sun*.

The *Sun* was the creation of a Massachusetts-trained printer, Benjamin H. Day, who remained with the new venture only four years but managed to make them both revolutionary and successful. The *Sun* was small—the actual type page was about eight inches by ten. The *Sun* cost only a penny a copy and was sold not by subcription but by newsboys, a novelty already successfully tried in London. Day sold the boys a hundred copies for sixty-seven cents, cash in advance, and they found a hundred readers and collected a dollar. It was a superb bargain for Day; the newsboys, darting through trains and steamboats, across crowded business districts, and up and down residential streets, kept the paper constantly before the public eye. The aggressive, shouting, pavement-wise little urchins with their armloads of *Sun*'s, were advertisements that money could not buy.

The *Sun* promised "to lay before the public, at a price within the means of every one, ALL THE NEWS OF THE DAY," and Editor Day immediately gave that promise a new and startling meaning. The first page of the first number contained a humorous sketch entitled "An Irish Captain" and a chatty article about famous objects of wonderfully small size (like the *Sun* itself, of course). The second page took note of a suicide and a few fires and burglaries, then threw in a maudlin sketch concerning a street waif, a joke about a man who cheated two shoemakers, and a long report of cases tried the preceding day in police court. The last two pages were taken up with advertising, which also claimed one of the three columns of the front page. The tone of all the writing was staccato; it took the reader by the elbow, promised not to keep him for more than a moment, and kept the promise.

It was nothing less than brazen to claim that four such pages contained "all the news of the day," or anything like it. The world of commercial respectability, looking up from the pages of the *Courier and Enquirer* or the *Evening Post* to take note of the new phenomenon, was inclined, with justice, to mutter "trash!" But Day had hit on something overlooked by commercial respectability. His penny-a-day customers— maids and hostlers, clerks and draymen, barbers and ship-caulkers, and all the thousands to whom the noisy streets belonged—had an insatiable fund of curiosity. Once this had been fed by village gossips; now it was frustrated by the conditions of urban living. A newspaper could feed that curiosity by taking the world for its beat. To do so, it should ignore nothing but should include:

> . . . bombastic panegyrics, jests, anecdotes, deaths, marriages, co-nondrums, enigmas, puns, poetry, acrostics and advertisements, of every shade, color and form, "from grave to gay, from lively to severe" . . . the "shread and patches" [*sic*] of all things on, within, above, or upon the earth—from the aerial ascension of Mr. Durant to the last downward plunge of cataract-leaping Patch; from the chase of the sea serpent and the grisly bear to the capture of Black Hawk and the horned frog; from the Siamese twins to the twins of Latona;—from the gold mines of Georgia to the gold vaults of the Bank—from Col. Crockett whipping his weight in wild cats to Maj. Downing bastinading the British at Madawaska—from Mr. Taney of the Treasury to Mr. Zaney of the Primer—from Alabama squatters to psalm-singing Puritans—from Carolina craceers [*sic*] to wooden nutmeg venders—from advertising bachelors to crim. con. elopements—from slander-poisoned paragraphs to pistol-shooting duelists—from Cincinnati pork to Brussels lace. . . .

A near impossible task it would be for any paper to cull from such chaos a dozen or so orderly columns each day, but the *Sun* undertook to try it. Day had possibly got some of his inspiration from "sporting papers" such as William T. Porter's *Spirit of the Times,* founded in New York in 1831, with their turf and ring news, tall tales, and squibs. But Day's paper was not, as some charged, mere entertainment for the vulgar. It avoided the kind of political discussion which filled the party papers, but its readers were not apolitical. They simply had no personal contact with their representatives, nor any sense of being immediately affected by turns of the political wheel, and therefore politics had to be made relevant to them through newspaper exploitation of its personalities and drama. They were not businessmen, but they were a tempting target for the advertisers handling the increasing flow of factory-made or processed products. Nor were they the lowest classes of society; indeed, the *Sun* invited them, in its police court reports, to enjoy their superiority over the wretched drunks and prostitutes who were made the victims of sardonic reporting.

Fanny Munrow, charged with taking up too much room on the side walk last night. . . . From the evidence of the watchman, it seemed that Fanny was one of those girls that "walk the night both when we sleep and when we wake"—and that last night, by some strange cause or other, she could not walk straight, but kept leaning over, first to the curb stone and then to the inside of the walk, as if she had something on her head, very heavy. The watchman observing her in this state, and thinking she might fall down and injure an elegant leg horn bonnet which she wore, very kindly brought her up. She was fined one dollar, but not having the right change about her, she was committed.

Day's catch-all sheet was, in short, a citified version of the colonial journal full of agricultural, literary, historical, commercial, and religious miscellany. It was aimed at a more restless and rootless audience than the farmers and artisans of the preceding century, but it filled much the same need. The *Sun*'s readers had a sharp instinct for what was alive in their hustling, pushing city world, from a dogfight in the street to the wedding of a rich merchant's daughter and an alderman, from a brawl between the Irishmen of two volunteer fire companies to a horsecar company's bid for a new franchise. They got out of Day's four pages a renewed sense of participation in a common life which urban growth had threatened to deny them. Best of all, from Day's point of view, God had made a very great many of them. The circulation of the *Sun* rocketed to 15,000 in 1834, and to 30,000 in 1837. Advertisers fell into line, and the owners of the more traditional journals looked afresh at Day's techniques and thought about adopting them.

In 1837 Day impulsively sold the paper to his brother-in-law, Moses Beach, and while Beach kept the *Sun* well up in the circulation race (in part through such "stunts" as a series of faked stories about a new super-telescope which revealed the existence of batlike living creatures on the moon), the leadership in penny journalism passed into other hands, specifically those of James Gordon Bennett, the founder, in 1835, of the *New York Herald*.

Bennett was, in a very real sense, the father of the modern newspaper. Like Day, he reached the popular audience through local news, trivia, sensation, even occasional plunges into outright vulgarity. His conceptions, however, were larger than Day's. Having won a mass circulation for the *Herald*, he also swept into its pages the political essays, the foreign intelligence, the commercial and financial news, and the specialized information which the party and mercantile and "class" organs had furnished separately. He made his paper a kind of department store of news and crowded his rivals with their special markets to the wall, forcing them to imitate him or be hopelessly outstripped in the race for readership.

To this task of consolidation, he brought matchless gifts of energy, business acuteness, literary talent, and showmanship.— as if in him had been combined qualities of Phineas T. Barnum, John Jacob Astor, and Lord Byron. A Scotsman born, Bennett had not come to the United States until he was twenty-four years old. As a young man he had read omnivorously in biography, history, and the English classics, and he knew as well the works of the Romantics who were his contemporaries. He could spice his editorial paragraphs with a constant sifting of apt quotations. He also possessed the twin keys to good journalistic prose: the eye for small but important details and the ability to compress material into short compass without sacrificing clarity. These assets he improved by working first for the *Charleston Courier* and then for James Watson Webb's *Courier and Enquirer*. He and Webb were Democrats together, but when Webb switched to the Whig side (an act which Bennett claimed was due to a bribe from the Bank of the United States, Jackson's mortal enemy), Bennett left his post as the *Courier and Enquirer*'s Washington writer and tried running a party paper of his own in Philadelphia.

But James Gordon Bennett was not cut out for party journalism. He could sting like an adder and be sharper than William Corbett's "Porcupine" when he chose, but he wanted to pick his victims regardless of their party affiliations. He had a contempt for politicians and their high-flown oratory. "The world has been humbugged long enough by spouters, and talkers, and conventioners, and legislators," he declared in an early *Herald* editorial. No longer need the masses of men rely on the power of "talkers" to mediate between them and complex events, for the 1830's were "the editorial age." He asked:

What is to prevent a daily newspaper from being made the greatest organ of social life? Books have had their day—the theatres have had their day—the temple of religion has had its day. A newspaper can be made to take the lead of all these in the great movements of human thought and of human civilization. A newspaper can send more souls to Heaven, and save more from Hell, than all the churches or chapels in New York—besides making money at the same time.

Bennett was intoxicated with the discovery that the newspaper could be a platform from which to address hitherto unreachable multitudes. He had no wish to use such a vantage point for the reformation of the world; he rather liked the world as bustling and noisy and sinful as it was. But he was convinced that it would be better managed if better informed. He would take it upon himself to enlighten "all ranks and conditions . . . the merchant and man of learning, as well as the mechanic and the man of labor." He began the task in the first number of the *Herald*, founded on a few hundred dollars and edited by Bennett from a basement office and a desk consisting of a plank laid across two barrels. Working doggedly from 5:00 A.M. until late at night, he sold subscriptions and advertising (the latter for short terms only without renewal, cash in advance); collected the information for excellent articles on the stock and money markets and shipping movements; supervised street sales; clipped exchanges and wrote rapid-fire editorial paragraphs; dropped in himself on police headquarters, courtrooms, theaters, and sporting events in search of items; "legged it" to fires, accidents, revival meetings, political rallies, and wherever else a story might be brewing. Inside of a year he had 20,000 readers and dared to raise the price to two cents. With his new opulence he enlarged both staff and paper and made the *Herald* a spicy, intimate, insistent morning visitor without which the day did not seem complete. Burned out by a fire in 1836, it was soon back in business, as Bennett said, "as saucy as ever."

Bennett's triumph lay in his whirlwind approach to journalism and also in his fantastic abilty to sell himself. An unabashed exhibitionist, not at all retiring on account of his hawk-nosed, cross-eyed homeliness, he described himself as the Napoleon, the Shakespeare, of the newspaper press, the man who had infused it with wit, humor, sentiment, and glowing taste. His editorials were frankly written in the first person and invited the reader to share his attitudes and triumphs. He announced his marriage under a heading, "Caught At Last," exclaiming: "I must fulfill that awful destiny which the Almighty Father has written against my name in broad letters of light against the wall of heaven. I must give the world a pattern of happy wedded life." When the terrible-tempered Colonel Webb beat him over the head with a cane in the street, Bennett rushed to his desk, bandaged, and wrote: "The fellow, no doubt, wanted to let out the never-failing supply of good humor and wit which has created such a reputation for the *Herald*, and appropriate the contents to supply the emptiness of his own thick skull."

No one could ignore this uncommon magnification of the common man's appetites and daydreams. Boycotted by churches as a mocker at religion and a spreader of vulgarity, Bennett trimmed only slightly and raced ahead in circulation once more. Condemned by fellow editors, he denounced them daily as buffoons and half-wits and gave every evidence, much to their chagrin, not only of getting richer in spite of them, but of enjoying himself hugely into the bargain. Like the biblical war steed, he rejoiced in the sound of the trumpet, and amid the thunder of the captains and the shouting, he said, "Ha, ha."

Yet all the showy fireworks of the *Herald* were launched from a solid platform of news, for which Bennett, romantic or no romantic, had a hard, canny sense. The *Herald* created its early sensations by covering the dominions of sin, from the city jail to the then-forbidden prize ring, but once established it never skimped on other news. Throughout the 1840's and 1850's Bennett hired the fastest news-boats and bought the greatest number of telegraphic dispatches. The *Herald* paid freely for correspondence from Washington, the gold fields of California, the battlegrounds of Mexico, the jungles of Central America, and the capitals of Europe. Abetting Bennett was Frederic Hudson, a Massachusetts Yankee who came to the paper in his late teens and as its managing editor lived for nothing but to fill its columns with the best and latest reports. The spirit he gave to the staff was exemplified by a nameless field superintendent of a group of *Herald* war correspondents in 1862.

The Federal Government was, to his eye, merely an adjunct of the paper. Battles and sieges were simply occurrences for its columns. Good men, brave men, bad men, died to give it obituaries. The whole world was to him a Reporter's district, and all human mutations plain matters of news.

This enterprising spirit had made the *Herald* an eight-page paper with a daily circulation of something like 60,000 in 1860. And this kind of circulation made the *Herald* the colossus among journals big enough to be independent at last. The thickest cluster of such papers was now in New York, which had become the nearest thing possible to a journalistic capital. Bennett's power was shown by the way in which all his competitors had to some extent given character to their own organs either by imitating or by consciously recoiling from the *Herald*'s style.

After 1841 the *Herald*'s foremost rival in New York and in the country was the *New York Tribune* of Horace Greeley. Begun in the aftermath of the "political revolution" which elected William Henry Harrison to the Presidency, the *Tribune* set its tone immediately by a proclamation that Harrison's elevation was a triumph of "Right, Reason and Public Good over Sinister Error and Ambition." That was the authentic voice of Greeley, a fascinating, mercurial, neurotic prophet crying aloud in a wilderness of slaveholders, rum-sellers, autocrats, and ignoramuses. No one in all of journalism was ever quite like this "incorrigible idealist," as one historian called him. Born of desperately poor parents in Vermont, Greeley was a prodigy who learned to read as a toddler and thereafter absorbed the printed word like a sponge. In a sense he always remained something of a precocious child, crying stridently for attention and flying into tantrums, but also inexorably pointing out the various emperors who really wore no clothes.

Greeley learned printing as a boy, drifted to New York in search of a place to ply his trade, tried his hand on a few papers, took an ill-fated flyer into penny journalism in 1833, managed to get a small weekly entitled the *New-Yorker* going in the next year, and finally achieved some recognition as owner-editor of the *Log Cabin*, a Whig campaign paper in 1840. Like Day, like Bennett, Greeley comprehended the enormous power of the new, low-priced daily paper to command mass attention. Unlike them, he wanted to use such a paper as a platform to publicize his favored schemes for uplifting mankind. As far as he was concerned, the "luxury" of journalism lay in lighting the path of progress. The *Tribune*, launched with a capital of some three thousand dollars, was dedicated to such ideas and projects as temperance, abolition, associationism (a plan for reorganizing society into small, co-operative communities), free gifts of land to bona fide farmers, trade-union congresses, scientific agriculture, women's rights, public encouragement of industry, and international peace. For three decades Greeley labored on behalf of these crusades, perched on a high stool in a small office and surrounded by stacks of foreign books, statistical publications, almanacs, government reports, reference volumes, and the litter of an omnivorous reader. His pen, racing over sheet after sheet of paper in a weird script that became a national joke, completed thousands of letters, editorials, pamphlets, articles, reviews, and books.

Greeley's real world was the *Tribune* office. Outside it he cut a strange-looking figure with his spectacles, white chin-whiskers, bald head, and costume of loose-fitting white coat and trousers, boots, and round, broad-brimmed hat. He mingled little in society and at the height of his success commuted from the city to a farm in Chappaqua, New York, where he felt at home among the fruit trees and breeds of poultry with which he liked to experiment. He ventured, inopportunely, into the world of politics from time to time. Firmly believing that democracy would flourish best under nationally encouraged industry, he was an ardent supporter of the protectionist-minded Whigs and later of the Republicans. Since he was never willing to concede any virtues of character or mind to his opponents, these party loyalties involved the *Tribune* in innumerable contradictions, for many of Greeley's beloved Whigs opposed his crusades. Moreover, while party leaders welcomed the paper's support, they were reluctant to reward its editor with the political offices in which he was interested, since his vulnerability to ridicule made him a liability to any ticket. As a result, his romances with Whig and Republican leaders like William H. Seward and Lincoln were constantly erupting in quarrels, reconciliations, recantations, and (for the editor himself) frustrations.

Yet the incongruous Greeley managed to make the *Tribune* an outstanding paper in its way. Its daily circulation always lagged behind that of the *Herald*, its news coverage was not quite so complete, and Greeley's financial management produced a succession of hairbreadth rescues from disaster until other stockholders in the owning company took over business matters. But the *Tribune* was a forum for intellectual discussion and moral challenge such as no other mass-audience journal ever has been.

Greeley surrounded himself with a talented staff. Charles A. Dana and George Ripley, philosophically literate defenders of associationism and veterans of its high-minded trial at Brook Farm; Solon Robinson, agrarian reformer; William Fry, musicologist and composer; Bayard Taylor, poet and traveler—these were only a few of the men who at some time held editorial posts with the *Tribune*. Greeley joined them in undertaking wide-ranging book reviews, examinations of current religious and scientific periodicals, reports of industrial and technical expositions, and accounts of conventions of every kind. The political correspondence of the paper was sharply biased, though well written, but the occasional contributors included intellectuals as diverse as Karl Marx and Margaret Fuller. Greeley, in short, respected his readers. His idealism was genuine, even if smudged by his impracticality, testiness, and innocent faith that politicians really shared his views. Deliberately, the *Tribune* stated its policy in retort to the gibes of Bennett at the self-righteousness, unreality, and extremism of the reformer. Greeley reminded the world that a newspaper had a duty to keep an ear

ever open to the plaints of the wronged and the suffering, though they can never repay advocacy, and those who mainly support newspapers will be annoyed and often exposed by it; a heart as sensitive to oppression and degradation in the next street as if they were practiced in Brazil or Japan; a pen as ready to expose and reprove the crimes whereby wealth is amassed and luxury enjoyed in our own country at this hour, as if they had only been committed by Turks or Pagans in Asia some centuries ago.

If the *Tribune* did not always live up to such pretensions, it was nevertheless illuminated by a courage and an eagerness to improve society to which other papers paid only lip service. For all its faults in coloring the news to suit its viewpoints, it had warmth and heart, and it won tremendous popularity in rural New England and the Middle West. Its weekly edition had an amazing circulation in those areas of nearly 200,000 in 1860, and to many farm families it must have been what it was to that of Clarence Darrow in his childhood, "the political and social Bible of our home." Despite his New York setting and his adventures among professional thinkers, Greeley remained at heart a countryman, and the countryside knew it.

The nearest thing to the *Tribune* in New York journalism was the *Post*, edited by William Cullen Bryant after 1829. Thanks to Bryant, it shared some of the *Tribune*'s literary interests and continued the long-standing newspaper practice of running occasional poems in its columns. In assistant editors like William Leggett and Parke Godwin it had a fiery pro-labor pamphleteer and an intellectual socialist, although both of them mellowed with time. In 1848 they were joined by John Bigelow, a dignified and conservative sponsor of civic improvements and a part-time diplomat. He and Bryant together gave the *Post* a genteel liberal tone. Believing in free trade and free banking, Bryant was a Democrat in the thirties and forties; believing in free labor and therefore opposing the spread of slavery, he was a Republican in the fifties and sixties; believing in honest and responsible government by citizens of intellectual if not monetary substance, he was a somewhat unhappy Republican in the corrupt seventies. The *Post* joined more popular papers in enlarging its news coverage and diversifying its features, but it was always a journal of high respectability and medium circulation, a spokesman for good causes in which open-minded gentlemen could believe.

The *Courier and Enquirer* and *Journal of Commerce* lived on, making adjustments to the new journalism where they had to and joined from time to time by other papers of greater and lesser prestige and length of life. In 1851 a new and important note was struck in metropolitan journalism, with the birth of the *New York Times*. The best-known man of the *Times* was Henry J. Raymond, a small, black-bearded Vermonter, quick in perception and enormously efficient at turning ideas into news copy. Raymond was a graduate of the University of Vermont who had purposely come to New York in 1840, diploma fresh in hand, to seek a career as a newspaper writer. He worked for both Greeley and Webb, diligently picking up a competence in all the branches of editorship, and in 1851 he saw a chance to strike out on his own. New York's half a million people could, he believed, use a cheap paper, newsier than the commercial sheets, calmer than the *Tribune*, and higher-toned than the *Sun* and *Herald*. Newspaper-founding was becoming expensive, and Raymond had to enlist the help of two rich friends, George Jones and Edgar Wesley, to commence operations. The *Times* corporation was capitalized at $100,000, of which better than half had to be put up in cash immediately. It was a portent of the age of big-business journalism. Once the initial investment to begin a newspaper grew to such proportions, publishing would no longer be a career open to any young man of talent. Raymond promptly turned the *Times* into a well-edited newspaper, cleanly made up, far-ranging in its coverage, and judicious in its selection and balance among political, economic, literary, and purely local news. By 1860 he had pushed its daily circulation to something slightly under the *Tribune's* estimated 45,000, and like both *Tribune* and *Herald* it commonly ran to eight pages, cost two cents, and was sold in the streets.

Raymond was not colorless, but it was the *Times* that gave him his importance, rather than the reverse. Although he took part in politics, was a lieutenant governor and a Republican congressman, and ranked among New York's business elite by virtue of the size of the investment which the *Times* represented, he was known first as an editor. Webb and Noah were figures who would have added yeast to any enterprise; Greeley was a Quixote tilting at windmills astride the *Tribune;* Bennett was a gaudy impresario who acted as his own press agent. But Raymond was an unspectacular professional, resembling not so much the other New York newspaper owners as their little-known managing editors—Hudson of the *Herald,* Dana and later Sidney Howard Gay of the *Tribune,* Godwin and Bigelow of the *Post.* Under Raymond's direction, the *Times* started on the road toward thorough newsgathering which set it finally among the foremost of the country's conservative, semiofficial, public-minded journals.

As 1860 approached, the trends visible in New York were transforming the newspaper scene in other places. Cheap, popular papers, dominated by aggressive editors, found their way into the market wherever cities had ripened enough for them. Three New York printers, William Swain, Arunah Abell, and Azariah Simmons began the *Public Ledger* in Philadelphia in 1836, and by 1850 it had a circulation of 44,000. The same trio introduced the *Baltimore Sun* to the penny readership of the Maryland seaport in 1837; by 1860 daily sales were estimated at something between 30,000 and 40,000. In Boston the *Times*, the *Mail*, and the *Herald*, all begun between 1836 and 1846, pursued the paths of low-cost, carrier-sold journals, and the *Herald*, at least, had passed the 50,000 mark in circulation by 1860.

All these papers were more or less cut to the same measure. They were still half-filled with advertisements, and they gave a reasonable amount of attention to whatever befell those in the seats of the mighty. But they dwelt at great length as well on the picturesque and sinful trivialities of existence in the human swarms that cities were becoming. In Boston or Philadelphia or New York the combined circulations of the cheap dailies ran as high as 200,000. One-fifth of a million people came to look forward to buying each morning a mirror of the times and an entertaining slice of life for a penny or two. The editors of the popular press of the fifties swelled with the consciousness of a new strength. They made their quarrels front-page stories, they talked opulently about the power of the press, they fended off libel suits with the happy consciousness that the resultant publicity earned them far more in circulation than any assessed damages might lose them, and they talked to politicians on new and secure terms. For, in the cities, a political party could no longer buy a paper with a few thousand dollars and install a "loyal" editor at its helm. It had to win over an already successful enterprise to reach the general ear. The newspaper was big enough to make its owner-editor someone to be courted, but not yet big enough so that he was lost sight of among his own staff. Thus it was an age of personal journalism. The American newspaperman who stood in the limelight was a captain of communication, a self-made hero who strutted on the public stage as the star in a popular national drama of success.

Away from the seaboard, the same pattern of vigorous personal leadership showed itself. In one sense it was not new, since the country and the western editors had always been completely identified with their papers. But now they felt the goad of enlarged ambitions and stretched themselves. In Springfield, Massachusetts, in 1844 Samuel Bowles III took over the management of his grandfather's *Springfield Republican,* energized by the belief that the "brilliant mission of the newspaper" was to be "the high priest of History, the vitalizer of Society, the world's great informer, the earth's high censor, the medium of public thought and opinion, and the circulating life blood of the whole human mind." He may not have achieved all that from Springfield, but he did make the *Republican* a paper of enormous rural circulation and influence, and in time a high priest and vitalizer of the Republican party. Bowles was confident that the Republicans were the guarantors of progress, that they marched in step with the marvelous measure of the railroad, the telegraph, the factory, the printing press, and the free school, and that he, as a newspaperman, was in the vanguard of the march.

In the West extravagant and picturesque personalities led the newspaper on toward horizons beyond the public printing contracts. In Louisville, George D. Prentice, begetter of that city's *Journal* in 1831, enlivened the city's political life with a razor-edged wit. He would comment of a rival owner: "The editor of the *Star* says that he has never murdered the truth. He never gets near enough to do it any bodily harm." Louisville would guffaw, and a week later the country would share the laugh as other papers reprinted the sally as an "Exchange." In Cincinnati and St. Louis, however, no strong leader emerged from the competition of half a dozen or more dailies in each town in the fifties. For a few years before the Civil War, Detroit had a tempestuous Democratic editor in Wilbur F. Storey of the *Free Press*, but in 1861 he moved to Chicago to begin a new career there at the helm of the *Chicago Times*.

Storey's move was a sign of the growing importance of the Illinois city, and of its lure for energetic newspapermen. In 1836 a gigantic young man named John Wentworth had walked into town, bringing with him a fresh Dartmouth diploma and a bone-deep addiction to Andrew Jackson, a low tariff, and westward expansion. Besides these assets, he had a hot temper and a sharp pen. Taking over the *Chicago Democrat* soon after his arrival, he made it a popular and important sheet, a leading publicizer of Chicago's multiplying advantages for investors, and his own springboard to Congress and to the mayoralty of the city. In 1855, Joseph Medill, Canadian-born and seasoned in small-town Ohio newspaper work, arrived on the scene to join the eight-year-old *Chicago Tribune*. Soon he was its leading editorial figure. The *Tribune* immediately took from him the vituperative, pugnacious, ultrapatriotic, proudly midwestern, crustily Republican, arrogantly Chicagoan tone which it maintained for more than a century thereafter. Medill, as brassy in his way as Bennett, filled the paper with news, titbits, and spice, fought hard to boost its advertising and circulation, and made it a power in Illinois public opinion that could not be ignored. In 1861 the *Tribune* absorbed the *Democrat*, as Wentworth retired to devote his full time to politics and successful real-estate speculation. The battle between

Wentworth and Medill thus ended, leaving the *Tribune* free to concentrate on the Civil War, which was in some ways less spectacular.

In such ways did the regional press fall into line with the new order. New York editors sometimes were tempted to refer to their contemporaries of the "provincial press," but they refrained from such airs in deference to their own out-of-town readers. In any case the term would have been a misnomer, since not even New York could overshadow the rest of the country as, say, London did all England. The most common kind of American newspaper in 1860 was still the country weekly. There were 3,173 of them, in contrast to 387 dailies. The coming of the railroad and the telegraph to prairie and mountain communities encouraged the founding of new rural papers, happy to tap the mighty currents of national communication. Further encouragement to country editors was furnished by the Post Office Act of 1851, which permitted delivery of newspapers within their home counties free of charge, a subsidy of a few hundred dollars a year which made a real difference to a small printer. The more vociferous newspapermen in the counties continued to enjoy party patronage, sometimes including free drinks, chewing tobacco, writing paper, and hotel accommodations at the state capitals. The special-interest papers of churches, reform associations, and professional groups pursued the even tenor of their somewhat narrow ways. There was even a foreign-language press of some 300 papers in 1860, five out of six of them German, all of them reaching limited groups. The average newspaper circulation in the nation, at the time of Lincoln's election, was still well under 4,000.

The American Newspaperman

Yet despite this diversity, big-time journalism, especially as it was practiced in New York, cast a potent spell over the land. The successful editors in other cities borrowed the techniques of the New York circulation leaders, and the small-town owners in turn modeled themselves on the Boston or Cincinnati or St. Louis counterparts of Bennett, Raymond, and Greeley. The high prizes of the editorial calling were in the metropolis, and the hearts of hustling young assistants in village printing shops yearned toward the *Tribune,* the *Herald,* the *Times,* and the *Sun.* By the 1870's the penny-paper formula of entertainment, sensation, and humorous miscellany was affecting the style of many a country pressroom. The onetime editor of the Lewiston, Maine, *Journal* remembered that in 1874 he

wrote editorials to fill up, devised paragraphs of alleged humorous impact under the heading "Brief Jottings," slept in a haunted house, reported poultry shows, lectures, murder trials, spelling-matches, hangings, and sermons, did the book-reviews, criticised current singers and dramatic invaders, constructed rebuses for the puzzle column . . . and even designed for the amusement of the farmhouse firesides a cryptic alphabet (with prizes for the correct interpretations of the entire series).

In one thing, however, the major city papers could not be imitated—in the growing extent of their newsgathering. The nation's thousands of rural journals did give it a number of newspapers per capita that exceeded any other country's, and substantiated American boasts of an enlightened populace. But when the newspaper's job was enlarged to include the rapid gathering of late intelligence from the world at large, only the wealthiest owners could meet the challenge. It was the cost of keeping up with the revolution in reporting that exerted the mightiest pressure toward keeping journalism's center of gravity in the greatest urban areas. Moreover, the effects of that revolution began to change the internal structure of the mass-audience papers themselves. As editing the news came to consist less and less of deft work with scissors among the exchanges, and as operations became more far-flung, the editors had to make room for specialists who shared their work. Among these was a new kind of professional journalist, the reporter.

The mercantile papers had pioneered in collecting European news quickly by sending boats out to meet incoming vessels offshore. In the 1830's the papers of the larger cities were making other efforts to speed information into print. The postal system obligingly provided in 1836 for certain "express mail" routes over which editors could send and receive—more rapidly than by the ordinary mail service and at no extra charge—clippings and proof sheets, letters from legislative correspondents, and texts of freshly released official documents and speeches. But private adventurers were ready to furnish even faster transmission. William F. Harnden of Boston began collecting English papers in 1839 from steamers touching at that port and rushing them by rail to newspaper clients in New York. At about the same time, Daniel H. Craig added a colorful note with a pigeon service operating from Boston headquarters. Craig's pigeon-handlers as far away as Halifax made quick digests of foreign news brought by ships which touched there, put them in the birds' leg capsules, and started them on the first leg of a trip which ended in newspaper offices of Philadelphia, New York, and Washington. These private agencies with multiple newspaper subscribers furnished the groundwork for co-operative newsgathering in the United States, although editors before the day of Craig and Harnden had been known to pool the expenses of a harbor boat or a private horse relay for collecting a particularly timely item (such as a presidential address) in a hurry. When the telegraph became available, a few enterprising souls, among them a certain Alexander Jones, arranged to have agents in centers served by the chattering wires forward to them brief telegraphic summaries of newsworthy events. They then sold these dispatches to interested editors. By 1848, Jones had built up something of a clientele and a reputation in New York, and this set the stage for significant developments in collecting news.

The New York papers had made great efforts to bring news of the Mexican War to their readers. The popular papers of Philadelphia and Baltimore, too, had recognized that battle action in the halls of Montezuma provided sensations tailor-made for the new journalism. All of them spent heavily for news taken from the New Orleans papers, closest to the theater of war, and rushed by horse express, railroad, and telegraph to the composing tables. Some of them joined in temporary arrangements to share both the stories and the expense, and it may have been with the idea of continuing this practice that six New York papers allied themselves, in May of 1848, in the nucleus of the "New York Associated Press." The associated journals arranged with a telegraph agent in Boston to receive, in one transmission, late news from steamships just arrived, at the rate of one hundred dollars for 3,000 words. Alexander Jones, the first supervisor of the service, was succeeded in 1851 by Daniel Craig.

From these small beginnings, great things grew. The original association made arrangements to sell its dispatches to journals outside New York and gradually required them to cut their ties with any rival telegraphic news services. Meanwhile, they bargained with competing telegraph companies, promising a monopoly of the association's traffic if those companies, in turn, would agree not to send wire news to "outside" papers. By the middle of the 1850's the original six members of the New York AP, now increased to seven by the addition of the *Times*, were in a commanding position. They controlled the wires from an increasing number of key points through exclusive priority arrangements with the owners of the wires. They sold the right to use their bulletins to other journals, but no paper could enter the charmed circle of subscribers without the consent of six of the seven associates. Once a paper undertook to receive the New York AP service, for weekly rates ranging from $7.00 to $120, it had to forswear the use of other news agencies and promise to share wired material from its own correspondents with other participants in the AP's news pool. No new paper could join the mighty seven without the consent of all of them. Craig was as industrious as any other nineteenth-century monopolist in his attempts to get a strangle hold on the news sent by telegraph, and he was close to achieving his goal by the end of the Civil War. Not until after 1865 was the New York AP seriously challenged.

As a result, regional journalism suffered a heavy blow. It was possible, of course, to publish a newspaper without telegraphic news, but as the country came to hunger for "the very latest," an editor who did not furnish the freshest copy available had to resign himself to a secondary position. It was also possible to station correspondents of one's own at the fountainheads of news, but only rich newspapers could do that, and rich newspapers were usually those which had built a large circulation by running, among other things, the latest telegraphic dispatches of the AP. There was no way out for the Pittsburgh or Cincinnati or Chicago or St. Louis or New Orleans editor but to subscribe—provided that the New York AP would let him, or provided that a local association of newspapers with which the New York AP had agreed to do exclusive business would admit him, on payment of a sizable entry fee.

In the nature of things, the AP was dominated by its New York founders, who tended to commission the gathering of news mainly of interest to themselves. In sorting and choosing among these AP items, the lesser clients became, willy-nilly, partial copies of the great New York organs. Even when the AP managers thought about the needs of their New England or Ohio Valley or Great Lakes subscribers, they were apt to ask the field agents for items most likely to have a national range of appeal. The papers which reached for a special geographic or class audience, therefore, were in a squeeze, unable to extract very much of value from the service and unable to thrive without it. Significantly, when the revolt against the New York AP did come in 1866, it was led by western papers demanding a voice in the management. The triumphs of the AP in speeding the flow of news were spectacular, but they pushed successful papers toward uniformity and foretold the eventual doom of the specialized organs.

Telegraphic coverage was only a part of the news-collecting operation of a successful journal. With the coming of the fifties, enterprising editors sensed an increasing value in letters from skilful observers on the scene of events. Aggressive editors were not content merely to wait for the Paris or London papers, or even for telegraphic digests of those papers rushed over the AP-controlled wires from Halifax. Bennett and Greeley began to arrange for regular letters from European residents whom they had come to know and trust through intermediaries or on their own travels. As the congressional skirmishes grew hotter with the deepening sectional crisis, capital correspondence also underwent a revolution. Coverage of Congress had been virtually a monopoly of the Baltimore and Washington papers until 1846. Thereafter, the leaders of the New York, Boston, Philadelphia, Cincinnati, St. Louis, and Chicago press saw to it that their own representatives sat in the galleries and filed regular letters. By 1859 two dozen reporters representing twenty-one newspapers and the AP covered the Senate; fifty-four writers kept an eye on the House for the benefit of forty-five papers and the omnipresent AP. In addition, the very largest owners, like Raymond or Bennett, were printing the reports of "specials" from such places as California, Central America, and other points of interest and tension.

The early correspondents were a curious group. Often they were young men of literary or political ambitions, hoping to win recognition through newspaper publication of their work. Some chose the papers for which they wrote on the basis of their political loyalties, and their news reports were mere forays in party warfare. Washington correspondents of Republican papers did not hesitate to punctuate reports of Democratic speeches in Congress with angry rebuttals and snide descriptions of the manners and morals of southern public officials. Reporters for Democratic journals caricatured Republican conventions and mass meetings as emotional orgies in which hotheads were aroused to frenzy by windbags. When in 1856 Kansas Territory was torn by political battle between pro-slavery and free-soil settlers, each trying to control the future state government, Greeley's *Tribune* sent half a dozen "specials" to the scene. Ardent abolitionists all, they sent back lurid accounts of proslavery villainy—stories fierce in their distortions and in their effects upon an already inflamed public opinion.

Through all these crises, reporters were getting practice in presenting news to the world, and editors were learning how to use them. The Civil War was a turning point for reporting. More than one hundred correspondents took the field with the Union armies, the bulk of them representing a dozen big-city journals. The *New York Herald* alone spent half a million dollars on its war coverage in telegraph tolls, salaries, and charter fees for horses, wagons, special trains, and steamboats. Bennett organized special bureaus and posted superintendents and reporters like a field marshal making dispositions—his Napoleonesque pretensions at last had a free rein. The correspondents themselves (for other papers as well as the *Herald*) included a sprinkling of brilliant young men, among them future chief editors of the *Chicago Tribune, New York Tribune,* and half a dozen other major papers, as well as a future railroad baron, minister to France, minister to China, and Librarian of Congress. In the course of four years they acquired a nose for facts and developed an *esprit de corps* and a kind of professional loyalty to the exacting task of getting full and accurate stories, all of which were vastly important to journalism's growth.

For with the emergence of the reporter as essential to the prospering newspaper, a new contender for the role of the "American newspaperman" was on the scene. It was becoming hard to say just who played that role. Once it had been the printer, but in 1860, in New York or Philadelphia or Cincinnati, the printer was a fifteen-dollar-a-week employee tending the

Democracy, Technology, and Profits

huge machines in the basement of the newspaper building. Nor was "the" newspaperman of the great city any longer the gifted writer, the party propagandist, or some counterpart of the small-town factotum. As a newspaper grew in size, subeditors inevitably took over many of the chores once performed by the jack-of-all-trades who had founded it. Greeley, Bennett, Bryant, Raymond, or Medill might still toss off the lead editorial of the day, but specialists did the paragraphs on the money market, municipal affairs, or European upheavals. No longer did the editor-in-chief make up the day's news columns by running through the exchanges while puffing on a cigar, punctuating his conversation with a snap of his scissors in the air, and pausing now and then to argue with the pressroom foreman over a deadline or to write up an advertisement for a customer who had dropped in. Managing editors sorted the telegraphic dispatches, handed reporters' copy to appropriate desk men for trimming, and scanned dummies for flaws in the work of the religion editor, the shipping editor, the city editor, and the other subordinate captains. The business manager wrinkled his brows over the avarice of newsboys and printers and dealt with the advertisers. With the coming of the first advertising agencies in the 1840's, he was even less likely to meet many of his customers directly. The businessman and the editor, once informal partners in the mercantile newspaper and often personal acquaintances, were now separated by intermediaries.

The great owner-editors, in short, were moving farther and farther away from immediate, active participation in the departments of their papers, whose value as investments crept steadily toward the million-dollar mark. They still had an important part to play in organizing and directing the journalistic revolution, and a group of them was to arise between 1865 and 1900 which lacked nothing in color or influence. Still, the successors of Day and Bennett and Greeley in the last forty years of the century were primarily publishers, not editors—generals far removed from the close-up shock of daily battle. The reporter, on the other hand, was becoming the foot soldier in journalism's front lines. He furnished the raw materials for the newspaper and shaped the attitudes of its readers. In their minds, he sometimes was the man who put the meaning into the daily press. Both publishers and reporters, each in their own way and from their respective vantage points in the working and governing ranks of newspaperdom, wrote important chapters in the story of American public life after Appomattox.

V

Empires in Newsprint: The Century Closes

In 1869 Henry Raymond, not yet fifty, died of a stroke. The next year saw the retirement of William Cullen Bryant, approaching his eightieth birthday, from the *Post*. In the summer of 1872 James Gordon Bennett was buried with pomp and ceremony. Horace Greeley was then campaigning for the Presidency on the Liberal Republican ticket, promising to drive the grafters from the government. In November, an avalanche of votes for Grant smothered him. A few weeks later Greeley was dead, too, his spirit finally broken by the frustration of his last political crusade. The passing of these four giants of the New York press signified the end of the era when modern journalism was founded.

A new cast took the boards. It was bigger and louder, but more disciplined, included fewer politicians and men of letters, and more millionaires. The drama it put on was a companion-piece to other spectacles on the national stage—the rise of the trust, the coming of the railroad barons, the conquest of the Far West. The stars of the new journalism shared the appetites, the successes, the laurels, and some of the catcalls which were the portion of their fellow magnates in rails, oil, steel, copper, lumber, meat, and grain. All of them profited by fantastic mechanical improvement and growth and stamped the institutions they managed into shapes which would endure into the oncoming twentieth century.

The marvels of mass production continued to transform the newspaper until the end of the nineties, when it assumed substantially its modern form. Web-perfecting and stereotyping presses were improved between 1870 and 1900 to the point where, by earlier standards, they were capable of prodigies. The cylinders grew wider to accommodate more pages simultaneously, and a series of clever devices for gathering and folding the pages made the four- and eight-page limits of the early days obsolete. By 1895 the Hoe firm was manufacturing an "octuple" press in which eight cylinders, each four pages wide, produced 24,000 thirty-two-page papers an hour. In 1902 a wealthy publisher could buy a "double octuple" Hoe which gave him 72,000 copies of a thirty-two-page journal in an hour, or lesser quantities of thicker papers. The problems of finding enough paper and type to feed these monsters were solved by methods as ingenious as they were important. Crude machines for making paper out of wood pulp had been patented before the Civil War, but in 1866 a Massachusetts firm, using equipment developed in Germany, began to produce pulp on a commercial scale. In another thirty years the production of newsprint had risen to something like half a million tons annually, the price had dropped from eight to two cents a

pound, and the industry could count on the immense re-
sources of the world's forests instead of an uncertain supply
of rags for stock. In 1886, after various prototypes had
tried and failed, Ottmar Mergenthaler's linotype machine had
its first successful practical test. Operated by a keyboard, it
arranged type matrices in a line automatically adjusted to the
correct length, cast a solid slug, and reshuffled the matrices
for the next line. It vastly increased the speed of composition,
and permitted the used type to be recast again quickly and
continuously.

These inventions broke down the last remaining barriers to
the spread of cheap publications, with all their unbelievable
power for mass organization, education, and propaganda. In
the nineties the circulation leaders among American papers
were reaching nearly 400,000 readers daily. Less than a hundred years after wooden hand presses were the only means
of publication, it was possible to gather the material for fifty
to eighty pages containing hundreds of thousands of words,
set them in type, and distribute them by the quarter-to-half-
millions of copies, all within twenty-four hours. The symbols
of this new publishing power were the great newspaper build-
ings—factories, really—which the successful owners put up to
house their behemoths. Thundering with the roar of the giant
presses, surrounded by wagons (and later, trucks) delivering
huge rolls of paper and carrying away bundles of finished
copies in a frenzy of motion, rising dozens of stories above
the streets, and showing lights in the windows of composing,
engraving, teletype, and editing rooms which were never
turned off, they represented the acme of controlled industrial
energy.

The contents of the enlarged newspaper also blossomed in

new forms under the sunshine of innovation. Stereotyping had broken the tyranny of column rules which held the type in place, so that headlines could go marching across two, three, four, and even eight columns at the century's end. Color presses were introduced about 1892, and the comics and Sunday supplements appeared in their wake. Photo-engraving techniques were sharpened in the seventies, and more and more line cuts, after first being transferred to the curved stereotype plates, were printed. The effects of these changes were felt in two ways. More pictures made the newspaper even more desirable to semiliterate readers, and advertisers could display their wares with a variety of eye-catching type sizes and illustrations. Quarter-page, half-page, and even full-page advertisements demonstrated the splendors of washing machines, vegetable compounds, soap that floated, baking powders, new fashions in dress, bicycles, baby buggies, and a thousand other items in the mass-production cornucopia. Line cuts were supplemented in the eighties by halftone engravings, which allowed photographs to be reproduced, and by the time of the war with Spain news pictures were beginning to appear in small numbers, although problems of technique in taking, developing, and transmitting photos delayed the full impact of picture journalism until the second quarter of the twentieth century.

All this meant that the owners had more scope for experimenting with their papers—adding features and supplements, providing Sunday and evening editions, increasing the volume of wired news if they chose, and testing varieties of makeup and headlining in the relentless quest for super-marketability. In one sense they had no choice, for just as in other industries, the firm that did not adopt new techniques was likely to be driven from the field. But the costs of modernization were formidable, and the publisher glorying in a new four-color press soon found that his debts multiplied faster than the best and latest "Hoe double-octuple" could spew out copies. The answer was to solicit more advertising, which could be done successfully only by getting more circulation, and more circulation could only be achieved in a sharply competitive field by reducing the price of the paper (which reduced income) or by new features and additions (which were expensive). The boasted independence of the non-party newspaper seemed to be a freedom to run a neck-and-crop race with bankruptcy. Beginning in the nineties, some publishers began to form chains in efforts to cut overhead, and consolidations of older papers, always a feature of the American newspaper scene, increased in number. A landmark was reached in the twenties when, among the dailies, failures and consolidations finally exceeded new starts. The number of dailies in the nation reached some 2,400 in 1919 and then began the slow decline which is still in process.

Despite the financial hazards, the owners had more or less given the newspaper its contemporary look as early as 1914. To the modern reader an 1860 copy of the *New York Times* or the *Chicago Tribune* is clearly antiquarian, exuding a dusty air of mummification. But the edition of either paper announcing the outbreak of World War I, nearly half a century ago, leaves *its* reader with a comfortable feeling of being at home. The large department-store layouts, the illustrated come-ons for nationally advertised products, the photographs, the head-lining, the women's and sports pages, the comics (in the case of the *Tribune*, at least) would scarcely seem out of place in 1961. Even the news, one reflects with discouragement, looks much the same.

The American Newspaperman

The publishers who were responsible for incorporating these changes in format were a varied lot. The wealth which they commanded put them in the ranks of the mighty, although their incomes did not approach those of the railroad and industrial leaders of the day and they were often forced to borrow from the real titans of finance. Whitelaw Reid, a chief editor of the *New York Tribune* at the time Greeley died, bought a controlling share of the paper's stock with the assistance of Jay Gould, the unscrupulous stock-market and real-estate speculator whose feats had once included an attempt to corner the country's gold supply. The *New York World*, begun in 1861, was owned until 1876 by Manton Marble, a practicing newspaperman, but when he tired of it and sold it, the power behind the purchasing syndicate was that of Tom Scott, master of the Pennsylvania Railroad. Five years later, Henry Villard, who had made millions promoting railroads in the Pacific Northwest, bought out the venerable *New York Post*. Papers on the financial rocks, indeed, had a way of drifting into the portfolios of big-time investors, who recognized the utility of having press spokesmen on their side.

Yet the very greatest editors were not bought outright, as some owners of country papers were, simply by generous advertisements, printing contracts, or cash subsidies. Their alliance with captains of industry was a natural one, for they shared with them a common faith in the glories of business expansion, the divine right of the individual to be master of his own property, and the uplifting power of wealth. What they said and did in defense of these abstractions, they did in their own way, and, for all the hugeness of their journals, they still made their personalities felt in their pages. The day of the shoestring printer and promoter was gone, but the leadership of the daily press until the era of the first Roosevelt remained entertainingly full of curmudgeons, civic uplifters, and ballyhoo experts.

Chief among the curmudgeons, in some respects, was Charles A. Dana. In 1868, after serving in the War Department and trying his hand at editorship in Chicago, he returned to New York and organized a company which bought the *Sun*. Both Dana and the *Sun* had changed since the 1840's. The paper, once the forerunner of cheap, impudent, successful journalism, had slipped badly in circulation. As for Dana, the youthful ardors which had led him to Brook Farm and then the *Tribune* office had burned away, leaving a brittle residue of cynicism. Dana had the paper filled with local stories of high life and low, always with an eye to the piquant, the offbeat, the drily comic. A succession of good city editors drilled cub reporters in the exactitudes of polished writing. One of those editors, John Bogart, earned a kind of immortality by coining the famous maxim that a dog biting a man was not news, while a man biting a dog was. The point of the advice, that only the unusual is newsworthy, tells much about *Sun* policy. A man-biting dog was simply a problem of public health and safety; a dog-biting man was a curiosity from which a clever writer could extract a high yield of amusement.

Dana's favorite vent for sarcasm was his editorial page. He wrote much of it himself, staring critically over his eyeglasses at his own copy before sending it off to press, and exchanging comments with assistants and visitors as he sat at his desk, wearing a black skullcap on his bald head. Sometimes his temper was up and he hit hard at targets like New York's Boss William Tweed, or President Rutherford B. Hayes, whose crime, in Dana's eyes, was in accepting the "stolen" election of 1876. But more often he poked fun, sometimes with more devastating effect on friends than on enemies. He supported Greeley in 1872, with tongue in cheek, dubbing him the "Woodchopper of Chappaqua." In 1880 he was behind the Democratic candidate, Winfield Scott Hancock, but he did little for Hancock's cause by referring to him as "a good man, weighing 240 pounds." In 1884 he claimed to favor the presidential candidacy of the Greenback nominee, Benjamin F. Butler, a slippery politician who changed parties almost seasonally, but this advocacy was clearly Dana's way of showing his contempt for the more orthodox candidates on the Republican and Democratic tickets. He was a pillar of the new journalism which was proud of its independence of party, but his own attitude showed that at least one reason for this emancipation was something other than a pride in impartiality. Like many businessmen of the postwar generation, the editors took little interest in national politics. The parties had become machinelike organizations for winning elections and getting jobs, and there was little to dictate a choice between them except sentiment and habit. Dana was skeptical of politicians, but he also distrusted foreign nations, labor unions, Socialists, farmers, and reformers in general. This put him in step with both parties and enabled him to boast that he wore the coat of neither.

Even more of a cynic than the aging Dana was Chicago's unbelievable Wilbur F. Storey, who controlled the *Times* of that city from 1861 to 1878. White-bearded Storey raged through life, breaking things to see who would shout. During the war he was a violent Copperhead, crying daily that the war was a failure, Lincoln a tyrant, and the boys in blue dupes of the Republicans. The military authorities padlocked his office for a short period and mobs threatened him almost regularly, and neither experience hushed him for a moment. He drank as he argued and lived, extravagantly, brazenly, and noisily, and he kept Chicago courts busy with his libel suits. He was publicly horsewhipped by a lady entertainer who could not put up with the law's delays in avenging slander. He kept a female spirit medium at his side for counsel and solace when his wife died, and was finally adjudged insane, without ever having yielded any quarter in his war on propriety.

The Chicago *Times,* under Storey, was distinguished for its tales of seduction and scandal and its verbal raids on city fathers. It also achieved notoriety for its pun-filled and alliterative head-lines—a story on Commodore Vanderbilt's will being captioned "The House that Vanderbilt," and accounts of hangings (a favorite *Times* topic) carrying such titles as "A Drop Too Much" and "Jerked to Jesus." Storey's paper appealed to par-ticularly urban groups—loafers and toughs who liked their news as they liked their whiskey, cheap and raw; clerks and laborers who found that the gossip and scandal of a great metropolis added spice to otherwise routine lives spent in its confines; and those who felt themselves sophisticated enough to enjoy flouting the conventional pieties, at least vicariously. All were drawn into a fraternity of *Times*-consumers, forming the kind of audience that sensational journalism could count on in the cities from that time forward.

In contrast to the Danas and Storeys who enjoyed the edi-torial prerogatives of puckishness, other prominent newspaper-men chose to identify themselves with the promotion of munic-ipal or sectional improvement. Henry Grady and Henry Wat-terson belonged to the latter camp. Grady was a poor boy from

Georgia who worked his way up through the ranks of country journalism and in 1880 managed to buy an interest in the *Atlanta Constitution,* then fifteen years old. He became its managing editor and remained at that post until his death nine years later. Grady's own experience had been as a reporter, and some of his nationally reprinted stories gave him a reputation that went far beyond Atlanta. He filled the paper with a wide assortment of news, but his outstanding talent was as a spokesman for the industrialization of the South. He was one of the greatest southern editors to preach the gospel of saving that region from poverty by importing the factory, and his invocation of the spirit of progress endeared him to the business mind of North and South alike. Thus he was a potent figure in laying the ghosts of the Civil War.

Watterson was of a more peppery temperament, which he had room to exercise in the Louisville *Courier-Journal,* owned by Walter Haldeman. Watterson loved the excitement of politics and became a power among the Democrats of the upper South, eminently visible and important at a succession of conventions. Gifted also in playing the role of the traditional southern gentleman, he entertained businessmen and politicians with bourbon, chuckles, and white-moustached charm at his home outside the city and conveyed some of the emotional prestige of the old South of broad-brimmed hats and frock-coat oratory to the new South of cigarette factories and iron mines. He lived on until the 1920's. Both Watterson and Grady were throwbacks, in a sense, to the regional promoter-journalists of the Thomas Ritchie era. They inherited the job of guiding southern middle-class opinion, which had belonged mainly to preachers and politicians before the war, and they were possibly more effective leaders than their predecessors. Southern politicians had a diminished national prestige at the end of Reconstruction, and southern preachers, though they kept a strong hold on the local mind, were out of step with liberalizing and modernizing movements in their churches. The newspaper therefore had a strong civic function in the South.

In the larger towns, where the old-time role of the paper in public affairs was fading, a determined editor could revive it and keep up in the race for circulation as well. William Rockhill Nelson was just under forty when he founded the *Kansas City Star* in 1880. He had made money in building contracting, and came to the editorial desk with the handicap of inexperience but the asset of vast energy—"a big, laughing, fat, goodnatured, rollicking, haw-hawing person who loved a drink, a steak, a story, and a fight," in the words of William Allen White, who once worked for him as a reporter. The *Star* was at first an evening paper, an idea fast becoming popular. Brought home on the way from work, the evening paper was read by the whole family and was a better advertising medium for retail stores than the morning paper. Thanks to time differentials and transatlantic cables it could often beat the morning papers with wire news from Europe, which, when filed in the evening there, hit American headlines in mid-afternoon. And since it could be outstripped on local and national news which broke late in the day, it tended to make the best of circumstances by concentrating more on assessing the value of local stories and hunting out colorful feature material. This turned out to be Nelson's forte.

He took it on himself to make the *Star* "the mentor and monitor of Kansas City." He prodded the raw meat-packing and rail center into civic pride. He demanded that it light its streets, widen its avenues, clean up its parks, ride herd on its traction and utility magnates, fire its boodling officials whenever the *Star* uncovered their peculations, paint its houses, fine its grasping landlords, and behave as if it had a conscience. Exposing the sins of an unruly Kansas City kept the *Star's* reporters busy and built for Nelson both a muckraking reputation and a big readership, touching 50,000 in 1893 and going past it soon after. Many of these crusades reflected simply the boosterism of the urban frontier, but they were something more, too. They gave the *Star* a personality and identified it with the "workingmen," whose two cents, in Nelson's view, entitled them to a friend and advocate as well as a newspaper. Nelson was trying to re-establish the organic link between the journal and the community which had existed in western towns a half-century before, when the editor was a political, social, and intellectual leader in the town as well as its gossip, raconteur, and advertiser. Hard as he fought the rings and bosses of his town, he was, like them, trying to win the loyalties of classes whose needs were ignored by more gentlemanly politicians and editors.

This kind of journalism was practiced elsewhere, too, a good example of it being the *Chicago Daily News*, founded by Melville Stone in 1875 and later carried on by Victor Lawson. It also specialized in crusades and deft local reporting, and its morning edition (issued as the *Chicago Record*) combined with the evening version to command over 200,000 readers by 1888. Lawson, like Nelson and like their imitators in many other cities, spelled out a worthy meaning for "independent journalism" by dedicating it to the service of the public at large. In such commitment lay the real power of the press. But it is noteworthy that this was not achieved, as the editors liked to suggest, by presenting "all the news" in nonpartisan fashion. The crusading editor had to catch his audience first. This required him not only to furnish plenty of the world-wide coverage that stamped a paper as one that kept up with the times, but also to provide a great many sporting, amusement, and advertising features having little to do with the news in any formal sense, as a record of momentous events. As for the local news, it was selected, shaped, and directed to a conscious end, just as it had been by the mercantile and party editors. The end might be more or less worthy than that served by political journalism, but it allowed editors to carry the serious, "objective" foreign and national news which could never hope to command mass circulation on its own.

There were, of course, papers which made the conventional kind of political and financial reporting the backbone of their offerings. The *New York Tribune* under Whitelaw Reid ran to politics, literature, and science, with an occasional dip into interesting scandal. The scandal could always be presented in the name of high moral purpose, if it happened to involve the saloon- and brothel-keepers who made up the rank and file of Tammany's voting platoons. Reid was only thirty-six in 1873 when he became the *Tribune*'s kingpin. A bright young graduate of Ohio's Miami College, with a good record as a war and Washington correspondent, he had come to the big city to make good, like Horace Greeley before him. Unlike Greeley, however, Reid did not aim to addle his readers by shouting their shortcomings in their ears. The *Tribune* stoutly defended all Republican candidates and every Republican policy. Reid himself was high in party circles, and its candidate for Vice-President in the unsuccessful year of 1892. He married wealth, served as minister to France for a time, and moved graciously and comfortably in an atmosphere of Anglo-Saxon friendship, banquets at Delmonico's, and a social milieu in which he could write easily of someone that he was "a liar as well as a trades unionist. In fact, the two things seem to go together." Reid could never be completely accepted as a high priest among the genteel, since he was running a daily newspaper instead of a literary monthly. But he came close.

The *Evening Post* also remained a paper for gentlemen and scholars. When Henry Villard bought it in 1881, he turned it over to a distinguished editorial triumvirate of Edwin L. Godkin, Carl Schurz, and Horace White. Godkin was the editor of the *Nation*, which Villard also purchased at that time. An English-born writer of laissez faire liberal persuasion, he had for years written distinguished, tart articles assailing the spoils system, the high tariff, monopolies, labor unions, and Socialists. He had at all times a high and firm sense of his own rectitude. Schurz was a reform politician of German background, and White was a former Washington correspondent and editor of the *Chicago Tribune*. All had taken some part in the Liberal Republican crusade which was in good part led by right-minded gentlemen-editors. They quarreled soon and often, and Schurz finally left the *Post* to White and Godkin, who used it to support hard-money policies nationally and to assail Tammany locally. Both the *Tribune* and the *Post*, holding to the three- and four-cent prices which had become common after the inflationary days of the Civil War, had modest circulations; both looked down on upstarts like the *New York Daily News* (the first of the city's papers so named), which sold, largely in the tenement house districts, for a penny, was loyal to Tammany, and reached between 100,000 and 200,000 people daily.

Municipal crusading, respectable reform, and sardonic sensationalism were all variations on the theme of successful editorship in the seventies and eighties. Another variation was showmanship, a pioneer in which was, appropriately enough, James Gordon Bennett, Jr. He was not the pushful worker his father had been, and he ran the *Herald*, after it was handed on to him, by cables from Paris to his managing editors. He knew more of yachts, champagne, and polo ponies than of financial statements and pressroom problems, but he did inherit one Bennett instinct: he knew how to *make* news. He was particularly grateful when the American Indians, the French and Prussians, or the Russians and Turks furnished a war which enabled him to carry on the great tradition of battlefield correspondence at any cost established by his father during the Civil War. But when no war was forthcoming, the younger Bennett financed exploring and archeological expeditions, creating artificial wars against time and nature. The most celebrated of these manufactured stories was the search of *Herald* man Henry M. Stanley in 1871 for the "lost" missionary, David Livingstone, ending with the dramatic confrontation in Ujiji, Tanganyika, and the celebrated query, "Dr. Livingstone, I presume?" The expedition cost thousands but made royal copy and filled the need for popular press drama.

The newspaper "stunt" of this kind was to have a long and hardy life after the 1870's. In part it arose naturally out of the age which produced Barnum. In part it furnished second-hand color and excitement to city dwellers whose jobs and lives were becoming ever more routinized. But some of it was due to the natural dynamics of the new journalism. A paper achieved rank and readers by being first with the news. If the stories it furnished could be not only early but exclusive, that was even better. But "beats" and "exclusives" could not be furnished daily or weekly, particularly when the most important events were covered by the co-operative newsgathering agencies.

Therefore, they had to be created by those who could afford to create them, which enhanced the lead of the already prospering sheets. The success of the spectacular report from the special correspondent, moreover, emphasized the degree to which the concept of news itself had come to embrace only the immediately exciting. No longer was there any pretense, as in early colonial papers, that the news should be a complete and continuous "history of the times." A general decline in crop prices in the West, an increase in bankruptcies in a given state, the emergence of new statesmen in European cabinets—these were not news but "background," possibly entitled to space only in the feature pages or Sunday editions of the more responsible papers. The craze for currency seemed to fit the accelerating tempo of city living, especially in the United States, where the present tense dominated almost all thought and the past was drawn on merely to justify, not retard, change. Yet the domination of the "hot" story gave the newspaper a May-fly character, with Monday's front-page earth-shaker being Friday's ten-line filler at the end of the second section. It also gave the newspaper readers a distorted view of the world as a theater in which sudden, violent acts succeeded one another with convulsive speed. The stunt was journalism's shot in the arm of history, when history moved too slowly between editions.

Then, in 1883, the curious talent of Joseph Pulitzer entered the scene. Like the great figures in any field, Pulitzer was able to create new patterns by synthesizing old ones. Day and Bennett, a half-century before, had taken advantage of the new mass literacy created by public education, the widespread tract and pamphlet distributions of the reform and religious associations, and the comic and sporting weeklies, to build their popular newspapers. Pulitzer now combined the sensationalism, the wit, the crusades, the stunts, the features, the wide coverage, and the public conscientiousness of such diverse men as Dana, Nelson, the younger Bennett, Stone, and Godkin and created a dazzlingly successful amalgam of them in the *New York World*.

Pulitzer's was a Horatio Alger story with a foreign accent. He came to New York from Hungary in 1864 as a skinny recruit for the Union Army. Broke and footloose after his discharge, he drifted out to St. Louis and kept alive by odd jobs. Pulitzer was, however, full of ambition. He made influential friends among the German community in St. Louis, studied law, and finally was hired as a reporter on the German-language paper, the *Westliche Post*. He got a journeyman's education in newspaper fieldwork, went into politics as a Republican, and was sent to the state legislature. He next bought a share in the *Westliche Post*, sold it, bought another small German paper and sold that, and meanwhile continued his political life, moving through the Liberal Republican and into the Democratic party. In 1878, he bought and consolidated two young and sickly St. Louis journals, the *Post* and the *Dispatch*, combined them, and began to find his true vocation. Aided by a skilful assistant, John Cockerill, Pulitzer threw the *Post-Dispatch* into a succession of crusades, brightened up its format, multiplied its features, and made it a scrappy circulation rival for the *Globe-Democrat*, which was ably run by Joseph B. McCullagh, a onetime Civil War correspondent for the Cincinnati press.

In 1883 Pulitzer invaded New York. He bought the limping *World* from Jay Gould, who in turn had got it from Tom Scott as part of a parcel involved in a railroad transaction. Tall, big-nosed, and red-whiskered, Pulitzer made no secret of his intention to dominate his new arena. The *World,* he announced in a ringing salutation, would be "not only cheap, but bright, not only bright, but large, not only large but truly democratic." This final adjective was meant to be taken both politically and socially. Pulitzer was in fact a fairly unorthodox Democrat by the 1880's, and he not only supported Cleveland but advocated the governmental curbing of monopolies, the right of workers to unionize, and the imposition of stiff taxes on incomes and inheritances—all of them then somewhat heretical positions. It was Pulitzer's conviction that the paper should also appeal to the taste of New York's heterogeneous mass of immigrants and workers, and if that taste was coarse by patrician standards, patrician standards would have to go the way of the whale-oil lamp in the age of electricity.

The *World*'s pages, therefore, presented a curious, intellectually piebald appearance to the reader, as Pulitzer cast his net for both serious and light-minded buyers. Cockerill and his helpers had a genius for provocative headlining that drew attention irresistibly to the story and made the paper hard to put down once it was begun. Here are the front-page items of a typical issue in 1884: "Ready To Visit Chicago" told of a meeting of Tammany to see how many members could attend the imminent Democratic convention. "A Boom for Cleveland," "The Illinois Democracy," "Carter Harrison's Candidacy," and "Blaine and Logan's Programme" were all straightforward political stories, but the makeup editor could not resist the sarcastic addition of "The Republicans Want Butler." It turned out that they did want the eccentric ex-general—as the Democratic candidate! Next came "Murdered on Shipboard," "Twenty-four Miners Killed," and "The Slugger

Empires in Newsprint

Laureate," the last-named an interview with John L. Sullivan while he lay in his hotel room nursing a gargantuan hangover. "Proofs of By-gone Murders" dealt with skeletons unearthed in the process of digging a foundation trench for a new building on the site of a saloon in Illinois. "Accident to Alderman Kirk" was followed by "Fighting the Cholera," and foreign news re-entered the picture with "The Annexation of Cuba" (the subhead explained, "Spain Officially Assured That the United States Does Not Want Her White Elephant") and "Revising the Constitution" (of France). In the last two of the seven columns, the Tabasco sauce was poured on freely: "A Brother on the War-Path; He Attacks His Sister's Dentist and Then Tries To Shoot Him"; "Another Murderer To Hang"; "Love and Cigarettes Crazed Him" (an account of a suicide); "He Barked like a Dog" (the tale of a man seized with hydrophobia); and "Love Stronger Than Money" (in which a man remarried, forfeiting $12,000 left to him by his wife on condition that he remain a widower); and finally, "A Vice-Admiral's Son in Jail"; "He Pawned the Diamonds: How an Enterprising Broker Managed to Fail for $50,000"; and "Did She Take the Diamonds? A Hotel Maid Accused of Stealing Jewels Which Were Mysteriously Returned." All these were continued on inside pages. If, as a later journalistic truism had it, the requisites for big circulation were blood, money, and sex, then the *World* entered the readership wars with no lack of ammunition.

The *World*'s success was dazzling. In about a year it was selling 100,000 copies daily; a Sunday edition reached 250,000 before 1890, and an evening edition was begun in 1887, which, combined with the morning *World*, accounted for 374,000 copies daily by 1892. And Pulitzer continued to pour it on. The

Sunday edition was a grab-bag of some forty-odd pages, half full of advertising, and half full of such diverse fare, according to one Saturday's promise, as "Lily Langtry's New Admirer," "Brooklyn Celebrities Illustrated," "Socialism and Its Meaning," "Monaco and Its Gambling," "A Sketch of Senator Bayard," and "Watering-Place Notes." When color presses appeared, the Sunday issue blossomed out with chromatic drawings, among them a cartoon illustrating the adventures of a group of ragamuffins from "Hogan's Alley." One of them, decked out in a wide, baby's nightshirt of brilliant yellow and nicknamed "The Yellow Kid," became a forerunner of comic-strip characters and the inspiration for the sobriquet "yellow journalism" applied to the Pulitzer (and later Hearst) formula.

Pulitzer's editorial column crackled with crusades—against aldermen who took bribes for favorable votes on a streetcar franchise that was a bad bargain for the city, against tenement contractors, against the Bell telephone monopoly and the Standard Oil trust, and against the conditions at Ellis Island, where hundreds of thousands of European newcomers were checked in by immigration authorities. When intellectual sympathy with popular causes was not enough to demonstrate the *World*'s love for the common man, Pulitzer went into open competition with the ward-heelers of Tammany (which, Democrat or no Democrat, he detested) and provided free ice, coal, picnics, and Christmas dinners for the needy. And when New York's citizens were not attending Pulitzer's civic parties or cheering his grapples with the "interests," they were paying wide-eyed attention to the *World*'s news, sporting, women's, and other feature sections (all plentifully illustrated) or laughing at its political cartoons or following some *World* reporter on a stunt in which he (or she) pretended to be a criminal or a lunatic or a contractor or an immigrant in order to write an inside account of conditions in the jail, the asylum, the legislature, or the sweatshop. One of Pulitzer's most celebrated coups was sending Elizabeth Cochran (who wrote over the byline "Nellie Bly") hurrying around the world on ships, trains, rickshas, sampans, and burros in seventy-three days, to beat the record of Jules Verne's fictitious hero, Phileas Fogg, who had turned the trick in eighty. Another was soliciting $100,000 from his readers, in nickels and dimes, to provide the money for the pedestal on which the Statue of Liberty was erected in the late eighties. In a sense, the familiar figure in New York's harbor is a monument to Pulitzer and the power of the new journalism as well as to freedom.

Pulitzer's triumphs and innovations successfully demonstrated the place of the popular paper in the United States. Despite the criticisms which rained about it, the *World* was not simply a lower-class scandal-sheet. In England, where sensational journalism was catching on in the eighties, and in France there was a wide and clear gap between the solid and informed journals of opinion or criticism and the lurid sheets aimed at the penny reader. But the *World*, together with its even more sensational imitators, was read by a population not so easily sorted out by class. Deacons and stockbrokers read it as well as their janitors and clerks, though a copy of it folded under the arm did not impart quite the tone of a copy of the *Post* or *Tribune*. The *World* sprinkled a good supply of the most respectable "hard" financial, political, and diplomatic information among its sordid vignettes, just as the most reverend and grave journals were not above reporting a murder trial or a particularly well-publicized sporting event. All the successful big-city journals embraced in themselves the many pasts of the American newspaper. Like fossils in the wall of a canyon the miscellany and advertising of the colonial gazette, the flamboyant editorials of the party and reform sheets, the special information of the business and mercantile papers, the stories and pictures of such popular quasi-magazines as *Harper's Weekly* and *Frank Leslie's Illustrated Newspaper* (both dating from the fifties) were all visible in the great newspapers of the Pulitzer heyday. The winning publisher learned that the laurels went to the man who did not confine himself to one appeal, that in American society the inexorable market test was passed best by the journal that resisted categorization. The American conviction that a reader might be simultaneously informed, challenged, diverted, and relaxed by the same paper might be irritating, might even be part of a national illusion that opposites could be reconciled without cost, but it was there, and the big, bargain-basement, mass-circulation journal was obedient to it.

The hallmark of the Pulitzer type of journalism was not its novelty but its paternalism. The *World* might well be friend, counselor, jester, and advocate for the great public, but it took these roles only when and insofar as Joseph Pulitzer directed. Pulitzer's liberalism might be admirable, but what sold the *World* was not its antimonopoly crusades but the simple excitement of crusades no matter at whom directed, plus the spice of the features and the timeliness of the news. Pulitzer could change policies with no depressing effect on his circulation. On the contrary, when he became rattled by the competition of William Randolph Hearst in 1898 and temporarily dropped his normal opposition to jingoism in favor of preaching war with Spain, the *World*'s sales climbed over the million mark. Editorials seemed to have little to do with the acceptance of a paper. Moreover, in providing the easy delights of sensationalism, Pulitzer conditioned readers to expect handstands on the high wire and other acrobatic shows before they would concede their attention to the press. They became not so much members of a thinking public as consumers of peppy newsprint, waiting to be told by the providers of that newsprint what was good for them. Once the institution of the big-time daily had oriented itself to popular taste, it tended to take its direction increasingly from its owners alone. If they sought to enlarge their power by lowering the level of their papers still further, there was little to stand in their way. Pulitzer and his predecessors had released forces which might go out of control in less scrupulous hands, the perennial danger of paternalism.

Pulitzer learned this himself when William Randolph Hearst came into New York in 1895 to beat him at his own game. The son of a mining millionaire, Hearst was a dynamic, dictatorial, arrogant baron of journalism whose career spanned forty years of muckraking, reaction, scandalmongering, empire-building, and fantastic spending. Although he liked to pose as the people's champion, he was never able to overcome his petulance when they voted against his wishes, and he made it clear in the editorial pages, whose contents he dictated, that he doubted their capacity to think in words of more than two syllables. He was initiated into the journalism of crusade and crime on the *San Francisco Examiner*, one of his father's incidental properties, which he took over at twenty-four after a wild and free-spending youth. New York was a prize he wanted badly, and he was accustomed to having enough money to gratify his desires. He bought the *New York Journal*, and then, with an inherited seven and a half million dollars at his disposal, bought the best talent in town to run it. He hired Pulitzer's entire Sunday staff, including the seasoned editors Morrill Goddard and his successor, Arthur Brisbane. He bought away such gifted reporters as Julian Ralph from the *Sun*, and he was able to engage Richard Harding Davis and Stephen Crane to write war correspondence for him and Mark Twain to cover such special events as Queen Victoria's jubilee. *Journal* reporters on limitless expense accounts dug gold in the Klondike, bribed their way past bodyguards to hold interviews with celebrities, and even tried their hand at solving murder cases, at least once successfully.

The *Journal* really hit its stride, however, in 1897 and 1898 when Hearst appeared to take over personal management of the drive for United States intervention on behalf of the Cuban rebels against Spanish rule. Here was a field for yellow journalism at its gaudiest—a continuing crusade, with violence and brutality in the raging guerrilla warfare and the repressions of the Spanish authorities; sex in the persons of beauteous Cuban girls villainously maltreated by the cruel Spaniards; patriotism in the constant reminder that autocratic, Catholic Spain was an intruder in the Western Hemisphere reserved by destiny for Americans. The *Journal* lavishly paid reporters to steal alleged documents illustrative of Spanish perfidy, to get on-the-spot stories from the fighting fronts, and to rescue Cuban revolutionaries. Homer Davenport drew cartoons pointing up the message that only pusillanimity kept Americans from going to the relief of the Cubans. Illustrator Frederic Remington concocted sketches of Spanish atrocities, such as the imaginary episode in which Spanish policemen boarded an American vessel in pursuit of a young Cuban woman sailing for the United States and stripped her naked in a search for messages from the revolutionaries. When the battleship "Maine" was blown up in

Empires in Newsprint

Havana harbor in February, 1898, the *Journal's* headlines shouted, in type several inches high, that the Spaniards had been responsible (an allegation for which no proof has ever been discovered) and that war must be waged. The cry was taken up throughout the country, and President McKinley was swept along on an implacable tide toward a declaration of hostilities in April. When the American campaign in Cuba got under way, the newspapers, the *Journal* chief among them, had a gloriously expensive time covering it, and the *Journal,* not without reason, printed "ears" in the upper corners of its front pages asking, "How Do You Like the *Journal's* War?"

Pulitzer, after initially holding back, had gone along with the jingo campaign, as the *Journal's* circulation crept past the *World's,* with each paper's morning and evening and extra editions selling over a million and a half copies on exciting days. By 1898, however, he was an absentee editor. Failing eyesight and poor health had driven him away from his desk in 1890. He spent twenty years thereafter cruising around the world in his yacht, issuing ukases from the Mediterranean or the South Atlantic to his editors in St. Louis and New York, being read to by a corps of secretaries, and contemplating in lonely magnificence what he had wrought. Hearst, too, eventually left New York and began to acquire more newspapers, so that the *Journal* became merely one child in the large family whose behavior Hearst supervised, finally, from a castle in California, surrounded by his purchased art treasures. Both men were among the last of the grandees of personal journalism, but both ended their lives (Pulitzer in 1911, Hearst in 1951) far from the direct, daily, shirt-sleeved participation in the papers which had lifted them to prominence.

The American Newspaperman

Despite the dominance of the great circulation giants, American journalism in 1900 showed enough variety to make the way of the generalizer dangerous. There were, according to one estimate, 2,190 daily papers in that year and no fewer than 15,-813 weeklies, with both figures on the rise. Some of the increase was accounted for by the creation of evening and Sunday editions, and much more by the fact that the Far West was still filling out; new townships, following the pattern of the past, produced new weeklies. The *average* circulation per issue of dailies in 1904 was still slightly above 12,000; of weeklies, about 8,000. Religious and agricultural weeklies continued to be read, although they tended to abandon all efforts to present general news and became harder to distinguish from magazines.

The small-town papers were often well managed, and their editors continued to be men of substance in the community. It was even possible, with luck, to shine in the national firmament from the desk of a modest journal. In 1895 William Allen White took over the *Emporia Gazette* in Kansas, and Josephus Daniels bought the Raleigh, North Carolina, *News and Observer.* From the prairie small town and the middle-sized southern factory city both White and Daniels rose into nationwide view through crusades against privilege, through personal charm, and, in White's case, attractive minor literary gifts. Daniels ultimately became a cabinet member and a diplomat, a genial southern Democratic grand-uncle. White was an important, if unheeded, figure in high Republican councils until his death in 1944.

Such men, however, were clearly exceptions to the general anonymity of country journalists. Many of the small-town publishers, struggling endlessly with the budget, yielded to the blandishments of bribers. When the legislature of New York brought Boss Tweed to bay in 1868, he confessed that rural

Empires in Newsprint

Republican editors had abandoned attacks against his operations on the city charter in Albany on payment of appropriate sums. How much? "Oh," growled the boss, "sometimes $5,000, sometimes $1,000, sometimes $500. It was a general dribble all the time." Other descendants of the country printer were much more subservient to pressure from advertisers than their metropolitan rivals. Bosses, bankers, and businessmen were too often the real powers behind many a country gazette that liked to spread itself editorially on the glories of a free press during patriotic holiday seasons.

In addition, the smaller papers were falling into a deadening uniformity under the increasing pressures of a new force, syndication. It was not really a new idea. When pre–Civil War editors filled their papers with gratuitous "exchanges," a particularly enjoyable joke or parody or poem was likely to appear simultaneously in a number of places, and the weekly editions "for the country" of the great newspapers were really separate papers filled with the news and feature services of the parent organ. Thus was appeased the hunger of the lonely but literate American countryside for more printed material than unskilled printer-editors could sometimes supply. After 1865, however, syndication put the old-time exchanges on an organized and widespread basis; in addition, tighter copyright laws in 1870 and 1874 made the freedom of the scissors harder to exercise safely. A. N. Kellogg, just at the end of the Civil War, conceived the idea of selling to rural editors hard-pressed for ideas newsprint already covered on one side with stories or material of an unspecialized nature. The purchaser took such a sheet and printed his local matter on the other side. When the paper was folded over, pages one and four contained the home-grown wisdom, pages two and three consisted of Kellogg's "patent insides," and the local editor had been saved half his usual labor, at a charge which became more modest as more papers subscribed. In 1871 an enterprising printer in New York discovered how to make thin stereotype plates which could be easily shipped and fitted to a variety of printing presses found in country newspaper offices. Like Kellogg's "readyprint," this "boiler plate" also made possible widespread distribution of already composed pictures and prose to hundreds of customers.

It was not surprising that syndicates soon formed for the widespread sale of writings aimed at public taste in the hinterlands. Kellogg democratically offered subscribers the choice of his "Story Department, or Miscellany, or Agricultural or Children's Reading" collections. The American Press Association, in 1882, reached out for the patronage of big dailies as well as little weeklies, with such popular humorists as Bill Nye and Eugene Field in their contractual net. In 1884 S. S. McClure overreached them by forming a syndicate which eventually attracted such writers as Kipling, Jack London, Conan Doyle, and Robert Louis Stevenson, all of them glad to get the prices for their work which McClure, combining the purchasing power of dozens of papers, could pay. Edward Bok, the Dutch immigrant, who proved later, as editor of the *Ladies' Home Journal,* to have an uncanny sense of what the "new" middle-class woman liked to read, began a successful syndicate in 1886. It was true that small papers which bought these made-to-order contents gave their readers something considerably better than local talent could furnish, but in the process the grass-roots press was likely to lose whatever individuality, good or bad, it possessed. The small-town paper continued to be the voice of the community, but now it also brought in the voice of the city, sometimes in deafening volume.

The New-York Times.

VOL. XIV....NO. 4230.   NEW-YORK, SATURDAY, APRIL 15, 1865.   PRICE FOUR CENTS

WFUL EVENT.

esident Lincoln Shot by an Assassin.

Deed Done at Ford's Theatre Last Night.

ACT OF A DESPERATE REBEL

empted Assassination of Secretary Seward.

This *New York Times* of 1865 was printed in the pattern made possible by the 847 press, although the *Times* was just beginning to acquire more modern equipment by that date. (Courtesy, University of Chicago Libraries.)

This *Chicago Tribune* announcing the victory at Manila Bay shows the variety of front-page makeup possible by 1898. (Courtesy, *Chicago Tribune*.)

Empires in Newsprint

The country editor might still be a power in the township, but like the country grocers and merchants he was getting to be more of a retail outlet for nationally made and nationally advertised products. In addition, he had to face the direct competition of the metropolitan dailies themselves. Special dealer associations like the American Newspaper Company, founded in 1864, bought bundles of papers directly from the big-city pressrooms, rushed them to trains, and had them in the hands of local agents fifty to one hundred miles away within hours. As early as 1890 twenty-one principal newspaper-distribution areas in the United States embraced twenty million people out of a national population of sixty million, a sharp instance of what one historian has called "urban imperialism in the cultural sphere." Long before radio and the movies, the newspaper played a part in infusing the countryside with urban attitudes and habits, dulling the edge of conflict between the two worlds but preparing the inevitable triumph of the city.

Among the bigger papers, too, the effects of standardization, powerful everywhere in American life, were felt. The syndicates served the large dailies as well as the small, and in fact spared them numerous woes in doing so, for as papers enlarged to attract more readers and more advertisements (which by 1910 furnished 65 per cent of all newspaper revenues), they developed nearly unappeasable appetites for material at low cost. An occasional paper might get by with a single-minded concentration on the news. The *New York Times*, for example, was taken over, after falling on evil days, by Adolph S. Ochs in 1895. Ochs magically pushed it toward its long-standing primacy in thoroughness of coverage without any disastrous sacrifice in circulation. But most papers were glad to have the stories, cartoons, popular scientific articles, columns of advice to women, sermons, and other assorted fare provided by an increasing number of feature services.

In the furnishing of the news itself, the press associations were increasingly dominant. The New York Associated Press battled with a number of competitors throughout the declining years of the century—among them the American Press Association in 1871; an early United Press, founded in 1882, which lasted until 1897; a Laffan News Bureau, in New York, which ran from the mid-nineties to 1916; and various services set up by large papers to ease the burden of newsgathering expenses by sharing their reporters' work with a select list of clients. The AP's two strongest challengers were initiated in the first decade of the new century by the owners of chains. Edward W. Scripps inspired the founding of the modern United Press in 1907, and Hearst's International News Service was born in 1909. Both were originally set up to serve the Scripps and Hearst papers but were later reorganized to take on other clients. The AP, however, continued to lead the field. As early as 1879 it began to lease wires for its exclusive use; by the end of 1900 it claimed 700 members, served 2,300 dailies, spent nearly two million dollars a year, and sent some 50,000 words a day buzzing over thousands of miles of leased wire. It was charged with being a monopoly, keeping franchises out of the hands of new papers, and serving as a funnel for propaganda through its exchange arrangements with European news services under the patronage of their governments. But whether or not these charges were true, the significant thing about the press associations was their tendency to standardize the contents of subscribing sheets. The owner of a paper in a small industrial city, with a circulation of 50,000, had the pick each day of thousands of words of news gathered and transmitted with miraculous efficiency—far more than his readers could hope to absorb. His only hope of variety lay in which items he selected and emphasized. Good editors managed to retain a judicious balance between local and wire-service news; hard-driven or careless ones piled in the syndicated features and the press association stories, and their papers grew to look like the front windows of chain stores, displaying the same canned goods in the same pyramidal heaps.

Although individual printers had sometimes been silent partners in a number of papers in the days of Benjamin Franklin and Isaiah Thomas, the modern newspaper chains, spurred on by the cost problem, were far more tightly organized. A mighty advocate of the chain was Edward W. Scripps, cantankerous and acute, who began newspaper work in Detroit in the 1870's but soon sought wider pastures. In the five years between 1878 and 1883 he scraped together the funds to buy or found papers in Cleveland, Cincinnati, and Covington, Kentucky. In 1895 he went into partnership with Milton McRae, establishing the Scripps-McRae League, which founded or purchased papers in such middle-sized-to-large towns as Kansas City, Akron, Des Moines, Toledo, Houston, and San Diego, with an occasional venture into a hard competitive market like Chicago. By 1914 the Scripps-McRae League was publishing twenty-three papers and had begun its own news service (later to become the United Press) and its own feature syndicate, the Newspaper Enterprise Association. Scripps was not fond of gigantism in individual papers; his technique was to send an agent to a city to commence operations on $50,000 or less, with a major (but not controlling) interest in the paper if he succeeded in building circulation and the threat of the ax if he failed. Like Pulitzer, Scripps assaulted the pieties of fellow millionaires by advocating public control of utilities, the strengthening of labor unions, and other policies of turn-of-the-century progressivism. His quarrels with associates and subordinates were on a grand scale, and so was his fortune at his death in 1926. While Scripps was pursuing his stormy career, Hearst continued to buy new properties. He had only seven papers by 1910, but twelve years later he owned twenty dailies and eleven Sunday papers, to say nothing of two wire services, a feature syndicate, six magazines, a Sunday supplement distributed with all his papers, a newsreel company, and a moving picture studio.

Others followed—though at a distance—where Scripps and Hearst led. The chains had irresistible advantages in bargaining with newsprint suppliers and advertisers and syndicates, competing for editorial talent, and reducing expenses generally. There were eight chains in 1900 controlling 27 papers and perhaps 10 per cent of daily circulation; by 1910 there were a dozen, with nearly 60 papers involved; in 1929 fifty-nine chains controlled 325 dailies, with more than a third of the country's total circulation; and by 1949 seventy chains controlled 346 dailies and some 40 per cent of all circulation.

The chains did not necessarily do away with the possibility of variety in the offerings of individual editors. Much depended on the chain owner. If, like Hearst, he wanted his papers united in speaking his prejudices, then the links in the chain were indistinguishable one from another. If the multiple publisher was interested principally in the balance sheet, he was willing to let his papers build circulation in whatever ways seemed best for the purpose. However it operated, chain ownership—being absentee ownership—destroyed the remaining vestiges of personal journalism in most of the country. And when the winds of economic crisis blew chill, chain owners had a tendency to consolidate or drop weaker members; the acceleration of chain-building in the twenties coincided with the beginning of the decline in the number of dailies.

The high priest of consolidation in twentieth-century journalism was Frank Munsey, who had made a fortune with a popular magazine and a grocery business but always yearned to be a newspaper publisher. From 1891 to 1914 he tried to build a successful chain and, failing in that, he was seized with an idea. "The same law of economics applies in the newspaper business that operates in all important business today," he wrote. "Small units in any line are no longer competitive," he added, and moved in to tidy up New York's unorganized newspaperdom with the same spirit he showed in his real-estate and banking investments. He bought the *Globe and Commercial Advertiser* (descendant of Noah Webster's *American Minerva*) and the *Sun* of Day and Dana, and merged them with the less renowned *Press*. He bought two evening papers, the *Telegram* and the *Mail*, and merged them as well. And he bought the *New York Herald* and sold it to the family which owned the *New York Tribune*, while the shades of Bennett and Greeley doubtless raised pandemonium in the afterworld. Still looking for new outlets for his peculiar energy, he died in 1925, and William Allen White wrote the obituary in his pungent style: "Frank Munsey contributed to . . . journalism . . . the talent of a meat packer, the morals of a money changer and the manners of an undertaker. He and his kind have about succeeded in transforming a once-noble profession into an eight per cent security. May he rest in trust!"

But Munsey, from the grave, had the last word, as the slow but sure pace of consolidation continued to reduce the numbers of dailies and weeklies in the post–World War I era. Journalism was an investment, and the major publishers had become businessmen, employers, and corporation owners indistinguishable from other magnates. Individuals in the group rarely stood out after 1900. No Hearst-Pulitzer wars filled the streets with cries of "Extra!" and the more lurid formulas of yellow journalism were generally abandoned in favor of a quieter kind of tawdriness, less likely to attract the attention of moral reformers. Occasionally an editor would appear like Robert R. McCormick, who by the sheer power of his personality made the *Chicago Tribune*, from 1914 to 1955, the widely known organ of his own xenophobia and arch-conservatism. The breed, however, was rare. Most owners preferred to enjoy their incomes quietly, away from the eyes of the popular press that they themselves sent prying into the lives of other notables. They also liked to face their problems collectively, through the American Newspaper Publishers' Association, founded in 1887. The ANPA's record in its first half-century was a curious one to be credited to an organization of professional descendants of Franklin, Bache, Bryant, Day and Greeley. It fought the Pure Food and Drug Act of 1906 on behalf of the advertisers; it fought the Post Office Act of 1912, which compelled sworn statements of ownership and circulation and thus threatened to reveal too much to the advertisers; it fought the proposed amendment of the twenties to regulate child labor because such regulation interfered with the control and exploitation of newsboys; it fought the American Newspaper Guild (the reporters' union) and the collective bargaining provisions of the National Recovery Act in the mid-1930's. The ANPA invoked the cry "Freedom of the press!" to protect journalism's grossest business practices, and its continuous defense of the largest propertied interests in society clearly illustrated that it was a trade association identical in spirit and outlook with those in other branches of industry.

The publishers had thus withdrawn from all but the largest business aspects of journalism by the time Dana, Nelson, Watterson, and Stone had departed. Business managers wrestled with immediate problems of cost; circulation managers carried on the free picnics and gifts of the old, crusading days, together with such puzzle contests and lotteries as their imaginations could devise—all in the name of revenue. Managing editors, often of great skill but little known outside the trade, directed operations cautiously or daringly as temperament, luck, or ownership dictated. But after 1900 the American who came at once to mind at the mention of the word "newspaperman" was likely to be the man with a byline—the humorous or serious columnist, the cartoonist, and, above all, the reporter. Personal journalism moved its residence from the editorial page to the news and feature columns. There, during the first half of the twentieth century, it settled down for what might prove to be a last stand.

Legmen, Wits, and Pundits:
The World of Reporting

Late in his teens, Henry Louis Mencken, the son of a successful German tobacco-manufacturer of Baltimore, was seized with an ambition. As he recalled it later, he had already embarked on a lifetime of omnivorous reading, but books were not enough. He wanted to lay in, as he put it, all the worldly wisdom of a shyster lawyer, a police lieutenant, a bartender, and a midwife. And he knew exactly where to apply. Early in 1899, he presented himself at the office of the *Baltimore Herald,* and after many days of cooling his heels unnoticed by the night editor, followed by a series of unpaid and dull assignments in the outermost suburbs, he was officially taken on as a cub reporter. Thus began "the maddest, gladdest, damndest existence ever enjoyed by mortal youth."

At a time when the respectable bourgeois youngsters of my generation were college freshmen, oppressed by simian sophomores and

Legmen, Wits, and Pundits

affronted with balderdash daily and hourly by chalky pedagogues, I was at large in a wicked seaport of half a million people, with a front seat at every public show, as free of the night as of the day, and getting earfuls and eyefuls of instruction in a hundred giddy arcana, none of them taught in schools.

Just as some boys of Mark Twain's generation had dreamed of standing in the pilot house of the "Natchez" or the "Eclipse," so adventurous youngsters of the nineties rolled the magic names of the *Sun,* the *Herald,* the *Record,* and the *Star* on their tongues and imagined themselves interviewing prime ministers, exposing grafters, trapping murderers, and rescuing kidnapped heiresses, all in the role of "star reporter."

While newspaper ownership in a large city had become an investment and the editorship of a big sheet a grinding executive job which tied a man to a desk for twelve hours daily, the romance was not yet capitalized out of reporting. There was a challenge in the job of actually *getting* the news, being on the scene of events as they happened, and racing the clock or calendar to get condensed, pungent, and newsworthy stories before the public. To be sure, the working reporter furnished only a part of the newspaper's contents. It was a small part, after the features, advertisements, and impersonal wire-service bulletins had been accounted for, but it was often the part that gave the paper its character. Some men rose to meet the possibilities of their craft and became writers of distinction. They carried their talents into the world of fiction or they became widely known special correspondents who took the nation or the globe for their beat or they became columnists dispensing wit, fancy, and opinion in the style of old-time editorialists like Prentice or Bennett. In all these capacities they demonstrated certain styles and attitudes which could be described as "American journalistic." The pace and tone of life in the United States were both reflected and molded by what the reporters said and wrote.

The city beat was for some, therefore, a literary academy. It was a curious one. The professors were tough city editors, the classrooms were docks, jails, morgues, and hospitals, and the dormitories were the cheap rooming houses which were all that salaries of five to fifteen dollars a week could command. Yet from the days in the sixties when Mark Twain and Bret Harte worked for California papers, many a worthwhile writer took a youthful turn at the journalistic pump handle. Stephen Crane and David Graham Phillips, Ring Lardner and Ernest Hemingway, George Ade and Samuel Hopkins Adams, Alfred Henry Lewis and Richard Harding Davis (whose newspaper reputation eclipsed his efforts at fiction) are only a handful of the novel- and short-story writers who had a taste of reporting. The daily search through the byways of the city, with its twenty-four-hour-a-day activity, its variety of noises, smells, sounds, languages, sacrifices, and sins, yielded much to the observant writer. The particularly strong emphasis in American literature on rendering the *details* rather than the inner qualities of experience—on shooting life on the wing, as it were—was reinforced in the work of those with newspaper training. If the antithesis between "redskin" and "paleface" in our fiction is represented by Walt Whitman and Henry James, as Philip Rahv suggests, it is worth recalling that Whitman was a Brooklyn editor in the 1840's, when editors still roamed the streets for their own stories. The newspaper offered a kind of quasi-literary form in which life was depicted in short snippets, to be forgotten after twenty-four hours. Perhaps this was suitable to a rapidly moving society whose producers and consumers of the printed word were varied in background and taste as in few other places. And perhaps the literature of a democratic nation that was, above all, always *busy*, had to be a kind of magnified newspaper account of existence.

Neophyte writers working under the command of a city desk learned how to describe what they saw accurately, with a minimum of words and a maximum of interest. In time, the form of the news story might become stereotyped, the insistence upon the captivating lead paragraph containing all the essentials of the account might be a form of restrictive tyranny. But even then, there could have been worse disciplines for a beginning writer. The value of this kind of big-city newspaper training was diminished somewhat, after World War I, by the increasing use of the telephone, which enabled reporters to call in a simple statement of facts to a rewrite man, who put them into shape. The observation and the writing of city news were divorced from each other in good part by this assembly-line procedure, to the disadvantage of both.

Until then, the reporter was in a unique position. In one sense, he was an insider, whose press pass admitted him behind the façade of respectability to the sweaty, dirty realities of municipal politics and society. Yet, in another sense, he was an outsider, too. The original reporters of the pre–Civil War era had been full of moral and party enthusiasms, which they were encouraged to pour into their stories. But with the coming of independent journalism, the correspondent was supposed to be bound to detachment. Sometimes this took the form of a cynical, bohemian pose. But some reporters with talent and consciences found that journalistic independence of party or sect (at the newsgatherer's, if not the publisher's, level) was not a mandate to indifference. It could simply mean replacing loyalty to separate creeds with loyalty to the public at large. With this viewpoint, and following the crusading tradition developed by Nelson and Pulitzer and Hearst and others, the reporter could be a profound force for good. No one could unearth a scandal as effectively as a man with no vested interest in any part of the scandal-making mechanism. It was not surprising, then, that the series of "muckraking" exposures which fed the Progressive movement in politics from 1900 to 1912 came in many cases from newspaper-trained writers. Jacob Riis exposed the nauseating conditions in New York's tenement houses; Lincoln Steffens lifted the lid off municipal corruption in the nation's major cities; David Graham Phillips described how the Senate had become a millionaire's club, faithful to the interests of the trusts; Samuel Hopkins Adams tore into the patent-medicine makers; Ray Stannard Baker wrote of the plight of the child laborer and the Negro. All these writers were newspapermen first.

Significantly, they wrote their exposures for magazines—*McClure's, Everybody's, Munsey's, Colliers, The American.* The daily paper did not allow enough display room for the fruits of long research, and it tended to drop a campaign of reform quickly if it was not topical or did not produce an immediate rise in circulation large enough to nullify any fears of offending advertisers. Yet many of the muckrakers owed much to their journalistic backgrounds. The newspaper had often been the first to show them the seamy side of urban life and shake them into awareness of what was happening in the unsullied republic of their schoolbooks. To communicate that awareness, to sound their alarms, they had learned by hard daily practice as reporters how to assemble facts clearly and completely and to present them with dramatic power and conciseness. The American newspaper of the muckraking era showed some of its best products in these writers, and some of its worst weaknesses in forcing them to do their most useful work elsewhere.

While the city beat might have its exciting side, the peak in reporting circles was reached when a writer could don a felt hat, riding boots, and a knapsack and swagger off to cover a war or a revolution. The Civil War itself had helped give birth to modern reporting. It provided a running subject of continued interest and gave hardy young writers a chance to do byline stories. They learned how to wrestle with the censorship and to cope with the seductions of press-agentry when some general offered inside tips in exchange for flattering accounts of his abilities. They also learned a good deal about the pleasant irresponsibilities and dreary horrors of life in camp, fort, and field; about the tricks of beating others to the wires or mails with dispatches; and about finding interesting leads and angles for their copy in quiet periods. The public, in turn, came to expect and generally like what the "specials" had to offer.

The twenty-five years after Lee's surrender did not offer much scope for war reporting. A correspondent for the *New York Herald*, with the improbable name of Januarius Aloysius McGahan, furnished exciting copy with the account of his escapes from Cossacks and Turkomans during Russian campaigns in central Asia in the 1870's; there was also some reporting of our own Indian wars for western papers. But the period beginning in 1890 offered a series of juicy assignments to the war correspondents, what with the Sino-Japanese War of 1895, the Cuban insurrection, our own campaigns in Cuba and the Philippines, a Greco-Turkish war in 1897, the Boer War in 1899, the Boxer Rebellion in 1900, and the Russo-Japanese War in 1905. In all these, Richard Harding Davis was almost a fixture, and Stephen Crane, Julian Ralph, and James Creelman among the better known of a large group of writers for newspapers, magazines, press associations, and syndicates. Their work was lively, thorough, and geared to the brash self-confidence of the newspaper world and, for that matter, of the nation at large. The romantic reporter, strolling with his notebook among Moros or Cypriots instead of the street-Arabs of an American slum, seemed to belong to that era when wars themselves were remote and exotic and could be enjoyed vicariously by Americans without disturbing their sense of isolation and security.

The energy and determination of the correspondents once more highlighted the technical skill of the newsgathering services. They chased their stories by horse, mule, and camel, steam launch and sampan. They spent freely and with the consent of their papers to hold wires open or to charter steamers. The public could be sure of getting the earliest and fullest accounts that money and sweat could provide. But always only the surface of events was reported. Few long background stories discussed the underlying causes of the insurrections and conflicts so colorfully described. That was left to other hands. The reporter, now taught to shun "interpretation," ignored forces, movements, and ideas in favor of tangible details that could be packed into a cabled dispatch. As a result, few Americans who confined their reading to newspapers realized that these wars were portents of the collapse of nineteenth-century international order. World war burst upon them as a stunning surprise.

Legmen, Wits, and Pundits

The nature of reporting had helped to create a paradox in which the American people had more information on world affairs at their disposal than ever before, yet seemed no more capable of understanding them than their relatively isolated ancestors had been.

World War I itself took much of the verve out of war correspondence. Its appalling, relentless slaughter did not lend itself to colorful prose, even though some of the country's best reporters—Davis, Will Irwin, Frederic Palmer, Irvin Cobb, and many others—were on the scene. In addition, the newsmen ran into censorship on a new and stifling scale. There was no point in a dramatic, hell-for-leather dash to be first in line at the telegraph office when French or British or Russian censors held up all outgoing messages for examination. When the United States entered the war, strict practices channeled front-line reporting into the service of the national propaganda effort. The job of writing war news became an exercise in playing safe variations on the themes stated in official communiqués and in enlivening them with personal and local color. The only dispatches to get through were those that the authorities were reasonably certain would neither discourage the home front nor leak information to the Germans. Criticism of the war's management and ghastly details of its horrors made their appearance later, in postwar books and Sunday supplements.

The return of peace opened a twenty-year period in which foreign correspondence faced the enormous challenge of explaining to Americans the significance of such grim realities as the rise of Stalin, Mussolini, and Hitler, the sickness of France and Great Britain, the collapse of stability in the Balkans, colonial uprisings, economic stagnation, and wars in Spain, Manchuria, and Ethiopia. The test was often well met by individual reporters, but it was questionable whether the press as a whole succeeded in preparing the United States for 1939 any better than it had been prepared for 1914. The wire services kept large staffs posted in Europe's capitals, and a few papers, like the *New York Times*, the *New York Herald-Tribune*, the *Christian Science Monitor*, and the *Chicago Daily News*, employed goodly numbers of regular overseas reporters of their own. London, for example, was covered by sixty-nine correspondents representing twenty-three agencies and papers in 1931; in 1929 no less than 20,731,000 words of press matter were received in the United States by transatlantic cable and radio. Certainly many of these correspondents were perceptive men who sensed the gathering tragedy around them and cried out eloquently in warning—Edgar Ansel Mowrer and Paul Scott Mowrer, Vincent Sheehan, Walter Duranty, John Gunther, Edmond Taylor, William Shirer, and Leland Stowe were among the better-known names. But it is noteworthy that many of these reporters were known to the nation, when World War II broke out, not for their newspaper dispatches but as the authors of popular books—Sheehan's *Personal History*, Duranty's *I Write As I Please*, Gunther's *Inside Europe* (and, after the fighting commenced, Taylor's *The Strategy of Terror* and Shirer's *Berlin Diary*). Just as the muckrakers had embodied their best observations in magazine-article and book form, so the ace European correspondents were best heard from the hard-cover platform. And some of the foreign news specialists, like Shirer or Raymond Gram Swing, were finding their audiences in radio broadcasting, to which they had switched.

By and large, however, the newspaper-reading public did not seem to be stirred by any sense of involvement in the foreign news provided for it, if the political climate of the isolationist thirties is any guide. Part of the reason for this lay in deep-seated attitudes which the press did not really touch, but part of it was due to the very nature of European coverage. The twenty million words of foreign cable news provided in 1929 sound impressive, until set alongside the fact that two million words were filed from the Tunney-Dempsey fight of 1926 alone. Nearly seventy journalists might be staked out in London in 1931, but three hundred covered the Hall-Mills murder trial in 1926, and an incredible seven hundred "reporters, photographers and communications men" filed millions of words on the 1935 trial of Bruno Hauptmann for the kidnapping and murder of Charles A. Lindbergh's son. The newspapers mobilized their best forces for special stories—disasters and crises in particular—but the day-to-day items confided to the cable offices in London, Paris, Rome, and Berlin were passed over by press-association subscribers or buried on inside pages. Only continuous, heavy coverage could build up a genuine understanding of complex events, and none but a handful of outstanding journals chose to invest space in stories whose significance would be apparent only in the long run. The reporter might hope to play the part of contemporary historian, but he was hobbled by the fact that he could get into print only those parts of a story which had immediate impact. The demands of editors for "hot" news, headline news above all, took much of the value out of the correspondent's insight and experience. As it happened, it also fitted in with the characteristic American reluctance to see European problems as continuous and insoluble. By way of contrast, the newsmen in Washington, which *was* on the front pages almost every day, were able to play a much more impressive part in shaping public attitudes.

The American Newspaperman

Until the 1840's, Washington correspondence was virtually a monopoly of the local papers. The coming of the wire service, the racing tempo of events just before the Civil War, and the transformation of the capital itself into a great military base as well as a center of fateful decisions, all brought outside reporters flocking. Washington never lost its primacy as a news source thereafter, and reports from the state capitals which had once been important items in a paper's political news now had a harder time finding their way into type. The machinery had been set in motion by which citizens would come to know much more of their national than of their local government—a fact of considerable import for a federal system based upon the idea that the reverse was the case. The rising tide of centralization was fed by streams of publicity from the White House and the Capitol.

The early Washington reporters were still branded with the marks of party journalism. Such men as Horace White and Whitelaw Reid produced columns of gossip through the favor of Republican congressmen; what they had to say was often shrewd and informed, but always partisan. They believed that a newspaper was the "right" party's pipeline to the public, and they took it for granted that part of their trade lay in moderating among party factions, floating trial balloons, mustering support for and against pieces of legislation, and expediting transactions between political leaders and their supporters. Young Henry Adams, back from England in 1869, hoped to assume the rightful place of an Adams in political life through journalistic work, and such onetime Washington reporters as White, Reid, and Murat Halstead believed themselves entitled to rank in the Liberal Republican party of 1872 because of their labors in the making of public opinion. As late as 1877, the

negotiations leading to the compromise which settled the dis-
puted Hayes-Tilden election were carried on by newspapermen
in the Western Associated Press. High dreams of political
wirepulling sweetened the rest of many an ambitious newspaperman.

But by the 1880's, this was changing. Independent journalism
demanded at least the semblance of neutrality from its reporters,
and the press-association men, with clients on both sides of the
fence, avoided entangling party commitments. The number of
correspondents accredited to Congress rose; there were 49 in
1867, 110 in 1890, and 180 by 1910. By 1952 that number had
nearly doubled—it was 350—and a Washington newsman himself estimated that in 1959 the gathering of information from
all branches and departments of the national government was
"a giant industry" occupying "upwards of twelve hundred"
reporters for individual papers, syndicates, press associations,
and magazines, domestic and foreign.

Many of these reporters were discovering that their power
was not diminished by the change in the formal relationship
between themselves and the parties. With the nationalizing of
the news, the importance of publicity dawned alike on congressmen and on those who had need of congressmen. Washington reporters linked both groups and secured for them the
popular attention they craved, while filling their own needs
for stories. Many of the press-corps members inhabited a
shadowy world where reporting, public relations, and lobbying
all met. They knew how to plant a rumor that would brighten
the prospects of a bill providing for a land grant or a public
undertaking, and a company with a bill in its pocket—for
example, the corporation which had bought the rights to the
Panama Canal route and wanted to sell the United States on a

The American Newspaperman

Panamanian instead of a Nicaraguan interoceanic link—knew enough to cultivate them. The reporters also had access to key senators and representatives whose doors did not open easily.

The congressmen, in turn, knew that modern journalism was important to them. A timely story in the Chicago press, for example, might throw more votes to an Illinois senator than half a dozen speeches in Ottumwa, Alton, Springfield, and Peoria. And all the legislators were aware that the building-up of a national reputation through the press was the indispensable prelude to serious consideration for the tantalizing high prize of the Presidency. Like the generals of the Civil War, some of them adopted pet correspondents, hospitably fed them leads, and reaped the rewards in newspaper flattery.

Ultimately this began to have an effect upon government itself. Congressional investigations had once been heavy-footed judicial affairs whose reverberations hardly rang outside the capital. But in the twenties the virtues of headline stories of villainy unmasked, both for the headline writers and the unmaskers, became increasingly obvious. The Teapot Dome scandal of 1923 (in which naval oil reserves had been corruptly sold to private companies) was probed by the Senate under the glare of a publicity spotlight which cast a glittering halo around the heads of the investigators. Thereafter, from 1930 through 1960, investigations made names for many a committee chairman—the Nye Committee, the Dies Committee, the Truman Committee, the Kefauver Committee, the Kennedy Committee—devoted to exposing alleged subversion, munitions lobbying, war profiteering, labor racketeering, and big-time crime. Incidentally (or not so incidentally) the investigations won home-state elections or nomination to national tickets for the legislators who conducted them. There was legitimate in-

vestigative business to be done by the Congress, but the tempta-
tion for reporters and lawmakers alike to grab front-page space
with dubious facts heavily wrapped in speculation was a mighty
one. Some investigations became pure drama, aimed at the re-
flexes, not the intellects, of the citizenry.

The most spectacular investigator of the twentieth century
was Senator Joseph R. McCarthy, who showed a dangerous
skill in using, as one Washington reporter put it, "a single issue
so as to dominate the channels of communication and to distract
a national audience." From his position as member and chairman of several committees inquiring into the operations of
government, he launched a series of charges intending to prove
that the national policy-making bodies were honeycombed with
Communist agents. McCarthy's charges were wild, sensational,
extravagant, irrational, reckless, and self-contradictory, but he
was a master at timing their release and phrasing them in such
a way as to capture the news media. Blazoned across the
country steadily from 1950 to 1954, they played on the in-
securities and hates of millions of Americans and placed an
awesome power of intimidation in the senator's hands. He knew
how to hold a press conference in which he made his accusa-
tions at an hour which would make it impossible for the denials
of his victims to reach the same edition as the charges, and he
had an instinct for spreading his "revelations" over several days
so as to make a week-long carnival of headlines that left an
impression of massive wrongdoing, when in fact there was
virtually no evidence to support him. The newspapers and reporters were on to him before long, but they were caught in
the toils of an "objectivity" which forbade them to evaluate
their news sources and forced into an irresponsible pattern of
stressing "hot" items, which made Monday's charge a front-

page matter and Wednesday's denial a back-page story. The blame for McCarthyism belongs not only to national neuroses but to the press which stubbornly ignored the possible effects of misuse of its publicity powers.

In other ways, too, the congressional reporter in the twentieth century assisted in the manufacture of news. He could pursue the author of a bill still pending and seek a statement of strategy; he could take the statement to rival politicians for comment; he could write an "overnight"—a story written in the evening to look as if it covered events of the next day—then ask a congressman a leading question (based on the overnight) to get a "lead" and secure a further comment from another government figure to furnish a "top" to the dispatch, giving to events an apparent sequence and meaning which they did not actually have. Yet once the story appeared, it might actually turn the course of a House or Senate debate into a new channel, as the public responded to the reporter's version of affairs. On a slow day a correspondent might conduct several interviews, select a routine item from his haul, and then build it into importance by securing reactions to it, "milking" it of news value. In short, the lawmakers were influenced in their courses not only by the power of public opinion but by the very nature of the means and agencies which they used to reach public opinion. The newspaper and the other mass media made the appearance of action sometimes as important as action itself. The full effects of this confusion of image and reality were yet to be tested as the decade of the 1960's opened.

If the newsman came to cast a shadow over the deliberations in the Capitol, his influence at the other end of Pennsylvania Avenue grew even greater, thanks to the evolution of the presidential press conference. The background to this institution was furnished by the rising stock of the Presidency itself in the first half of the twentieth century. The emergence of the United States as a great international power amid the alarums and excursions of two world wars and dozens of diplomatic crises did much to put the White House at the focus of events, since the President's is the commanding voice in foreign and military affairs. Then, too, as the problems of American society outgrew the federal system and were increasingly referred to Washington for amelioration, the President played a greater role in domestic affairs. He represented a national viewpoint rather than the collection of local outlooks represented in Congress, and, once he was given legislative authority to act, his agents ran the network of administrative bodies which coped with the dilemmas of the modern age. Congress, under the Constitution, created the tools of power, but the President *used* them, which was a much more eye-catching performance.

As the Chief Executive's office called forth new energies, the bolder occupants of the presidential chair discovered a need to explain their acts to the public and to rally the support which would make the way smoother in conducting their proliferating affairs. The press gave them the platform they needed to reach all market places of thought, all areas of consent and discord; and the press, in turn, welcomed the opportunity to concentrate its scrutiny on a single man. Thus evolved the press conference, which was patterned after a mode of communication conceived by daily journalism—the interview—and became both an instrument for the President himself and an almost constitutional device for public questioning of the President.

Jackson, thanks to his friendship with Blair, had been able to count on a journalistic friend through whom he could reach the public with his ideas; Andrew Johnson had been (according to some reports) the first President interviewed by a reporter in the modern sense of the term; Grover Cleveland had been badgered by curious newsmen who followed him to his honeymoon retreat. But Theodore Roosevelt was the first master of publicity, as created by the new journalism, in the White House. He was a magnetic figure to his generation partly because he was equal to the role he chose for himself as an embodiment of the "American" virtues of patriotism, hard work, and clean living. The "strenuous life" was a morality play in which he starred; it was neatly divided into scenes—T. R. dashing off a historical volume or an article for *Outlook;* T. R. shooting a water buffalo; T. R. chopping wood at Oyster Bay; T. R. shaking his finger at the malefactors of great wealth *and* the Socialists; T. R. in a hundred ever changing poses, all bristling. Small wonder that he charmed the reporters, for whom he made gorgeous copy. Besides, as police commissioner in New York he had known some of the more eminent members of the fraternity and had shared some of their midnight rambles through the streets to watch his patrolmen at work. And he was far more literate and better company than most men in political life. The upshot of all this was that he pioneered in using the press to make news in which he was the central figure, close to the popular heart and always in the popular eye. Communication, however, was mostly one-way. T. R. occasionally permitted a favorite reporter like Lincoln Steffens to the White House, and now and then met correspondents in small groups, but he rarely interrupted his high-pitched, machine-gun flow of opinions on art, politics, football, war, poetry, conservation, literature, and bronco-busting long enough to allow questions.

Woodrow Wilson more or less systematized the conferences.

Legmen, Wits, and Pundits

He found them useful as a kind of lecture platform from which he could explain the workings of constitutional government as he had once done in Princeton classrooms, and he knew that the "students" would be attentive to what they read in the papers. According to the memories of some participants, he grew annoyed and distant when the reporters tried to change the tone of the meetings with intrusive questions. Harding was ill at ease in press gatherings; his small-town editor's *bonhomie* could not help him explain the workings of an office in which he was miserably lost. Coolidge and Hoover were both taciturn and unwilling to be drawn out. They preferred formal meetings, with pre-submitted questions and prepared statements to be distributed. Then, in 1932, Franklin Roosevelt appeared on the scene and proved to be a master of the conference. He loved to josh the correspondents, with whom he built up an informal comradeship; he could turn sharp questions aside with a witticism (although he occasionally snapped at an unwary interrogator who hit at a weak spot); he liked to explain problems and policies in simple homilies, thus tailoring a Lincolnesque habit to the needs of mass communication; above all, he knew what made good copy, and he could make a quiet newsday a red-letter one by holding back an announcement until press conference time, giving the corps of reporters its story "lead" for the day. Ironically, he was the first to break the total dependence of the President on the press for publicity. By popularizing the informal, radio "fireside chat" to "sell" himself to the people, he opened new vistas in the use of mass media. He was thus able in part to circumvent the hostility of the great majority of newspaper publishers, whose editorial pages damned him even while their reporters concentrated public attention on him. He took full advantage of the split between the editorial-writing and news staffs of the press, too, knowing instinctively that as a news-making public figure he could use the news columns to muster interest in programs officially deplored by the owners of those same columns. In the world of mass readership the editorial pages might carry on the motions of rational argument, but real persuasion was achieved in the news, advertising, and feature departments.

Truman and Eisenhower enlarged the press conferences, regularized their routine, and relied increasingly on press secretaries who, as former newspapermen themselves, were adept at timing and preparing handouts which would give the White House news a desired emphasis. But if the press conference was a great device for bringing the president close to the public, it was also a unique forum for questioning the Chief Executive. It filled the need for the sort of interrogation provided in some other democratic countries by the custom of having the prime minister appear in Parliament to defend his policies. It was a more searching kind of interpellation in some ways, because there were no limits to the subjects on which it might touch; also, since the reporters were in close touch with public reaction to events, it furnished an important chance for the President to learn at first hand of popular discontents which might not otherwise filter to him through his immediate entourage.

The press conference was not a perfect channel from the President to the nation. He could refuse to answer questions (although the refusal was itself a matter of record, for the public to judge), or obfuscate or evade issues, or distract attention from serious business by grandstand performances. He could be baited into unwise statements on undeveloped policies, making life difficult for his department heads. The newspapermen, too, had a dangerous power. They could distort the record by selective emphasis in their accounts, covering up for an ineffective President or bringing out the worst in one whom they did not like. Nevertheless, the conference was an important institution which actually modified the form of American government. It tied the Presidency more firmly, for good or ill, to rapid movements of public sentiment, and it gave a really well-liked President an important public opinion advantage in any battle with Congress. For the newspaperman himself it had a curious outcome. Once, the press writer had played an essential political role because he was a party insider, as in the days of Seaton, Blair, or Ritchie. Now he carried weight in the political process as a party outsider, but one who controlled the approaches to the electorate.

The reporter's job, in Washington or elsewhere, could develop into another important kind of newspaper work, the writing of syndicated columns. By the 1950's, the various feature services supplying "insides" to weeklies and dailies had reached a total of some 150. As the services were always on the lookout for usable material, any writer or cartoonist who caught on with a single journal stood a chance of blossoming forth in a dozen or a hundred if he was lucky. A history of features, both syndicated and local, would reveal a colorful array of changing social attitudes through the years. It would also run the danger of becoming a mere muster roll of well-known names, because so many men (and women) have, in their time, gained a national audience through the few hundred words of a signed daily column. Lasting reputations have been built on the foundations afforded by these brief and ephemeral pieces. Too short to be called essays, they were (and are) "letters to the world," inseparable from the public personalities of the writers. There are, however, general patterns of column-writing, and the changes in those patterns have been, to some degree, an index to the shifting concerns of American life in the twentieth century.

The newspaper humorist flourished particularly in the period covering the ten-year spans before and after World War I. Eugene Field's sardonic "Sharps and Flats" and the slangy fables of George Ade, reworking the classics into the *patois* of the knowing city cockney, were both appearing in Chicago papers before 1900. The Illinois city's papers could also boast that they had first shown the world the political humor of Finley Peter Dunne's "Mr. Dooley"—by far the best short political satires in America, full of genial but devastatingly accurate thrusts, in brogue, at the foibles of government in the Progressive era, as seen through the eyes of the vigorous city-bred Irish. Another Chicago columnist, whose fame remained more purely local, was Bert Leston Taylor. Taylor's column in the *Chicago Tribune*, "A Line o' Type or Two" began in 1901 and ran for years. A miscellany of jokes, riddles, epigrams, and short poems, many contributed by readers, it was a survival of the old country paper's editorial page, full of short observations and the effusions of local sages and scolds. Franklin P. Adams' "The Conning Tower," begun in 1914 and carried in several New York papers, was the same kind of semicomic gathering of odds and ends; so was Don Marquis's *New York Sun* column known as "The Sun Dial" later taken over by H. I. Phillips. Adams, Taylor, Phillips, and Marquis (whose typewriter-pounding cockroach, Archy, became a folklore figure of the 1920's), all were hosts to a variety of youthful talents, welcoming readers to meet the company and share a few laughs each day. All four had crowds of devoted followers through the twenties; perhaps only the poems of Edgar Guest were more often clipped and folded into wallets than their columns. The humorous column atrophied by the thirties, however, and efforts to keep it alive through enlisting such popular writers as Will Rogers were unavailing. Possibly the depression had dimmed the taste for humor; more likely, the function of providing Everyman with his periodic dose of laughter had passed to the radio.

Political humor was kept alive in the newspaper, to some extent, by the cartoonists. John T. McCutcheon was another *Chicago Tribune* star; his political jibes alternated with drawings full of nostalgia for the vanishing America of the countryside—milking cows in the morning, collecting maple syrup in the fall, skating on the pond in the winter. Such "ole-swimmin' hole" life seemed all the more appealing because it was so remote from the world of the city dwellers who read the *Tribune*. Jay N. Darling and Rollin Kirby were noted cartoonists of the twenty or thirty years after 1914; Darling's style was full of linear flourishes and squiggles, but effective; Kirby, who cartooned for the liberal *New York World*, was more acid, and millions of Americans in the twenties came to recognize his caricature of the Prohibitionist—a gaunt, hatchet-faced, top-hatted figure epitomizing the spirit of "thou shalt not," the repression against which young rebels were battling to be free. In the period after World War II, Daniel R. Fitzpatrick earned national recognition with his *St. Louis Post-Dispatch* drawings, usually featuring dark-shadowed backgrounds, suggesting a certain grimness in his themes, a technique also effectively used by C. D. Batchelor, of the *New York Daily News*. Herbert Block, better known by his sig-

nature "Herblock," proved a deft political satirist in his cartoons for the *Washington Post;* and Bill Mauldin, of World
War II fame, seemed to be following in the tradition of liberal
political caricature as the sixties dawned.

As for political columns, they came in many shapes and
sizes and engendered a wide range of emotional response.
There were the grave and learned analyses by Walter Lippmann, who, after a brilliant career as an editor of the *New
York World*, settled down to conducting a column, "Today
and Tomorrow," for the *New York Herald-Tribune* and, via
syndication, for other papers. Lippmann went through cycles
of conservatism and liberalism, always proudly independent
but always seeming to brood magisterially over a political scene
in which the actors did not understand their roles nearly so
well as did Lippmann himself. Joseph Alsop maintained a
similar serious air throughout the fifties in a syndicated column,
although he first became famous in the thirties as a Washington
gossipmonger, rather like Drew Pearson, who specialized in
capital "inside" information. Heywood Broun, Samuel Grafton,
and Max Lerner carried on a battle for the humanitarianism of
the New Deal in their columns in the thirties and were quoted
enthusiastically by many liberals. On the other side, Mark
Sullivan dispensed a mellow but firm conservatism in his
columns in the thirties, and David Lawrence was further to the
"right." Extreme haters of the New Deal could rejoice in the
perennially boiling Westbrook Pegler, who nursed a consum-
ing hatred for all things emanating from Franklin D. Roosevelt
and expressed it often, in a picturesque vocabulary reminiscent
of the sports arenas where Pegler had done his apprenticeship
in journalism. But, by the 1950's, while Pegler, Lawrence, and
the equally right-wing George Sokolsky lingered on, they

178

Legmen, Wits, and Pundits

shared the limelight with men like William L. White and Roscoe Drummond, pre-eminently reporters, whose opinions, if strong, were nevertheless couched in moderate terms, whatever side of the argument they might take.

The sports desk also showed signs of the changing times. Grantland Rice had been the best-known sports writer of the "Golden Age" of sport in the 1920's, with his heroic invocations to the backfield of Notre Dame and his epic tales of World's Series contests and Dempsey prizefights. The sportswriter best known in the fifties was Red Smith, whose attitude was more often tongue-in-cheek, reflecting a growing acceptance of sport as a part of commercialized entertainment in a prosperous society. The pose of detachment, in short, seemed to have been adopted by the chroniclers of sport as well as by the political observers.

Entertainers of stage, screen, and airwaves furnished meat for the gossip columns. Louella Parsons and Hedda Hopper thrilled a certain class of star-gazing readers by giving them the illusion that they were being admitted to the private lives of the great and glamorous. Walter Winchell acted to the hilt the role of the sardonic, wisecracking, drinking newsman and coined new words for the American language, but essentially he remained a New York street boy bursting to tell the latest secrets gathered from the lips of the mighty in strictest confidence.

There were also the "guest stars"—such figures as Eleanor Roosevelt, Norman Vincent Peale, and Billy Graham—people who became columnists because in some non-journalistic field they had achieved a fame that newspaper syndicates were eager to market. Nor would the tale be complete without some reference to the purveyors of advice on bridge, medicine, love, and cooking; or the experts on war, education, and economics; or the critics of music, books, and radio and television programs. All of these filled an appetite for popular self-education which had, in an earlier time, spawned lyceums and the Chautauqua movement. Millions sought personal guidance but also enjoyed peeping through the curtains of their neighbors' homes and listening in on domestic quarrels by reading the "lovelorn" and "family" columns of Dorothy Dix in the thirties, or Mary Haworth, Abigail Van Buren, and Ann Landers in the forties and fifties. So real did these counselors become to millions that their names were preserved as authors of the columns even when a succession of different writers took over their tasks. Countless invalids were comforted or examined themselves intently for symptoms of new ailments in response to the counsel of such syndicated medical advisers as Dr. Walter Alvarez. A generation of home-front newspaper buyers during World War II debated the prospects of a second front or the virtues of strategic bombing with the analyses of Hanson Baldwin and George Fielding Eliot.

A list of feature writers would, finally, be woefully incomplete without the names of the comic-strip artists, whose productions bore a varied content of laughter, sensation, violence, and sentimentality and whose characters—more alive to many readers than people of their actual acquaintance—managed to mirror the fantasies, folkways, and preoccupations of machine-age culture in the United States.

All the millions of words and pictures produced by these artists and writers furnished much of the content of the newspaper after it grew to its modern size. They were of infinite variety in quality, and their enormous quantity showed the voracious appetite of the mass media for material that would

LINER TITANIC SINKS; 1300 DROWNED, 866 SAVED

GIANT OF SEA RAMS ICEBERG IN ATLANTIC

Women and Children Taken Into Lifeboats While Men Remain.

RESCUE SHIPS TOO LATE

Wireless Calls Summon Help, but It Arrives After Disaster.

NOTED PERSONS IN PERIL

Women and Children Saved.

Boston, April 16—(2 a. m.)—A wireless message picked up late tonight, relayed from the Carpathia, says that the Carpathia is on her way to New York with 866 passengers from the steamer Titanic aboard. They are mostly women and children, the message said, and concluded:

"Grave fears are felt for the safety of the balance of the passengers and crew."

Wireless from Olympic Confirms Extent of the Disaster.

New York, April 15—(Special)—Confirmation of the horrifying extent of the disaster to the Titanic came late tonight in a wireless message from the Olympic which also expressed the opinion that 1,800 lives were lost

The Olympic's dispatch is as follows:

"Carpathia reached Titanic position at daybreak. Found boats and wreckage only. Titanic sank about 2:20 a. m. in 41:16 N; 50:14 W. All her boats accounted for containing about 675 souls saved, crew and passengers included. NEARLY ALL SAVED WOMEN AND CHILDREN. Leyland liner Californian remained and searching exact position of disaster. Loss likely to total 1,800 souls."

THE TITANIC AND ITS CAPTAIN.

Prominent People on the Titanic.

Mr. and Mrs. John Jacob Astor of New York.
C. M. Hays, president of Grand Trunk railroad.
Mrs. Hays and Miss Hays.
Maj. Archibald Butt, aid de camp to President Taft.
W. T. Stead, noted English author.
J. G. Widener, traction magnate, Philadelphia.
Mr. and Mrs. Isadore Straus, New York.
J. P. Thayer, vice president Pennsylvania railroad.
Mr. and Mrs. Arthur Ryerson, and two daughters, formerly of Chicago.
Mr. and Mrs. J. Clinch Smith of New York.
Henry B. Harris, theatrical manager.
Col. Washington Roebling, builder of Brooklyn bridge.
Clarence Moore, formerly of Chicago.
E. G. Lewy, jeweler, of Chicago.
Benjamin Guggenheim, of New York.
Mrs. Ida S. Hippach and daughter Jean, 7360 Sheridan road, Chicago.

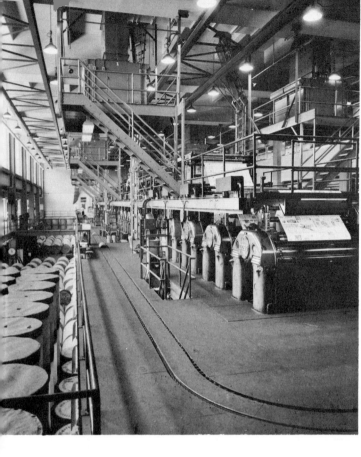

A portion of the printing plant (*top*) and the city room (*bottom*) of the *Chicago Sun-Times* today. (Courtesy, *Chicago Sun-Times* and *Daily News*.)

always appear fresh. Because of their wide circulation, they tended to nationalize American culture. Because they were offered in short "takes" of a few hundred words to an audience of widely varied background, they inevitably aimed at an undemanding common level of taste, thus tending to freeze the culture in a standardized, "middlebrow" pattern. They existed in a newspaper without being affected by, or in turn affecting, its local personality. Indeed, in a curious sense the political columns lent a kind of objectivity to the increasingly conservative press, for they often appeared on the editorial page next to statements of owner opinion which they flatly contradicted. The very nature of large-scale urban journalism, therefore, worked toward its homogenization. Long before television existed and radio was widespread, the daily newspaper began to experience the powers, problems, achievements, and evils of mass communication.

Somewhere along the path of this evolution toward a daily paper which was a bargain-counter of syndicated packages, the feature writer passed the reporter as the most conspicuous supplier of the newspaper's contents. The growth of the wire services in addition tended to throw the burden of providing "individualized" stories on the shoulders of the city reporter. But the twentieth-century machinery of depersonalization ground on. The coming of news syndicates and the tendency to make the reporter a "facts-only" legman, feeding the rewrite desk, reduced the numbers and fame of the byliners who covered the town from city hall to city morgue. As late as the mid-1950's the *New York Times* might employ a man like Meyer Berger, who was a genius at extracting interest from accounts of his rambles on the sidewalks of New York, but the breed was declining. Moreover, the great rush to the suburbs which began almost with the century and appeared to be turning into a stampede after World War II reduced readership interest in municipal coverage. Suburbanites were not as concerned as their grandfathers had been with the problems of the metropolis except when they concerned automobile traffic. Suburban weeklies were launched occasionally, promising to revivify journalism at the grass roots, but they were often composed almost exclusively of retail advertising and syndicated features, hardly the ingredients of a newspaper revolution. The glory of the city-room was departing, as smaller staffs wrote up the local political news, occasionally took a fling at a minor crusade (against traffic offenders, say, or poor street lighting) or went through the motions of furnishing the once-bright but long-since-shopworn feature stories—the interviews with parents of murdered children, the reactions to the first warm day of spring or the first snowstorm, or the stories of grandmothers belatedly completing high school, policemen delivering babies, and taxicab drivers returning thousand-dollar bills left in the back seat. The reporter's job had become far more a matter of routine.

In a sense, too, the professionalization and unionization of journalism, whatever their merits (or whatever the contradiction between the two ideas) had a standardizing effect on the life and work of the newspaperman. The first independent school of journalism was organized at the University of Missouri in 1908, although separate departments and curriculums for journalism instruction had already appeared in several places. By 1945 there were over seventy such schools and departments. Veteran newspapermen continued to debate whether or not the "trade" could be taught, and educators disagreed about the propriety of vocational training institutions on university campuses. Wherever the truth might lie in these encounters, two things were certain about academic training for journalists. It could not improve the deficiencies in the daily press which were due to the size, ownership, investment, and audience of that press—particularly when the training was partially financed by the owners. Second, like all academic work, it tended to some extent to yield its prizes to the hard worker and to discourage the extremes of laziness and brilliance. Managing editors could hire journalism graduates and be confident that they were not acquiring the vagrant, cynical tosspots of the "bohemian" era. On the other hand, it was impossible to imagine a graduate school of journalism adding anything to Walter Lippmann or Heywood Broun, or keeping a grip on such intellects long enough for them to finish a degree program.

The American Newspaper Guild, born in 1933 in the canyon of the depression, had some 26,000 members in 1954, serving 180 papers, mainly in metropolitan areas, as well as press associations, syndicates, news magazines, and broadcasting companies. Its effect in raising the living standards of newspapermen who had been paid in "glamor" instead of cash was admirable, but it unquestionably made the working journalist a more conventional-appearing white-collar employee.

Thus, in the public imagination the reporter was fading as the symbol of the newspaper's romance and power. He had succeeded the editor as "the newspaperman," as the editor had succeeded the printer. In the 1930's, 1940's, and 1950's, the question was who would succeed *him?* And that question was made harder by the fact that the newspaper itself was still changing—some even said "disappearing." Its position was threatened by other forms of mass communication which had waxed great by imitating it. Was it conceivable that the mighty daily press, seventy years after reaching its maturity in the days of Pulitzer, no longer had a future? Or was its future merely obscured by the fogs of a confusing time and society?

VII

The Vanishing Newspaperman?

In the six years following American entry into World War I, symptoms of new revolutions in communication made their appearance. A week after the United States joined the battle, President Wilson appointed a Committee on Public Information, in charge of a former newspaperman, George Creel. The CPI's job was twofold: to inform editors of the workings of the censorship and steer them into voluntary co-operation with its requirements, and to furnish them with "safe" news of the war effort. The second of these tasks, bluntly stated, was in effect to act as the national propaganda agency, and Creel threw himself into the work with vigor, issuing a stream of releases to the news services, arranging interviews with government officials, cozening free advertising for conservation, war-bond, and recruiting drives, and providing copy, mats, boiler-plate, and photographs for thousands of papers. Among the 150,000-odd Americans who helped in the execution of these chores (at a total cost of some five million dollars) were

The American Newspaperman

Edward L. Bernays, Carl Byoir, and Ivy Lee, key men in the infant industry known as "public relations." The CPI inaugurated the first really full-scale program using the press not merely to inform but to manipulate public opinion. In the words of Newton D. Baker, the Secretary of War, the public prints, under Creel's guidance, "fused the heterogeneous elements that hitherto constituted our citizenship . . . into one homogeneous, liberty loving people." What Bernays was later to call "the engineering of consent" had undergone its first real trial, the success of which was to have a profound influence on the newspaper world thereafter.

Then, in June of 1919, a new daily broke into the rough-and-tumble New York City market. First known as the *Illustrated Daily News* (it later dropped the *Illustrated* from its title), it was the brain-child of Joseph Patterson, cousin of Robert R. McCormick and another stormy member of the newspaper dynasty begun by Joseph Medill. Patterson was an unorthodox millionaire—like Hearst before him, or Marshall Field, Jr., after—full of ebullient notions of rendering service to the "common man" by creating a paper that would reach him through an appeal to his gamier tastes. The *Daily News* was to be a tabloid in format, but its greatest novelty was to lie in the quantity of photographs it offered, particularly those of corpses and lightly clad girls. There was nothing strikingly new either in tabloids or in pictorial papers. Both had American ancestors, and what was more, Patterson was familiar with the fact that Alfred Harmsworth, Lord Northcliffe, had enjoyed an enormous success with cheap papers tailored to this formula in Great Britain. But Patterson's magic in combining the ingredients was sensationally suited to the age of Prohibition, jazz, and sports and movie celebrities. The cut of a camera appearing between the words of its title signified its highly successful exploitation of the news photographer's power to attract the semiliterate when he chose. In ten years the *Daily News* had a thumping circulation of 1,320,000 and imitators abounded.

In November, 1920, radio station KDKA of Pittsburgh broadcast, for the first time, the results of a national election. There had been a few scattered attempts in the preceding year to transmit news to the public by radio, but KDKA was the innovator in carrying a story of nationwide significance to listeners as it broke. Not even the most desperate efforts of reporters, printers, and distributors, with all the technology at their command, could inform a newspaper reader of those voting returns as quickly as KDKA told the owners of crystal sets within its range. A whole new dimension had been added to the dissemination of news, literally at the speed of light.

Then, in 1923, two Yale graduates, Henry Luce and Briton Hadden, published the first number of a new magazine known by the stark monosyllable *Time*. *Time* was to be something more than a daily newspaper, and more than a weekly review like the *Literary Digest*, which had been on the market since 1890 and which itself followed the half-century-old tradition of *Harper's Weekly*. *Time* would organize, categorize, and explain the meaning of the week's news for "busy men" who were unable to spend hours leafing through numerous papers and magazines to "keep informed." It offered to guide readers quickly and expertly through what Benjamin Harris had long ago called the "glut of occurrences." In the process *Time* developed a nervous, compressed style, a set of firm opinions controlling every verb, noun, adjective, and participle in its stories, and an enormous circulation, which was near two million by the middle of the 1950's.

Inside a handful of years, therefore, a wide-reaching public relations operation, picture journalism, electronic news-hawking, and the news magazine had been either born or revitalized. By the thirties, it was clear that each one invaded areas once almost exclusively the preserve of the newspaper. Together, they toughened the struggle of many dailies to stay alive, and for those who survived the new competition, they changed the terms, the direction, and the impact of the newspaperman's work.

The early papers that survived on photographs were mainly designed to appeal to "lewd fellows of the baser sort." The *Daily News* was followed in New York by the *Daily Mirror*, a Hearst bantling which was soon racing Patterson's organ to see who could pry the most circulation out of pictures of slaughtered gunmen, traffic victims, and leggy mistresses of the great and powerful. Bernarr Macfadden, until then a publisher of "body-building" and "true confession" magazines, leaped into the fray in 1924, with the *New York Daily Graphic*. When the *Graphic* could not get pictures of what the tabloids called "slayings" (which often took place in "love nests"), it faked them, and although the depression killed it off in 1932, it left a lurid trail through a segment of American publishing history.

Yet despite these gashouse beginnings, photo reporting was capable of serious work and growth. In 1935 Luce expanded his operations with *Life*, a weekly devoted entirely to pictures of current interest. After twenty years, it was circulating over

The Vanishing Newspaperman?

five million copies of each issue. It had outlasted and outdistanced a number of rivals, of which the only one to show any real competition was *Look*, begun in 1937. It had also brought the photographic essays of the notable camera artists Gjon Mili, Margaret Bourke-White, Carl Mydans, Alfred Eisenstadt, and many others to public attention. But above all, it presented a challenge to reporting. The essence of good news-writing, from the days when John Bogart, Selah Clarke, Carr Van Anda, and other great managing editors were coaching the staffs of such papers as the *Sun*, *Herald*, *World*, and *Times*, had been terseness and graphic realism. The crack journalist had been able, in his handful of words, to convey the essence of a scene through a minute description of its details, so vividly captured in prose that the reader actually experienced the emotion of the moment. But a good cameraman did this with a flick of his finger. No story could match the impact of some of the great news pictures of the twentieth century—Mayor Gaynor of New York, mortally shot by an assassin, being led away to medical aid; Woodrow Wilson, his face ravaged by illness, riding down Pennsylvania Avenue next to Warren Harding at the latter's inauguration; the panic-stricken crew of the sinking freighter "Vestris" struggling on the slanting deck; the towering, hydrogen-gas funeral pyre of the dirigible "Hindenburg." The camera rendered obsolete the "star reporter" whose talent was in bringing disasters to the breakfast table with the force of a punch in the stomach.

There was, however, one edge that the reporter still held. The photograph could only explore the surface of events. It still required a human intelligence (aside from the cameraman's) between the event and the reader to develop the meaning of the facts, the nuances of human reaction to them, the part that they played in the context of the day's news as a whole. Because the camera eye did a far better job of presenting certain kinds of "facts" than the reporter's pencil, the real test of journalism now was to do something effective with those facts.

The "threat" to journalism from radio news services and, after 1945, television, was basically that they could outrace the newspaper with the up-to-the-minute story, just as the newspaper, in turn, could beat the magazine. The newspaper publishers were uncertain of how to treat radio in its early days. Was it an enemy or an ally? It was tentatively treated as both. As early as 1922 the Associated Press warned its members neither to broadcast news nor to permit others to do so. But at that time, more than one hundred newspapers had already invested in radio stations, considering them useful as a means of advertising the wares of the press to a new audience. Their idea seemed to be that an appetizer of news served from the loud-speaker would send the listener downstairs to the newsstand to get the rest of the feast.

By 1933, however, the American Newspaper Publishers' Association had become frightened by the growth of the new medium with its lusty bid for the advertising dollar which, in the hard times of the thirties, was shrinking swiftly. The Association recommended that newspapers owning stations restrict their broadcasts of news to the barest bulletins and that press associations refuse to sell or give news to radio channels until after publication in the press. This proposal to keep a monopoly on the news for its members was a rather curious way to secure the "freedom of information" which the ANPA professed to cherish above all things. The Associated Press, followed by the United Press and the International News Service, dutifully refused to sell news to the networks, and the broadcasters responded by organizing their own news services. In 1935 the UP and the INS recognized the virtue of the adage that if you can't beat them you had best join them and began selling news to the radio stations, with the AP following in 1940 and admitting station operators to associate membership. By that time the airwaves had carried the familiar voices of H. V. Kaltenborn, Lowell Thomas, Gabriel Heatter, and other news commentators into millions of homes. The newscasts and comments of wartime made national reputations for Elmer Davis, William Shirer, Edward R. Murrow, and Eric Sevareid. Television, when it came, inherited the news practices of the radio networks as well as the experience of their public affairs and current events departments. By 1960 some Americans knew the faces and tones of Walter Cronkite, John Daly, and others as well as people had once, in smaller communities, known their neighbors. They also accepted with a certain aplomb the privilege, accorded to them by the TV cameras, of looking directly at World's Series, royal weddings and coronations, political conventions, and countless other scenes in the pageant of events which they had once been able at best only to read about. In a mass society with declining opportunities for genuine intimacy, people enjoyed, to an unsurpassed extent, a vicarious intimacy with history in the making.

Again, for the daily journalist, a subtle and not always recognized change in the character of his undertaking was implied by these developments. The "extra" disappeared from the newspaper scene, and the urgent race to break stories into print as quickly as possible had less meaning. The newspaper had thrived on speed from the day of the telegraph. In a country where things were always on the move and no one wanted to be left behind, the question "What's new?" had demanded an immediate answer, which the late edition had provided. Now the radioed or televised bulletin could skim the cream off the immediate news. Editors and reporters were challenged to provide the context which would give the spot news of the airwaves some local relevance, some significance in their own communities, some meaning that escaped in the staccato rush of the announcer's sentences. And this, too, in a way, might be the newspaper's answer to the news magazine. The national current events weekly was inescapably tied to the "big picture," the development of over-all significance. The newspaper, if it wished, still had the power to speak, to exhort, to explain to the specialized interest group or to the individual community.

There were, however, difficulties in the way of the newspaper's exerting this power. It could offer outlooks and make inquiries impossible for *Time* or its competitors—like *Newsweek*, founded in 1933, *U.S. News and World Report*, dating from the late 1940's, and *The Reporter*, a fortnightly of thoughtfully interpretive articles on current events, begun in 1950. Properly led, it could offer an individualized style that went to the core of a reader's interest far more surely than any telecast or broadcast packaged for national consumption. What it could *not* do, however, was resist the steady munching process by which the competing mass media, particularly radio and television, took bigger and bigger bites out of its share of the national advertising revenue. And this declining revenue— or at least proportionately declining revenue—in the face of rising costs for newsprint, labor, and services after 1945 led to a brisk increase in the pace of newspaper consolidations.

The Vanishing Newspaperman?

Until 1935 newspapers received more than half of all sums spent on national advertising. But the picture began to change after World War II. In 1949, when more than five billion dollars were paid for advertising of all kinds, the newspapers had slightly under two billion dollars' worth, or some 37 per cent of the total. By 1954 the newspapers' share of total advertising expenditure was down to 33 per cent, and by 1959 the newspapers received less than 32 per cent of approximately eleven billion dollars in total payments for advertising. The share of television in total advertising revenue had climbed from almost nothing, in 1949, to nearly 14 per cent ten years later. These figures do not reveal the full measure of the problem, for the bulk of newspaper advertising continued to be local. The daily papers' share of national advertising in the mass media was variously estimated, in 1959, to be something less than 25 per cent, depending upon what various statisticians meant by "national." The actual volume of newspaper advertising revenue rose from 1945 onward to over three and a half billion dollars in 1959, but the increase was in inflated postwar dollars, and, in any case, rising costs matched it, step for step.

The bell, accordingly, began to toll for many a daily. Between 1937 and 1944 there were 362 suspensions or mergers of newspapers, and the total number of dailies had sunk to a low of 1,745. (In 1919, there had been 2,604.) Fifteen years later, in 1959, despite an increase in population from approximately 140 million to 175 million, the total number of dailies was still almost at the same level, with 1,751. Figures varied slightly from almanac to almanac owing to some ambiguity in the definition of a daily newspaper, but the relative and absolute shrinkage was nonetheless plainly visible. New papers had been almost exactly offset by those that had died. But significantly, while the new ones were in suburban or other small communities, the deaths were in the large cities.

Some of these casualties were great names in American newspaper history. The depression of 1929 had already claimed some distinguished victims, among them Pulitzer's *New York World*, which was merged in 1931 into the *New York World-Telegram* and became part of the Scripps-Howard chain, and the *Philadelphia Public Ledger*, one of the pioneering "penny papers" of the 1830's. Although an evening edition of the *Public Ledger* lasted until 1942, its glory departed when it ceased to appear on Philadelphia breakfast tables in 1932. The consolidations during and after World War II also brought a touch of sadness to many readers of newspapers which had become virtual institutions. The *Boston Transcript* died in 1941—the only paper in history to be the subject of a poem by T. S. Eliot—and a certain Bostonian way of life satirized in *The Late George Apley* lost one of its props. In 1947 the *Springfield Republican*, a great organ of nineteenth-century liberalism under Samuel Bowles, was reduced to Sunday appearance only. In 1950 the *New York Sun* was merged with the *World-Telegram*, and thus the paper founded by Benjamin Day and made great by Charles A. Dana—a paper which had been a part of the comforting routine of daily life for millions of New Yorkers for more than half a century—joined the long list of deceased journals. A newspaper was a community institution, and to many Americans who could not think of particular cities without certain newspapers there was something sad in the growing casualty list produced by the new economics of mass communication.

More and more American urban areas were served by only one paper. By the middle of 1959 fewer than 90 cities in the entire nation had more than one newspaper ownership—and of 106 cities with a population greater than 100,000, 66 were either served by one paper or by two under a single ownership. Even such metropolitan giants as Cincinnati and New Orleans had become newspaper monopoly towns. And only 10 cities in the nation had more than two ownerships.

Even total circulation was slacking off, relatively speaking. The total circulation of dailies in 1941 amounted to 41 million, when the entire population was slightly over 132 million. Circulation reached 54 million by 1954, while the population curve had risen to something like 160 million—that is, the sales of dailies had increased by almost one-third, while the population had gone up only one-fifth. But between 1950 and 1958, when the population pushed well beyond 170 million, circulation rose only to 58 million. Even so, a total daily readership of better than 58 million did not seem to indicate a state of sickness. But in the larger setting it was cause for alarm. Cities with monopolies of newspaper ownership could receive exactly as much variety of information as the publisher's good will and integrity allowed, which was asking a good deal of normally fallible mortals. Although monopolists pointed out that the new order reduced the temptations felt by competing newspapers to truckle to advertisers or indulge in sensationalism in order to beat the "enemy," it was equally true that without rivalry there was less of a spur to furnish more and better news. The arguments for "responsible monopoly" also rang strangely in gatherings of publishers whose editorial columns vaunted the virtues of "free enterprise." But above all, at a time when the newspaper's only answer to competing media might lie in diversification, its control was slipping into fewer, not more, hands.

The American Newspaperman

If the news was, in the phrase of one contemporary observer, "like fluid, to be portioned out in bulletins, and leads . . . capable of being bottled in any quantity," it might be said that the number of containers was getting smaller all the time. Even if the containers held more, and more people took them off the shelves, this meant that fewer men were needed to fill and handle them and fewer new ideas were likely to crop up for improving their shape and usefulness. If this metaphor had any truth, it could also illustrate another current problem for the newspaperman: the source of the "fluid" was in danger of pollution by a growing army of press agents trying to affect its flavor.

A history of the press agent would be strewn with gaudy and sometimes moderately larcenous characters. The brassy genius of Phineas Barnum for planting "news" stories about the marvels exhibited in his "museum" opened new paths for others to follow. As early as the Civil War friends and associates of leading editors as well as advertisers attempted to have the merits of their products and services made the subject of editorial comment, instead of occupying the advertising columns, where the reader was forewarned. By 1876 political parties had established "press bureaus" which saw to it that announcements of speeches, campaign progressions, and meritorious deeds by their candidates were sent, broadside, to newspaper offices for insertion in the "regular" columns. Actors, theatrical managers, and circuses were among the early employers of press agents—often sporty, ex-newspaper types, in derbies, canes, and fur-collared coats, whose crude and simple techniques consisted of supplying free passes to reporters who wrote about their clients or of threatening business managers with the withdrawal of advertising if performances were handled too uncharitably by critics. The railroad managers, too, before the Interstate Commerce Commission frowned on the practice, dealt free passes generously to editors and reporters, leading Eugene Field to write sardonically that cash was much more welcome and that for "the setting forth of virtues (actual or alleged) of presidents, general managers, or directors, $2 per line" would be the standard rate. But it was with the coming of Ivy Lee that modern press relations took form and substance. Recognizing, at the height of the muckraking era, that the largest corporations badly needed to counteract the growing notion that they were predators feeding on the vitals of democracy, he organized a firm in 1905 to act as a "literary bureau" for companies in need of benign publicity.

Lee had had experience as a press agent for the Democratic party and had helped to promote several public enterprises, such as the St. Louis World's Fair of 1904. His vision lay in recognizing that simple, forthright propaganda defeated its own purpose. In a note to city editors, he informed them that he intended "frankly and openly, on behalf of business concerns and public institutions, to supply the press and public of the United States prompt and accurate information concerning subjects which it is of value and interest to the public to know about." No editor could object to such an agency or, on a slow day, fail to be happy to get stories concerning Lee's clients. Those clients included such corporations as the Union Pacific and Pennsylvania railroads and (most notably) such individuals as John D. Rockefeller, and the stories stressed their charities, their good works in the community, the nature of their public services, the magnificent scientific progress achieved in their technical departments, and their essential place in creating national power and prosperity. Lee had divined the importance of creating a proper public "image" for those whom he served and getting the newspapers to present it by capitalizing on their never-ending need for making each day's issue surpass the previous day's in interest, significance, and circulation. There was nothing so sordid as payment involved for the printing of these notices; thus Lee escaped the indignities of being a simple advertising agent, bidding for column space with other tradesmen. He also evaded the restrictions of the Post Office Law of 1912, which insisted that any matter for the printing of which money was accepted should clearly be labeled "Advertisement." And since Lee's releases were not transparent "puffs" but were, indeed, interesting and provocative according to their fashion, he did not bring upon himself the obloquy usually bestowed by publishers upon "space-grabbers."

The forty years after the close of World War I witnessed a sensational flowering of the public relations business. Trade associations, aided by their publicity experts, formed "institutes" to promote the use and understanding of oil, rubber, tin, lumber, paper, railroads, tin cans, and all the innumerable products that industry and ingenuity could devise to snare the consumer dollar. Universities, labor unions, baseball clubs, charitable agencies, professional groups, and almost any collection of people with a scheme to promote, an institution to defend, or a message to propagate, hired public relations counsels and specialists. Even the agencies of the government followed the fashion. In 1910 Congress was surprised to learn, while investigating the Bureau of the Census, that it employed "a person whose principal duty [was] to act as what might properly be called . . . a press agent." By 1959 one Washington reporter conjectured that the number of government information officers who stood ready to "brief" him was close to three thousand, or about twice the size of the capital press corps itself. As many as three hundred of their mimeographed handouts, containing over 200,000 words, representing "the government's own idea of what the news should be" stuffed his mailbox in a week.

The effect of the public relations boom was that a cascade of "releases" poured over the desks of editors, bureau chiefs, and correspondents every day. Each release carried a cargo of manufactured news—a contest to determine the tomato catsup queen of the nation, a breakthrough in the "vitaminizing" of dog food, the inspiring speech of a suspenders manufacturer on the perils to health involved in wearing belts, the triumphant return of a popular recording star to the town of his boyhood. Dipping into this flood of words to fill his column, the best-intentioned newspaperman in the world could not hope to exercise much critical discrimination in separating fact from fancy.

The press agents argued their case persuasively—persuasion was, after all, their business. Much of their material was legitimate news, they said, which any enterprising reporter should be grateful to have prepared for him. In an increasingly complex world the multifaceted organisms that carried on the world's work needed specialists to explain their functions to the public. Where would a newspaperman seeking an article on automotive progress go for his insights if not to the press relations departments of the great companies, which kept abreast of the work of dozens of subdivisions? How could the complicated operations of far-flung government agencies be understood by the press if the public relations officer did not make it his task to sort out and give some meaning to the mass of reports from suboffices and bureaus? What of the work of the publicizers in mobilizing the support of the nameless multitudes for worthy causes? And wasn't it true that public relations counselors encouraged a high standard of behavior from clients attempting to live up to the image created for them?

Despite these rationalizations, public relations work was a major threat to the role of the newspaperman, and by its very nature would always remain one. The "independent" newspaper had broken away from mercantile and party control in order to assume a pose, at any rate, of presenting the news in the interest of the public at large, not simply one portion of it. The basic premise of objective journalism was that news *happened*, that the press presented it impartially, and that the people then had the facts at their disposal to render a free judgment on the performance of their institutions. The creator of public images in the public relations firm, however, worked on the assumption that news was *managed*, in order to create an impression. The impression did not have to be untruthful, but it could not be unfavorable to the client. The editor who printed a handout without rigorously scrutinizing, checking, and criticizing it as he would have any other news story— and without indicating its source—was giving the public the picture of an institution as drawn by the institution itself. The newspaper filled with such handouts was no longer an independent vantage point from which to observe institutional performance. It was performing a secondary service, merely choosing from the prepared paragraphs provided for it and displaying them to the readers. Yet it was clear in the 1950's that few newspaper staff members really investigated the pre-

The Vanishing Newspaperman?

packaged goods from which they wrote a good part of their "news." For this failure they had the excuse of the inexorable pressure of the deadline. There was no excuse for the almost universal failure to indicate what material had been provided by someone other than the newsman himself.

Indeed, in the frightening world of the mid-twentieth century, with its gigantic corporations, gigantic government agencies, gigantic organizations of every kind, the citizenry needed an uncommitted friend in the newspaperman more than ever. But standing amid the flood of manufactured news, the reporter could no longer render service simply by following the old rules—to get the statement from the authorized source, get it in full, spell names correctly, and leave comments out. To do this in dealing with some men in public life was to be a pushover for a McCarthy; to do it with some spokesmen for organized groups was to become an unpaid salesman. The press agent or the popular leader who cultivated the reporter, with a free drink in one outstretched hand and a prepared statement in the other, eager only to "help him do his job of public information," was baiting a trap which canny newsmen avoided.

> How cheerfully he seems to grin,
> How neatly spreads his claws,
> And welcomes little fishes in
> With gently smiling jaws.

Thus, some three hundred and seventy years after the publication of *Publick Occurrences,* the newspaper press in America faced a series of dilemmas. It had prospered on furnishing information quickly, fully, and correctly, and it was challenged by competitors who could match its performance in those departments, forcing it to look elsewhere for appeal. It had worked hard to develop an independent stature, basing its claim to merit (though not its finances) on unbiased accounts of life, and it was currently beset by those who wished only to make its columns showcases for what they had to sell. It had been small, flexible, and tied to communities; now it was large and costly, and its weaker members were being gobbled by its larger in the struggle to survive.

The newspaper claimed to be the public conscience, yet it had become dependent on mass readership and could rarely risk alienating customers by prodding them as a conscience should. The newspaper claimed a passionate interest in freedom of information about the conduct of public matters but rarely printed a twentieth of the quantity of such information already available to it. The newspaper claimed to be the voice of the locality, but except for advertisements, scandal, and crime was almost completely filled with matter that bore no relation whatever to the paper's home city. The newspaper claimed to be an educator, but except for the *New York Times*, *Christian Science Monitor*, and *Wall Street Journal*, its information of any intellectual weight was drowned in a flood of trivia. The newspaper claimed to be the lively literature of the commonalty, but its relentless quantitative demands filled it with banalities and formulas. To stay alive, it had had to become a commercial success in an America which was awed by size and efficiency.

But if it was supported on nothing but market acceptance, perhaps a change in market fashions would start it down the road to oblivion. For the generally honest and competent working members of the press, that would be a tragedy. And it would be a tragedy for the nation, too. The newspaper, like popular government itself, might not always live up to its great promises, but society was the gainer from even its crudest, most stumbling efforts to make those promises good.

There was no need for despair. The way of the journalist had never been smooth, and unexpected social or technical change, combined with brilliance and hard work, had lifted him out of ruts before. The little gazette of the 1780's seemed bound forever to the form it had adopted in 1719, but it was the nucleus of the hundreds of important papers of half a century later. To their limited audiences the blanket sheets of the 1830's seemed to represent the ultimate in growth. Yet the great age of newspaper expansion had been on the verge of birth in that decade. So, in the 1960's it would be foolhardy to insist flatly that the makers and molders of journalism will never break through the limitations of the mass-communication newspaper to answer the challenges of the age. A new American newspaperman may yet emerge, wielding some unforeseen cost-cutting mechanism, reaching for some as yet unsuspected audience, shouting, shaping, innovating, and carrying on the traditions of a calling which, all in all, has had many things to boast of.

Important Dates

1690   Benjamin Harris of Boston publishes *Publick Occurrences,* first attempt at an American newspaper

1704   John Campbell establishes *Boston News-Letter,* first successful, continuous paper in colonies

1719   Founding of *Boston Gazette* and Philadelphia *American Weekly Mercury* in the same week makes Boston the first two-paper town and spreads the newspaper outside Massachusetts

1732   Birth of the short-lived Philadelphia *Zeitung,* first foreign-language newspaper in United States

1735   Zenger Case

1765   Stamp Act, followed by Townshend tax on paper in 1767, enlists many papers in Patriot cause

1775   Revolution begins; thirty-seven newspapers in existence in the colonies

1783   *Pennsylvania Evening Post and Daily Advertiser* becomes first American daily

1786   Founding of *Pittsburgh Gazette,* first newspaper west of the Alleghenies

1789   John Fenno's *Gazette of the United States* launches partisan journalism on national scene

1798   Alien and Sedition Acts

Important Dates

1811   Samuel Topliff establishes a service for gathering news quickly from ships entering Boston harbor

1814   Steam-powered cylindrical press developed in England by Koenig; various improved versions reach United States in next fifteen years, making daily press runs up to 4,500 possible

1833   *New York Sun*, first successful "penny daily" aimed at popular audience, is launched

1844   Introduction of the telegraph for transmission of newspaper dispatches

1847   Hoe "rotary press" developed, raising circulation potentials above the 50,000 level

1848   New York Associated Press formed by six papers (*Sun, Herald, Tribune, Express, Courier and Enquirer,* and *Journal of Commerce*)

1851   Post Office Act of 1851 provides for free delivery of papers within county of publication, a great asset to growth of the country press

1863   Stereotyping and web-perfecting presses begin to appear in United States, eventually lifting circulation potentials to the million mark

1864   Formation of American News Company, to distribute city papers en masse in rural districts; beginning of serious competition between big-city journals and rural papers, to great disadvantage of latter

1865   A. N. Kellogg founds one of the earliest syndicates for providing ready-printed materials to newspapers

1872   Foundation of Western Newspaper Union, feature syndicate specializing in supplying weeklies and small dailies; by 1917 it enjoys a virtual monopoly in its field

1878   E. W. Scripps starts career as chain-builder by founding *Cleveland Press*

1883   Joseph Pulitzer takes over *New York World* and brings "new journalism" to the national unofficial journalistic capital

1889   Formation of American Newspaper Publishers' Association, the newspaper owners' trade association

1893   Color presses find their way into major newspaper plants

1897   Perfection of halftone engraving process from stereotype plates makes photography feasible for newspaper use

1900   Reorganized Associated Press, after fighting off various competitors, establishes virtual monopoly in co-operative news-gathering field

1907   United Press founded to serve Scripps chain of newspapers and dilute (though not combat) the AP monopoly

1908   Organization of first separate school of journalism, at University of Missouri, a step in the training of newspapermen as "specialists"

1909   International News Service formed to render same service to Hearst chain as UP renders to Scripps; both later assume other clients and a more independent role

1917   Coming of World War I brings strict sedition laws drastically limiting press freedom, and Committee on Public Information, massive public-relations and propaganda effort involving manipulation of news and newspapers

1920   First broadcast of election returns by radio station KDKA breaks newspaper monopoly of "hot" news

1922   Beginning of American Society of Newspaper Editors, an attempt to set "professional standards" for editorship

1923   Emergence of *Time*, the weekly news magazine, signalizes another kind of competition for newspapers

1933   Founding of American Newspaper Guild, the newspaper writers' union; printers' unions already in existence since the 1790's

1945   Supreme Court rules that AP restrictive membership practices are in restraint of trade; forces grant of an AP franchise to *Chicago Sun*, previously blackballed by *Chicago Tribune*

1958   Merger of United Press and International News Service shows trend toward consolidation in newsgathering services; major press associations reduced once again to two

1960   Merger of *Detroit Times* and *Detroit News* under one ownership becomes latest in a series of continuing consolidations and creation of chains, concentrating newspaper ownership in fewer hands and readership in fewer urban areas

Suggested Reading

The task of learning something of the history of journalism is made easier by Warren C. Price's *The Literature of Journalism* (Minneapolis, 1951), an annotated bibliography. While I disagree with most of Price's evaluations of books which I have read, his work is undeniably useful and a necessary point of departure. Journalistic history of the past half-century or so is also to be quarried out of several periodicals. *Editor and Publisher*, in existence since 1884, is rich in information on business and mechanical phases of newspaper operation, while *Journalism Quarterly*, published since 1924, is a mine of articles and reviews on all aspects of newspaperdom. Since 1947 the Nieman Alumni Council, representing those newspapermen who have enjoyed a year of graduate study at Harvard at the expense of the Nieman Foundation, has issued a quarterly, *Nieman Reports*. *Nieman Reports* consists of commentaries on the current press scene —sometimes affectionate, sometimes chastising, usually frank. Since 1923 the American Society of Newspaper Editors has issued a bound volume of the proceedings of its annual conventions, under the title *Problems of Journalism* followed by the year of issue, and a great variety of problems is dealt with in these volumes.

Details of ownership, circulation, and management are to be found in N. W. Ayer and Son, *Directory of Newspapers and Periodicals*,

The American Newspaperman

issued annually from New York since 1880, and in the yearly *Editor and Publisher Market Guide*. Almost any information concerning newspapers before 1820 may be gathered from Clarence S. Brigham's *History and Bibliography of American Newspapers, 1690–1820* (Worcester, Mass., 1947). Winifred Gregory's *American Newspapers, 1821–1936: A Union List of Files Available in the United States and Canada* (New York, 1936) not only locates holdings of almost every newspaper in the country but has much condensed data on changes of title, period of issue, and like matters.

General histories of the American newspaper press are hard to classify. I have found most useful Frank L. Mott's *American Journalism: A History of Newspapers in the United States through 260 Years, 1690–1950* (rev. ed.; New York, 1950). Edwin Emery and Henry L. Smith, *The Press and America* (New York, 1954), is less detailed than Mott and more ambitious in its attempt to set journalism against a broad background of "communications." There are several earlier studies of the American newspaper, of which three rate special mention. Alfred M. Lee's *The Daily Newspaper in America* (New York, 1937), a sociological study, has material not found elsewhere on such matters as syndication, distribution, press associations, and the relationship of newspapers to urban growth, though it is presented piecemeal. Willard G. Bleyer's *Main Currents in the History of American Journalism* (Boston, 1927) is now dated, but Bleyer had a certain perception, a feel for personality, a nose for issues, all of which make his book more readable than its successors. A curious pioneer history is Frederic Hudson's *Journalism in the United States from 1690 to 1872* (New York, 1873). Hudson was the managing editor of the *New York Herald*, and his book is based partly on personal recollections, partly on stories by others, partly on newspaper clippings. It is rambling, opinionated, and often inaccurate; yet it sizzles with the enthusiasm of a man convinced that journalism was the queen of callings in a progressing age and thus gives a "feel" of the journalistic situation late in the nineteenth century which is hard to come by elsewhere.

Histories of printing tell much about newspapers. The colonial press is well depicted in Isaiah Thomas' *The History of Printing in America* (2 vols.; Albany, 1874). Thomas himself originally issued this work in 1810 to commemorate the printing and publishing arts in which he had been outstandingly successful, and it has worn well.

Suggested Reading

It can be usefully supplemented, for the colonial era, by Lawrence Wroth's *The Colonial Printer* (New York, 1931). Douglas C. Mc-Murtrie, author of several sound monographs on printing's past, planned a four-volume history of the part played by the press in America's beginnings but was able to issue only a single volume of his *History of Printing in the United States* (New York, 1936) before his death. Harold Innis, in *The Bias of Communication* (Toronto, 1951), discusses the social effects of cheap, mass-produced newspapers and develops arguments which he set forth earlier in *The Press, a Neglected Factor in the Economic History of the Twentieth Century* (New York, 1949).

There are numerous histories of individual newspapers, but most of them are "house products," done by staff members to commemorate anniversaries and composed mainly of anecdotes and clippings. Honorable exceptions are Allan Nevins' *The* Evening Post: *A Century of Journalism* (New York, 1922) and Elmer Davis' *History of the* New York Times, *1851–1921* (New York, 1921). A sampling of newspaper histories chosen for sectional diversity would include: J. Cutler Andrews, *Pittsburgh's* Post-Gazette: *First Newspaper West of the Alleghenies* (Boston, 1936); Erwin D. Canham, *Commitment to Freedom: The Story of the* Christian Science Monitor (Boston, 1958); Gerald Johnson, Frank R. Kent, H. L. Mencken, and Hamilton Owens, *The Sunpapers of Baltimore, 1837–1937* (New York, 1937); Frank O'Brien, *The Story of the* Sun, *1833–1928* (New York, 1928); and Eugene J. Smith, *One Hundred Years of Hartford's* Courant: *From Colonial Times through the Civil War* (New Haven, 1949).

Mainly, however, the story of the American newspaperman is told in biographies. Going more or less chronologically, one may begin with Benjamin Franklin's *Autobiography*, which, in any one of several editions, has wise comments on the printer's calling and stature in colonial America. John C. Oswald's *Benjamin Franklin, Printer* (New York, 1917) is a useful supplement. Other studies of colonial newspapermen are Anna de Armond's *Andrew Bradford: Colonial Journalist* (Newark, Del., 1949) and Annie Marble's *From Prentice to Patron: The Life Story of Isaiah Thomas* (New York, 1935). Several useful books illuminate the story of the press in the era of Federalist-Republican warfare. Bernard Fay's *The Two Franklins: Fathers of American Democracy* (Boston, 1933), despite its ambitious title, is a lively biography of Benjamin F. Bache. Lewis Leary's *That Rascal Freneau: A Study in Literary Failure* (New Brunswick, N.J., 1941) deals with the editor-poet-sailor, and G. D. H. Cole's *The Life of William Cobbett* (New York, 1924) sets the background against which the American experiences of the "fretful Porcupine" can be better understood. There is much to be learned about editors of the period from 1790 to 1830, especially in New England, from Joseph T. Buckingham's *Specimens of Newspaper Literature, with Personal Memoirs, Anecdotes, and Reminiscences* (2 vols.; Boston, 1852).

For the period following the War of 1812, William E. Smith's *The Francis Preston Blair Family in Politics* (2 vols.; New York, 1933) deals with the forces behind the editor of the *Globe,* just as Charles H. Ambler's *Thomas Ritchie: A Study in Virginia Politics* (Richmond, 1913) shows the connections between Democratic politics and Virginia journalism and Glyndon Van Deusen's *Thurlow Weed: Wizard of the Lobby* (Boston, 1947) throws some light on the newspaper operations of New York's Whigs. John T. Flanagan, in *James Hall: Literary Pioneer of the Ohio Valley* (Minneapolis, 1941), tells something of the many-sided nature of an early western editor, and Don E. Fehrenbacher, in *Chicago Giant: A Biography of John Wentworth* (Madison, Wis., 1957), shows the tempestuous side of western editorship, business, and politics. Isaac Goldberg's *Major Noah: American-Jewish Pioneer* (Philadelphia, 1936) is the story of an uncommonly lively figure in mercantile journalism. Norval N. Luxon's Niles' Weekly Register: *News Magazine of the Nineteenth Century* (Baton Rouge, 1947) is in part a biography of Hezekiah Niles, the newspaper's prophet of progress through industry.

The abundance of material on the thirty-year period of expansion prior to the Civil War is difficult to winnow. No single biography of Greeley, for example, really presents a full picture of the man. Glyndon Van Deusen's *Horace Greeley: Nineteenth Century Crusader* (Philadelphia, 1953) is adequate but has less flavor than Greeley's own *Recollections of a Busy Life* (New York, 1868) or the surprisingly durable work of Greeley's contemporary, James Parton, *The Life of Horace Greeley, Editor of the* New York Tribune (New York, 1855). There is no biography of Benjamin Day. Oliver Carlson's *The Man Who Made News: James Gordon Bennett* will

Suggested Reading

do as a study of the *New York Herald*'s founder until something better comes along. Don C. Seitz, in *The James Gordon Bennetts, Father and Son* (Indianapolis, 1928), covers the activities of the younger Bennett. Parke Godwin's heavy *Biography of William Cullen Bryant, with Extracts from His Private Correspondence* (2 vols.; New York, 1883) helps to tell the tale of the *New York Evening Post* through the years of rapid change, and Margaret Clapp's *Forgotten First Citizen: John Bigelow* (Boston, 1947) shows the civic spirit as it moved a *Post* editor. Francis Brown's *Raymond of the* Times (New York, 1951) is a competent study of Henry J. Raymond; if it is not exactly stirring, neither was its subject. Interesting gossip concerning all the major journalists of New York is in Augustus Maverick's *Henry J. Raymond and the New York Press for Thirty Years: Progress in American Journalism from 1840 to 1870* (Hartford, 1870). This rambling, reminiscent work is akin in spirit to Hudson's *Journalism in the United States*, mentioned earlier; a counterpart to it for the world of Washington correspondence in its "primitive" era is Benjamin Perley Poore's *Perley's Reminiscences of Sixty Years in the National Metropolis* (2 vols.; Philadelphia, 1886). Looking to the West again, John Tebbel's *An American Dynasty* (Garden City, N.Y., 1947) is a colorful study of the founder of the *Chicago Tribune*, Joseph Medill, and of his grandchildren, Robert R. McCormick, Joseph Patterson, and Eleanor Patterson.

For the closing four decades of the nineteenth century, many biographies are available, widely varied in temper. Solid and dignified, as befits their loftily principled subjects, are Claude Fuess, *Carl Schurz, Reformer* (New York, 1932), Rollo Ogden, *Life and Letters of Edwin Lawrence Godkin* (2 vols.; New York, 1907), and Royal N. Cortissoz, *The Life of Whitelaw Reid* (2 vols.; New York, 1921). A somewhat livelier work is Candace Stone's *Dana and the* Sun (New York, 1938), best of the crop of Dana biographies. George S. Merriam's *The Life and Times of Samuel Bowles* (New York, 1885) is a good study of the *Springfield Republican*'s greatest editor, showing how successful journalism and Republican politics were practiced outside the major cities. A saucy, impertinent book is Franc B. Wilkie's *Personal Reminiscences of Thirty-five Years of Journalism* (Chicago, 1891), which consists in part of a long sketch of Wilbur F. Storey of the *Chicago Times*. Charles H. Dennis' *Vic-*

The American Newspaperman

tor Lawson: His Time and His Work (Chicago, 1935) is a semi-official study, and the story of the *Chicago Daily News* in its early years can also be gathered from Melville E. Stone's *Fifty Years a Journalist* (Garden City, N.Y., 1921). Icie F. Johnson's *William Rockhill Nelson and the Kansas City* Star (Kansas City, 1935) is the only Nelson biography of any substance. Two competent lives of editors in the New South are Joseph Wall's *Henry Watterson: Reconstructed Rebel* (New York, 1956) and Raymond Nixon's *Henry W. Grady: Spokesman of the New South* (New York, 1943), though both of them, like most studies of editors in politics, deal heavily in party matters and issues and less thoroughly in the mechanics of newspapering.

One treads on dangerous ground in approaching Pulitzer and Hearst. James W. Barrett's *Joseph Pulitzer and His World* (New York, 1941) and Don C. Seitz's *Joseph Pulitzer: His Life and Letters* (New York, 1924) must be used together for a three-dimensional picture of Pulitzer. Hearst is still too close to our time to be evaluated objectively. Among a mass of studies marked by transparent sycophancy or palpable venom, John Tebbel's *The Life and Good Times of William Randolph Hearst* (New York, 1952) is worthy of mention. Gerald W. Johnson's *An Honorable Titan: A Biographical Study of Adolph S. Ochs* (New York, 1946) is a tribute to the man behind the modern version of the *New York Times*. The independent mind of Edward W. Scripps, who begot both chains and chain lightning in the world of journalism, is reflected in *Damned Old Crank: A Self-Portrait of E. W. Scripps*, edited by Charles R. McCabe (New York, 1951). Regional and small-town journalism still had possibilities and personalities at the century's end, and these are illustrated in such books as Josephus Daniels' *Editor in Politics* (Chapel Hill, N.C., 1941), containing the reflections of a Raleigh editor who knew his people and his politics shrewdly, and William Allen White's *The Autobiography of William Allen White* (New York, 1946), a good-natured tour of the twentieth century with the Sage of Emporia, Kansas. The last-named book can be enjoyed even more by reading, along with it, Walter Johnson's *William Allen White's America* (New York, 1947), a biographical study of the cheerful, middle-class world in which White lived and moved and had his being.

Reporters and managing editors have left many a memoir, some

Suggested Reading

worthy of special note. Samuel L. Clemens' *Roughing It,* in any of its many editions, is not only vintage Mark Twain and a fine account of California and Nevada mining camps but a sprightly recalling of frontier journalism as well. Edward P. Mitchell's *Memoirs of an Editor: Fifty Years of American Journalism* (New York, 1924) shows some of the inner workings of a big, successful paper like the *New York Sun.* George W. Smalley's *Anglo-American Memories* (New York, 1911) is a recollection of things past by a highly successful *New York Tribune* war and foreign correspondent who became something of an Anglophile in later life. John Russell Young's *Men and Memories: Personal Reminiscences* (2 vols.; New York, 1901) in an interesting fashion tells of war correspondence, editorship, and political life in Philadelphia and New York.

Muckraking reporters also wrote testaments of faith as they grew older. *The Autobiography of Lincoln Steffens* (New York, 1931) is a classic, and *The Making of an American* by Jacob A. Riis (New York, 1901) is a good story of the city beat in the days of Charles A. Dana and Whitelaw Reid and of what it taught a big-hearted immigrant about the underprivileged of New York. Ray Stannard Baker, in *American Chronicle* (New York, 1945), recalls how legwork as a Chicago reporter in the 1890's introduced the author to the problems of American industrial society. Different books by reporters illustrate the varieties of attitude possible among the newsmen. Some memoirs affect the romantic pose, combined with Horatio Alger–like exhortations to hard work and daring as the keys to journalistic success; such a one is Julian Ralph's *The Making of a Newspaperman* (New York, 1903). Some recollections show good-humored cynicism, after the fashion of H. L. Mencken in *Newspaper Days* (New York, 1941), while others show bad-tempered cynicism infused with a "bohemian" spirit, like Ben Hecht's *A Child of the Century* (New York, 1954), much of which deals with life among Chicago city-room minions between 1910 and 1925. The task of foreign correspondence between two world wars and during the second of them made some reporters speculative and pessimistic in their recollections. Three examples of such remembrances would be Vincent Sheean, *Personal History* (Garden City, N.Y., 1935), William Shirer, *Berlin Diary: The Journal of a Foreign Correspondent, 1934–1941* (New York, 1941), and Eric Sevareid, *Not So Wild a Dream* (New York, 1946).

The American Newspaperman

Turning from biographies and autobiographies to monographs on particular topics, one finds a large literature, the scope of which can only be indicated by particularizing. A study such as Arthur M. Schlesinger's *Prelude to Independence: The Newspaper War on Britain, 1764–1776* (New York, 1958), is a rare example of skilful, intelligent investigation of a special topic in the history of the press. John C. Miller's *Crisis in Freedom: The Alien and Sedition Acts* (Boston, 1951) and James M. Smith's *Freedom's Fetters: The Alien and Sedition Laws and American Civil Liberties* (Ithaca, N.Y., 1956) are further samples of the kind of study in depth which must be undertaken in many areas before we can really understand the past of the newspaper. Wesley Rich's, *The History of the United States Post Office to the Year 1929* (Cambridge, Mass., 1924) reveals much of what the government thought about the importance of the press, as shown in mail subsidies. In the field of the rural and specialized newspaper, Milton W. Hamilton's *The Country Printer, New York State, 1785–1830* (New York, 1936) is a good (and lonely) state study. Thomas D. Clark's, *The Southern Country Editor* (New York, 1948), dealing with the period after the Civil War, illustrates the importance of the newspaper in regional history. Albert L. Demaree's *The American Agricultural Press, 1819–1860* (New York, 1941) shows what can be learned by close examination of a limited-readership press, and Robert E. Park's *The Immigrant Press and Its Control* (New York, 1922) is another example of the fruitful examination of one segment of the newspaper field.

Victor Rosewater's *History of Co-operative News-gathering in the United States* (New York, 1930), remains the standard on its subject. Frank Presbrey's *The History and Development of Advertising* (Garden City, N.Y., 1929) is an account of an institution whose past is closely entwined with the newspaper's. It should be supplanted some day by a modern work. The story of syndication, as a whole, has not yet had its historian, although Elmo S. Watson's *A History of Newspaper Syndicates in the United States, 1865–1935* (Chicago, 1936) makes a beginning. Nor has anyone gathered various monographs on distribution, pricing, and marketing policies into a readable history of the newspaper as a business enterprise.

The political complexion of the newspaper has been dealt with in many histories of individual organs, but the role of the newspaper as a factor in the making of political institutions has less often been

Suggested Reading

assayed. Three important works which attempt to explore this subject are Leo Rosten's *The Washington Correspondents* (New York, 1937), James Pollard's *The Presidents and the Press* (New York, 1947), and Douglass Cater's *The Fourth Branch of Government* (Boston, 1959), the last-named an excellent account in a very brief compass. Fauneil J. Rinn, in an unpublished Ph.D. dissertation, "The Presidential Press Conference," submitted to the Department of Political Science, University of Chicago, in 1960, offers an interesting analysis of that particular meeting ground of government and journalism.

Ever since Lambert A. Wilmer issued *Our Press Gang; or, a Complete Exposition of the Corruptions and Crimes of the American Newspapers* (Philadelphia, 1859), criticizing the press has been the prerogative, obligation, and sometimes the pleasure of various writers. Examples of this kind of appraisal within the last forty years are Upton Sinclair's *The Brass Check: A Study of American Journalism* (Pasadena, Calif., 1920), George Seldes' *Lords of the Press* (New York, 1938), and Silas Bent's *Ballyhoo: The Voice of the Press* (New York, 1927). The books by Sinclair and Seldes are mainly concerned with the conservatism of the publishers and the influence of "big money" on the newspaper's outlook, while Bent's has more to say about sensationalism, misleading advertising, and other sins of the racier tabloids and the "yellows." Less strident than these, and therefore more devastating, are two books by A. J. Liebling, *The Wayward Pressman* (Garden City, N.Y., 1948) and *Mink and Red Herring: The Wayward Pressman's Casebook* (Garden City, N.Y., 1949), consisting of reprinted articles from the *New Yorker* in which Liebling pokes fun effectively at many aspects of the daily press's daily show. The years just after the Second World War were fruitful in critical studies of the newspaper. Morris L. Ernst, in *The First Freedom* (New York, 1946), expresses concern over the effects of concentration of ownership. More facts and figures on such control are to be found in "Local Monopoly in the Daily Newspaper Industry," *Yale Law Journal*, Vol. 61 (1952), 948–1009. The Commission on the Freedom of the Press, financed in part by Henry R. Luce and headed by Robert M. Hutchins, issued *A Free and Responsible Press* (Chicago, 1947), which was a thorough plumbing of many sins committed by the daily press. Articles in various periodicals took up the burden of these criticisms, and possibilities are not yet exhausted; just at this writing, Carl Lindstrom has come out with *The Fading American Newspaper* (Garden City, N.Y., 1960), in which he takes a sorrowful view of the present state of journalism based on long experience as a Connecticut editor and a teacher of newspaper work. There are no formal, booklength rebuttals to the critical works listed above, but almost all the studies mentioned at the beginning of this reading list make a case for the importance and public service of the newspaper. The editors and publishers also express their candid opinions of their critics in the trade publications and, of course, in the newspapers themselves. So long as the newspaper appears every day, it will always have the last word, and it has never in all its history suffered from modesty.

Acknowledgments

I am grateful, as always, to friends, colleagues and students for ideas and suggestions, and to the librarians of the University of Chicago Libraries and the Newspaper Division of the Library of Congress for their help. My deepest thanks go to the American Council of Learned Societies for providing a year's fellowship during which much of the material that went into this book was gathered.

Index

Abell, Arunah, 107
Adams, Franklin P., 176
Adams, Henry, 166
Adams, John, 37
Adams, Samuel Hopkins, 158, 160
Ade, George, 158, 176
Advertising: in colonial papers, 8, 17, 24; in mercantile papers, 74–75; revenue from, 75, 149; development in post–Civil War era, 124; newspaper's declining share of, 193–94
Agricultural newspapers, 85–86, 146
Albany (N.Y.) *Argus*, 82
Albany (N.Y.) *Evening-Journal*, 35, 83
Alien and Sedition Acts. *See* Sedition Act
Alsop, Joseph, 178
Alvarez, Walter, 180
American Farmer (Baltimore), 85
American Newspaper Company, 149
American Newspaper Guild, 154, 183
American Newspaper Publishers Association (ANPA), 154, 190

American Press Association, 148
Associated Press: beginnings, 114–16; growth in latter part of nineteenth century, 150–151; reaction to radio newscasts, 190–91
Atlanta Constitution, 130

Bache, Benjamin F., 44–46, 47
Baker, Newton D., 186
Baker, Ray Stannard, 160
Baldwin, Hanson, 180
Baltimore Herald, 156
Baltimore Sun, 107
Batchelor, C. D., 117
Beach, Moses, 97
Bennett, James Gordon, 77, 97–101, 107, 121
Bennett, James Gordon, Jr., 135
Benton, Thomas Hart, 68
Bernays, Edward L., 186
Bigelow, John, 105, 107
Blair, Francis P., 80–82
"Blanket sheets," 74
Block, Herbert, 177–78
"Bly, Nellie." *See* Cochran, Elizabeth
Bogart, John, 127, 189

Index

"Boiler plate," 148. *See also* Syndicates, feature

Bok, Edward, 148

Boston: *Chronicle,* 29; *Columbian Centinel (Massachusetts Centinel),* 36; *Continental Journal,* 35; *Courier,* 76; *Daily Advertiser,* 76; *Evening-Post,* 13, 23, 35; *Gazette,* 6, 9, 26, 27, 30, 35; *Herald,* 108; *Independent Chronicle,* 35; *Mail,* 108; *Massachusetts Spy,* 9; *New-England Courant,* 6; *New-England Weekly Journal,* 7, 23; *News-Letter,* 3, 4, 5, 6, 35; *Post-Boy,* 35; *Publick Occurrences,* 1–2; *Times,* 108; *Transcript,* 93, 194; *Weekly Rehearsal,* 23

Bourke-White, Margaret, 189

Bowles, Samuel, III, 109

Brackenridge, Hugh Henry, 66

Bradford, Andrew, 7, 11, 13

Bradford, Fielding, 67

Bradford, John, 67

Bradford, William, 7

Bradford, William, III, 25, 28

Brisbane, Arthur, 144

Brooker, William, 5–6

Broun, Heywood, 178

Bryant, William Cullen, 39, 105–6, 121

Buckingham, Joseph T., 76

Byoir, Carl, 186

Callender, James T., 58, 60

Campbell, John, 3, 48

Cape Fear Mercury, 9

Cartoonists, 177–78

Censorship: of first newspaper, 1–2; in colonial era, 12–16; in World War I, 163. *See also* Freedom of the press; Libel

Centinel of the Northwestern Territory, 67

Chain ownership: forces behind, 125; growth and patterns of, 151–53; recent, 194–95

Charleston: *Courier,* 70, 76, 77, 98; *Mercury,* 70; *South Carolina Gazette,* 8

Chase, Samuel, 60

Chicago: *Daily News,* 132, 164; *Democrat,* 110; *Record,* 132; *Times,* 110, 128–29; *Tribune,* 110, 154, 176, 177

Christian Advocate (Methodist), 84

Christian Examiner (Unitarian), 84

Christian Science Monitor, 164, 202

Circulations: colonial and revolutionary, 25, 31; of mercantile papers, 73–74; of *N.Y. Sun* (1834), 96; of *N.Y. Herald* (1860), 101; of weekly edition of *N.Y. Tribune,* 105; of *N.Y. Times* (1860), 107; of various "penny" papers, 107–8; average (1860), 111; average at end of nineteenth century, 123, 145–46; of *Kansas City Star* (1893), 132; of *Chicago Daily News* (1888), 132; of *N.Y. World* (1890's), 139; of *N.Y. Daily News* (1929), 187; total for all newspapers in recent years, 193, 195

Civil War, effect on newspapers, 118

Clarke, Selah, 189

Cleveland, Grover, 172

Cobbett, William ("Peter Porcupine"), 46–48

Cochran, Elizabeth ("Nellie Bly"), 141

Cockerill, John, 137, 138

Coleman, William, 39

Color presses, 124, 140

Columnists, 175–80

Comics, 140, 180

Committee on Public Information, 185

Congress, effect of press upon, 167–70

Congressional investigations. *See* Congress

Connecticut Courant, 9, 31

"Conning Tower, The," 176

Index

Consolidations. *See* Newspapers

Coolidge, Calvin, 173

Cooper, Thomas, 59

Cosby, William, 14

Country newspaper: early, 51–55; competition with urban papers, 105; in 1860, 111; and Associated Press, 115–16; after Civil War, 146–49

Craig, Daniel H., 113–15

Crane, Stephen, 144, 158, 162

Creel, George, 185

Creelman, James, 162

Cronkite, Walter, 191

Croswell, Edwin, 82

Croswell, Harry, 61

"Crusades," newspaper, 132

Daily newspapers: beginnings of, 35, 40; number of, 125, 193–95

Daly, John, 191

Dana, Charles A., 104, 107, 127–28

Daniels, Josephus, 146

Darling, Jay N. ("Ding"), 177

Darrow, Clarence, 105

Davis, Elmer, 191

Davis, Matthew, 77

Davis, Richard Harding, 144, 158, 162, 163

Day, Benjamin H., 93–97

Daye, Stephen, 10

Detroit Free Press, 110

Detroit Gazette, 62, 68

Dix, Dorothy, 180

"Dooley, Mr." *See* Dunne, Finley P.

Doyle, Conan, 148

Drummond, Roscoe, 179

Duane, William, 46, 56, 60

Dunne, Finley P., 176

Duranty, Walter, 164

Edes, Benjamin, 9, 27, 30

Editor: Franklin's description of qualifications for, 22; emergence of (1790's), 38; in early nineteenth century, 108–9; and specialization, 113, 119; in post–Civil

War days, 127–45; and publisher, 154

Editorials: in mercantile papers, 72; in politically sponsored papers, 81; loss of personal touch in, 155

Eisenhower, Dwight D., 174

Eisenstadt, Alfred, 189

Eliot, George Fielding, 180

Emporia Gazette, 146

Essex Gazette, 9

Evans, George Henry, 86

Evening papers, introduction of, 124

Fenno, John, 40–41, 45

Fessenden, Thomas G., 85

Field, Eugene, 148, 176, 197

First Amendment. *See* Freedom of the Press

Fitzpatrick, Daniel R., 177

Fleeming, John, 29

Fleet, Thomas, 13, 23

Foreign correspondents, 163–65

Foreign language newspapers, 10, 111

Foster, John, 10

Frank Leslie's Illustrated Newspaper, 142

Frankfort (Ky.) *Argus of the Western World*, 81

Franklin, Benjamin: as apprentice, 6; and *Pennsylvania Gazette*, 7; trains printers, 10; and *New-England Courant*, 13; as "Busy Body," 13; as joint deputy postmaster, 19; as "Silence Dogood," 21–22; opinions on newspaper, 22–24; as postmaster general, 29; on press freedom, 56

Franklin, James: and *Boston Gazette*, 6; and *New-England Courant*, 6; and *Rhode Island Gazette*, 8; and censorship, 12–13; and Mathers, 20–21

Free Inquirer, 86

Freedom of the press: in Zenger

Index

Freedom of the press (*continued*)
case, 16; in post-Revolutionary
state constitutions, 31; and debate on First Amendment, 55–
63. *See also* Censorship; Libel
Freneau, Philip, 35, 41–43
Fry, William, 104
Fuller, Margaret, 104

Gaine, Hugh, 11, 29
Gales, Joseph, Jr., 79
Garrison, William Lloyd, 86
Gay, Sidney Howard, 107
"Gazette," significance of as title,
8, 68
Genius of Universal Emancipation,
86
Georgia Gazette, 9
Gill, John, 9, 27, 30
Glen, James, 10
Goddard, Morrill, 143
Goddard, William, 28–29
Godkin, Edwin L., 134
Godwin, Parke, 105, 107
Gould, Jay, 126, 137
Grady, Henry, 129–30
Grafton, Samuel, 178
Graham, Billy, 179
Greeley, Horace, 102–5, 107, 121
Green, Bartholomew, 4, 6
Green, Duff, 80
Green, Samuel, 10
Gridley, Jeremy, 23
Guest, Edgar, 177
Gunther, John, 164

Hadden, Briton, 187
Hale, Nathan, 76
Hall, James, 68
Hall, Joseph, 66
Halstead, Murat, 166
Hamilton, Alexander: and founding of newspapers, 38, 39, 40–41;
as defense attorney (1804), 61;
on freedom of the press, 62
Hamilton, Andrew, 14–15, 60
Harnden, William F., 113

Harper's Weekly, 142, 187
Harris, Benjamin, 1–3, 12
Harte, Bret, 158
Haworth, Mary, 180
Hearst, William R.: and *N.Y. Journal,* 143–45; founds International
News Service, 150; as builder of
a chain, 151–52
Heatter, Gabriel, 191
Hemingway, Ernest, 158
"Herblock." *See* Block, Herbert
Hill, Isaac, 81
Hoe, Robert, & Son: and Napier
press, 73; and rotary "lightning"
press, 90; and post-1865 presses,
122
Holt, John, 28
Hopper, Hedda, 179
Hoover, Herbert, 173
Hudson, Frederic, 101, 107
Hudson (N.Y.) *Wasp,* 61
Hunter, William, 19

Illinois Emigrant, 68
Illustration, 17, 124
Indiana Gazette, 68
International News Service, 150,
191
Irwin, Will, 163

Jackson, Andrew, 80–82, 171
Jefferson, Thomas: sponsors *National Gazette,* 41–44; and freedom of press, 57–58, 60–61
Johnson, Andrew, 172
Johnson, Marmaduke, 10
Jones, Alexander, 11
Jones, George, 106
Journalism, schools of, 182–83

KDKA (radio station), 187
Kaltenborn, H. V., 191
Kansas City Star, 130–31
Kellogg, A. N., 147
Kendall, Amos, 80–81
Kentucke Gazette, 67
Keimer, Samuel, 7, 11, 23
Kipling, Rudyard, 148

Index

Kirby, Rollin, 177
Kneeland, Samuel, 6–7, 22
Knoxville (Tenn.) *Gazette*, 67
Koenig, Frederick, 73

Laffan News Bureau, 150
Landers, Ann, 180
Lardner, Ring, 158
Lawrence, David, 178
Lawson, Victor, 132
Lee, Ivy, 186, 197
Leggett, William, 105
Lerner, Max, 178
Lewis, Alfred Henry, 158
Libel: in Zenger case, 14–17; suits against William Cobbett, 48; actions to restrain press, 56, 58, 60–61. *See also* Censorship; Freedom of the press
Liberator, 86
Life, 188
"Line o' Type or Two, A," 176
Linotype, invention of, 123
Lippmann, Walter, 178
Literary Digest, 187
London, Jack, 148
London Gazette, 5
Louisville (Ky.) *Courier-Journal*, 130
Louisville (Ky.) *Journal*, 109
Luce, Henry, 187
Lundy, Benjamin, 86
Lyon, Matthew, 59–60

McCarthy, Joseph R., 169–70
McClure, S. S., 148
McCormick, Robert R., 154, 186
McCullagh, Joseph B., 137
McCutcheon, John T., 177
MacFadden, Bernarr, 188
McGahan, Januarius Aloysius, 161
McKenney, Thomas L., 64
McRae, Milton, 151
Marble, Manton, 126
Marquis, Don, 176
Marx, Karl, 104
Maryland Gazette, 8, 25
Mauldin, Bill, 178

Mechanics' Free Press, 86
Medill, Joseph, 110, 186
Mein, John, 29
Mencken, Henry L., 156–57
Mercantile newspapers, 70–77
Mergenthaler, Ottmar, 123
Mili, Gjon, 189
Mississippi Gazette, 67
Missouri Gazette, 68
Mowrer, Edgar Ansel, 164
Mowrer, Paul Scott, 164
Munsey, Frank, 153
Murrow, Edward R., 191
Musgrave, Philip, 6
Mydans, Carl, 189

Napier, David, 73, 90
National Intelligencer, 78–79
Nelson, William Rockhill, 131
New England Farmer, 85
New Hampshire Gazette, 9
New Hampshire Patriot, 81
New York: *American Minerva*, 38; *Commercial Advertiser*, 38, 70, 153; *Courier and Enquirer*, 71–72, 77, 98, 106; *Daily Graphic*, 188; *Daily Mirror*, 188; *Daily News* (1870's), 134; *Daily News* (founded 1919), 177; *Evening Post*, 39, 105, 126, 134; *Gazette*, 7; *Gazetteer*, 29; *Globe and Commercial Advertiser*, 153; *Herald*, 97–101, 153; *Herald-Tribune*, 153; 164, 178; *Illustrated Daily News*, 186; *Independent Advertiser*, 34; *Journal* (colonial), 26, 28; *Journal*, 143–45; *Journal of Commerce*, 71–72; *Log Cabin*, 102; *Mail*, 153; *Mercury*, 29; *New-Yorker*, 102; *Press*, 153; *Royal Gazette*, 29; *Sun*, 93–97, 127–28, 153, 176, 194; *Telegram*, 153; *Times*, 79, 106–7, 149, 164, 202; *Tribune*, 101–5, 126, 133–34, 153; *Wall Street Journal*, 76, 202; *Weekly Journal*, 7; *Weekly Post-Boy*, 28; *World*, 126, 136–43, 145,

Index

New York (*continued*)
177, 178, 194; *World-Telegram*,
194
New York Associated Press. *See*
Associated Press
News, concept of: in colonial journals, 5, 17–18; in early nineteenth
century, 49–50; in early Western
papers, 67–68; in politically supported papers, 82–84; in religious
papers, 84–85; as affected by new
communications methods, 92; in
"penny press," 96; in major urban
papers, 133, 136; as affected by
new forms of competition, 191–
92
News magazine, 187, 192
Newsboys, first use of, 93
Newspaper Enterprise Association,
151
Newspapers: establishment of in
colonies, 8–9; physical appearance of early, 17–18; acceptance
of, 23–26; and Revolution, 30–31;
evolution of in early national era,
49–51; growth and popularity of
in 1830's and 1840's, 65; tendency
to become general in appeal, 88–
90; growth in size, complexity,
and investment represented, 120–
25; post–Civil War changes, 124–
25; American as contrasted with
European, 141–42; status in 1900,
146; consolidation and decline in
numbers of starts, 153–54; new
competition after World War I,
188; consolidations and decline
in numbers of since 1919, 192–
95; problems and prospects as of
1961, 201–3
Newsweek, 192
Niles, Hezekiah, 75
Niles' Weekly Register, 75–76, 79
Noah, Mordecai M., 72, 107
North Carolina Gazette, 9
Northcliffe, Lord (Alfred Harmsworth), 186
"Nye, Bill," 148

Observer, Presbyterian newspaper,
84
Ochs, Adolph S., 149

Palmer, Frederic, 163
Paper, 17, 122
Parker, James, 28
Parks, William, 8
Parsons, Louella, 179
Parties, political, and newspapers:
in early national period, 34, 40–
47, 50; in Jacksonian era, 78–84
"Patent insides," 148
Patterson, Joseph, 186
Peale, Norman Vincent, 179
Pearson, Drew, 178
Peck, James H., 62
Pegler, Westbrook, 178
"Penny press," 93–94, 107–8
"Personal journalism." *See* Editor
Philadelphia: *American Weekly
Mercury*, 7; *Aurora* (*General
Advertiser*), 44–46; *Gazette of
the United States*, 40–41; *National
Gazette*, 35, 41–44; *Pennsylvania
Chronicle*, 28; *Pennsylvania Eve-
ning Post*, 40; *Pennsylvania Ga-
zette*, 7, 23; *Pennsylvania Jour-
nal*, 25; *Pennsylvania Packet and
Daily Advertiser*, 40; *Porcupine's
Gazette*, 46–48; *Poulson's Ameri-
can Daily Advertiser*, 70; *Public
Ledger*, 107, 194
Phillips, David Graham, 158, 160
Photographs, 124, 188–90
Pittsburgh Gazette, 66
Pleasants, John H., 69
Plough-Boy (New York), 85
Porter, William T., 95
Post Office Act: of 1792, 52; of
1851, 111; of 1912, 154, 198
Postal system: colonial, 4, 5, 19–20;
in Revolution, 29; in early na-
tional period, 52–53
Prentice, George D., 109
*Present State of the New-English
Affairs*, 2

Index

Presidential press conference, 170–75

"Press boat," 77, 100, 114

Presses: colonial, 17; improvements in hand-operated, 52; steam and cyclindrical, 73–74; improvements, 90, 122

Printer: in colonial society, 10–12; in early republic, 52; decline of to employee status, 118–19

Providence (R.I.) *Gazette*, 9

Public printing, 12, 68

Public relations, 196–201

Publick Occurrences Both Foreign and Domestick, 1–2

Pulitzer, Joseph, 136–43, 145

Radio: and news dissemination, 185, 190–92; as competition for advertising, 193

Raleigh (N.C.) *News & Observer*, 146

Ralph, Julian, 144, 162

Raymond, Henry J., 106–7, 121

"Readyprint," 148

Reform newspapers, 86, 111

Reid, Whitelaw, 126, 133–34, 166

Religious newspapers, 84–85, 111, 146

Remington, Frederic, 144

Reporter: emergence of, 113, 116–20; in modern journalism, 156–76, 183

Reporter (magazine), 192

Revolution, American, 3, 26–31

Rhode Island Gazette, 8

Rice, Grantland, 179

Richmond (Va.) *Enquirer*, 68–69, 82

Richmond (Va.) *Examiner*, 58

Richmond (Va.) *Whig*, 69

Riis, Jacob, 160

Ripley, George, 104

Ritchie, Thomas, 69, 82

Rives, John C., 80–82

Rivington, James, 29–30

Robinson, Solon, 104

Rogers, Will, 177

Roosevelt, Eleanor, 179

Roosevelt, Franklin D., 173

Roosevelt, Theodore, 172

Rural newspapers. *See* Agricultural papers; Country papers

Rush, Benjamin, 48

Russell, Benjamin, 35–37, 55–56

St. Louis Enquirer, 68

St. Louis Globe-Democrat, 137

St. Louis Post-Dispatch, 137, 177

San Francisco Examiner, 143

Schurz, Carl, 134

Scott, Tom, 126, 137

Scripps, Edward W., 150, 151–52

Scripps-Howard chain, 194

Scripps-McRae League, 151

Scull, John, 66

Seaton, William W., 79

Sedition Act of 1798, 58–60

Sevareid, Eric, 191

Sheehan, Vincent, 164

Shirer, William, 164, 191

Signs of the Times (Adventist), 84

Simmons, Azariah, 107

Skinner, John, 85

Smith, "Red," 179

Smith, Samuel Harrison, 78

Sokolsky, George, 178

Southern Agriculturist (Charleston), 85

Southwick, Solomon, 85

Sower, Christopher, 10

Spanish-American War, 144

Spirit of the Times, 95

Sports writers, 179

Springfield (Mass.) *Republican*, 109, 194

Stamp Act, 25–26

Stanley, Henry M., 135

Steffens, Lincoln, 160

Stereotype printing and presses, 90, 122

Stevenson, Robert Louis, 148

Stone, Melville, 132

Storey, Wilbur F., 110, 128–29

Stowe, Leland, 164

"Stunt," newspaper, 135

Index

Subscription prices, 75
Sullivan, Mark, 178
Sunday editions, 124, 140
Swain, William, 107
Swing, Raymond Gram, 164
Syndicates, feature, 147–48, 151, 175. *See also* American Press Association; Bok, Edward; McClure, S. S.; Newspaper Enterprise Association; Western Newspaper Union
Syndicates, newsgathering, 77, 113–16, 150–51. *See also* Associated Press; International News Service; United Press

Tappan, Arthur, 71
Taylor, Bayard, 104
Taylor, Bert Leston, 176
Taylor, Edmond, 164
Telegraph, 91–92, 114–15
Television: and news presentation, 190–92; as competition for advertising, 192–93
Thomas, Isaiah, 9, 11, 27–28, 35, 55
Thomas, Lowell, 191
Time, 187, 192
Topliff, Samuel, 77
Townshend taxes, 17
Truman, Harry S., 173
Twain, Mark, 144, 158
Tweed, William M., 146
Type: first efforts to found, 17

United Press, 150, 151, 191
U.S. News and World Report, 192
United States Telegraph, 80

Van Anda, Carr, 189
Van Buren, Abby, 180
Villard, Henry, 126, 134
Virginia and Kentucky Resolutions, 59

Virginia Gazette, 8

Wall Street Journal, 76, 202
Walter, Lynde M., 93
Walter press, 91
War correspondents, 118, 135, 161–63
Washington correspondents: on congressional debates, 56; in mercantile papers, 72, 77; in official party papers, 79; on eve of Civil War, 117–18; in modern times, 166–75; and public relations officers, 198–99
Washington Globe, 80–82
"Washington" hand press, 52
Washington Madisonian, 91–92
Washington Post, 178
Watchman and Reflector (Baptist), 84
Watterson, Henry, 129–30
Web-perfecting press, 91, 122
Webb, James Watson, 72, 98, 107
Webster, Noah, 37–38
Weed, Thurlow, 35, 83
Wentworth, John, 110
White, Horace, 134, 166
White, William Allen, 131, 153
White, William L., 179
Whitemarsh, Thomas, 8
Whitman, Walt, 158
Willington, A. S., 76
Wilmington (Del.) *Courant*, 9
Winchell, Walter, 179
Wilson, Woodrow, 172–73
Worcester (Mass.) *Spy*, 9, 35
Workingman's Advocate, 86
World War I, 163, 185–86
Wright, Frances, 86

"Yellow journalism," 140

Zenger, John Peter, 7, 14–17

THE CHICAGO HISTORY OF AMERICAN CIVILIZATION

Daniel J. Boorstin, Editor

Edmund S. Morgan, *The Birth of the Republic: 1763–89*

Marcus Cunliffe, *The Nation Takes Shape: 1789–1837*

*Elbert B. Smith, *The Death of Slavery: The United States, 1837–65*

John Hope Franklin, *Reconstruction: After the Civil War*

Samuel P. Hays, *The Response to Industrialism: 1885–1914*

William E. Leuchtenburg, *The Perils of Prosperity: 1914–32*

Dexter Perkins, *The New Age of Franklin Roosevelt: 1932–45*

Herbert Agar, *The Price of Power: America since 1945*

*   *   *

Robert H. Bremner, *American Philanthropy*

Harry L. Coles, *The War of 1812*

Richard M. Dorson, *American Folklore*

John Tracy Ellis, *American Catholicism*

Nathan Glazer, *American Judaism*

William T. Hagan, *American Indians*

Winthrop S. Hudson, *American Protestantism*

Maldwyn Allen Jones, *American Immigration*

Robert G. McCloskey, *The American Supreme Court*

Howard H. Peckham, *The War for Independence: A Military History*

Howard H. Peckham, *The Colonial Wars: 1689–1762*

Henry Pelling, *American Labor*

*John B. Rae, *The American Automobile: A Brief History*

Charles P. Roland, *The Confederacy*

Otis A. Singletary, *The Mexican War*

John F. Stover, *American Railroads*

*Bernard A. Weisberger, *The American Newspaperman*

* Available in cloth only. All other books published in both cloth and paperback editions.